1000 essential words that often appear on the TOEFL

토플에 자주 나오는
TOEFL
1000 단어

정연재

중앙대학교 영어영문학과와 같은 학교 대학원 영어영문학과를 졸업하였다.
고등학교 영어교사, 토플·토익 강사로 여러 해 영어를 가르쳤고,
도서출판 고려원 부설 「고려원어학연구원」 원장으로 재직하면서
많은 영어 교재들을 연구하고 개발하였다.
저서로는 《좋은 지문 다 모은 테마영문독해》(전7권)
《좋은 지문 다 모은 주니어 테마영문독해》(전6권)
《쉬운영어운동 회화과정》(전3권) 《처음문법 40단계》
《TOEFL 초보를 위한 기본독해》 《시험대비 영문법》 《영미문화사전》 등이 있다.

TOEFL에 자주 나오는 1000단어

2010년 1월 5일 발행

편저자・정연재
발행인・김대현
발행처・영어포럼

서울시 영등포구 영등포동 6가 147-7
대표전화・02-323-7901 팩스・02-323-7902
홈페이지・www.englishforum.co.kr
등록번호・제 318-1999-000125 호
등록일자・1999년 2월 2일
TOEFL Vocabulary 1000 ⓒ English Forum 2008
ISBN 978-89-88891-06-3

값 14,000원

저자와 출판사의 사전동의 없이 책 내용의 전체 또는 일부를 어떤 형태, 어떤 방법으로도
발췌 또는 저장, 복사, 전파할 수 없습니다.

토플에 자주 나오는

TOEFL
1000단어

VOCABULARY

정연재 편저

영어포럼
ENGLISH·FORUM

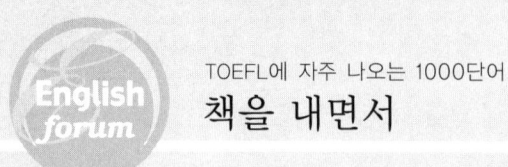

TOEFL에 자주 나오는 1000단어
책을 내면서

TOEFL이란?

토플은 영어권 국가에 유학하려는 학생들을 대상으로 하는 시험으로, 미국의 ETS라는 기관에서 주관한다. 예비 유학생들의 영어 사용 능력을 테스트하는 것이 목적이다. 만점은 iBT120(PBT677)점 이고, 보통 미국의 일반 대학은 88(570)점 전후의 점수를 요구하고, 상위권 대학은 100(600)점 이상의 점수를 요구한다. 토플은 영어에 대한 기본적인 소양만을 묻는 시험이기 때문에 토플 성적자체가 합격 여부를 결정하지는 않는다. 단지 대학의 입학 허가 조건일 뿐이다. 국내 대학에서는 영어 특기자를 선발하는 기준으로 토플 점수를 활용하기도 한다.

TOEFL의 활용

토플이 영어에 대한 기본 소양을 묻는다는 것은 토플이 어떤 분야의 전문성을 평가하는 시험이 아니라는 것을 의미한다. 토플은 영어에서 기본적으로 알아야 할 것을 미국의 전문가들이 시험이란 형식을 통해서 제시한 것이라고 할 수 있다. 다시 말해서 토플은 유학을 준비하는 사람뿐만 아니라, 영어를 공부하는 사람이라면 누구나 자신의 학습 성과를 가늠해 볼 수 있는 잣대로 삼아도 좋다는 것을 뜻한다.

TOEFL에 자주 나오는 1000단어

토플에 자주 나오는 단어를 엄선된 예문과 함께 공부하는 것은 토플에 가장 빠르게 접근할 수 있는 방법이다. 《TOEFL에 자주 나오는 1000단어》는 책 제목 그대로, 토플에 자주 나오는 단어 1,000개를 엄선된 예문과 함께 싣고 있다. 이 책의 1,000단어는 필자가 오랜 기간 토플에 출제된 어휘를 분석하여 간추린 것이다. 이것은 토플의 기본단어라고 할 수 있다. 기본단어 정도는 토플에 입문하면서 익히는 것이 좋다. 기본단어를 익히는 것은 영어의 기본을 다지는 일이다. 짧은 기간 동안에 집중적으로, 그리고 확실하게 익히기 바란다. 이 책의 입체적인 구성은 여러분들이 토플 기본단어를 효과적으로 익히는 데에 많은 도움을 줄 것이다.

이 책의 특징과 활용

1. 토플에 자주 나오는 1000단어를 난이도별로, 품사별로 나누었다.

　　이 책에 수록된 1,000단어는 토플을 준비하는 학습자라면 반드시 알아야 하는 필수 단어들이다. 이들 단어의 난이도를 따져서 5 STEP으로 나누었다. 각 STEP은 다시 동사, 명사, 형용사·부사 등 품사별로 나누었다. 난이도별, 품사별 분류는 학습자 개인의 취향이나 수준을 고려한 것이다. 토플 초보자들은 1-2 STEP의 단어를 먼저 익히는 것도 좋다.

2. 단어는 엄선된 예문과 함께 익힐 수 있게 하였다.

　　엄선된 예문이란 현재 미국에서도 자연스럽게 유통되는 문장이란 뜻이다. 단어는 반드시 엄선된 예문과 함께 학습해야 한다. 단어 자체만을 익히는 것은 의미가 없다. 특히 동사나 형용사는 문장에서의 쓰임새를 살피는 것은 중요하다.

3. 각 단어는 3-4개의 동의어와 반의어를 함께 실었다.

　　PBT(Paper-based Test) 토플의 어휘 문제는 의미와 동의어를 묻는 문제였다. CBT(Computer-based Test) 토플에서는 반의어 찾기가 추가되었다. 특히 이 책에서는 iBT(Internet-based Test) 토플의 새로운 경향에 충분하게 대비할 수 있도록 동의어와 반의어를 함께 실었다. 중요한 동의어와 반의어는 파란 색으로 구분하였다.

4. 많은 연습문제를 통해서 이미 학습한 단어를 반복하여 익힐 수 있게 하였다.

　　이 책의 가장 큰 특징은 많은 문제를 통하여 단어를 되풀이해서 익히게 하였다는 점이다. 문제 풀이 과정은 시험에 대한 준비 과정이며, 또 단어의 쓰임새를 정확하게 익힐 수 있는 과정이기도 하다. 각 STEP 뒤와 품사별 분류 뒤에 〈동의어 찾기〉, 〈반의어 찾기〉, 〈문장 완성하기〉 등의 문제를 실었다.

5. 혼동되는 단어를 부록으로 실었다.

　　혼동되는 단어는 한번에 정리하는 것이 좋다. 이 책에 수록된 단어는 혼동되는 단어뿐만 아니라 잘못 쓰기 쉬운 단어들도 포함하고 있다.

1000 essential words that often appear on the TOEFL

Contents

책을 내면서   4
이 책의 특징과 활용   5

STEP 1

Verb	11
- Practice Test 1	24
Noun	27
- Practice Test 2	38
Adjective & Adverb	41
- Practice Test 3	53
Mastery Test 1	57

STEP 2

Verb	65
- Practice Test 4	78
Noun	85
- Practice Test 5	95
Adjective & Adverb	99
- Practice Test 6	111
Mastery Test 2	116

STEP 3

Verb	123
- Practice Test 7	135
Noun	141
- Practice Test 8	151
Adjective & Adverb	155
- Practice Test 9	170
Mastery Test 3	175

STEP 4

Verb	187
- Practice Test 10	196
Noun	201
- Practice Test 11	209
Adjective & Adverb	213
- Practice Test 12	226
Mastery Test 4	232

STEP 5

Verb	241
- Practice Test 13	249
Noun	253
- Practice Test 14	264
Adjective & Adverb	269
- Practice Test 15	283
Mastery Test 5	288

Commonly Misused Words	298
- Practice Test 16	320
Mastery Test Answers	325

ENGLISH FORUM

1000 essential words that often appear on the TOEFL

Step 1

STEP 1

verb 동사   vocabulary 1000

abate
[əbéit]

감소시키다, 값을 내리다, 기세를 누그러뜨리다

\<syn\> decrease, reduce, moderate
\<ant\> increase, intensify, magnify

The wind *abated* after the storm.
태풍이 지나고 바람이 누그러졌다.

abide by
[əbáid bai]

결정에 따르다, 규정을 지키다

\<syn\> live up to, submit to
\<ant\> abandon, avoid, shun

We will *abide by* the decision of the court.
우리는 법원의 결정에 따를 것이다.

abolish
[əbáliʃ]

없애다, 폐지하다, 철폐하다

\<syn\> do away with, eliminate, eradicate
\<ant\> establish, institute

Slavery was *abolished* in Massachusetts shortly after the American Revolution.
매사추세츠주에서는 노예제도가 미국독립전쟁이 끝난 직후 곧 없어졌다.

abridge
[əbrídʒ]

줄이다, 축약하다

\<syn\> shorten, digest, abbreviate, cut down
\<ant\> expand, enlarge, extend, increase

The paperback book is an *abridged* edition.
문고판 도서는 축쇄판이다.

abstain
[əbstéin]

삼가다, 금주하다, 금연하다

<syn> refrain, desist, forbear, avoid
<ant> partake of, indulge in, give in to

Alcoholics must *abstain* from any indulgence in alcoholic drinks.
알코올 중독자들은 알코올 음료에 빠지는 것을 삼가야 한다.

accede
[æksíːd]

동의하다, 따르다

<syn> consent to, agree to, concede, approve
<ant> refuse, reject, oppose, object to

He *acceded* to their request.
그는 그들의 요구에 동의하였다.

accelerate
[æksélərèit]

속도를 높이다

<syn> increase in speed, speed up, go faster
<ant> slow down, decelerate, retard

Going downhill, a vehicle will naturally *accelerate*.
언덕 아래로 내려가면, 자동차는 자연히 가속도가 붙게 될 것이다.

accept
[æksépt]

받아들이다

<syn> take something offered, receive, admit
<ant> refuse, deny, reject

They *accepted* their responsibility to meet the deadline.
그들은 마감시한을 넘긴 책임을 받아들였다.

accustom
[əkʌ́stəm]

익숙해지다, 적응시키다

<syn> get or be used to, acclimate, adapt, adjust

The supervisor was not *accustomed* to having her instructions ignored.
그 감독은 자기가 내린 지시가 무시되는 것에 익숙하지 못했다.

affect
[əfékt]

영향을 미치다

<syn> influence, impinge on, act on
<ant> leave unmoved

The judge did not allow his personal feelings to *affect* his judgment of the case's legal merits.
판사는 그 사건의 법률적 시비를 판단함에 영향을 미칠 수 있는 자신의 개인 감정을 허용하지 않았다.

affix
[əfíks]

붙이다, 부착하다

\<syn> attach, fasten, stick
\<ant> detach, unfasten, take off

A price tag was *affixed* to each item.
가격표가 각 품목마다 부착되었다.

allocate
[ǽləkèit]

할당하다, 배분하다

\<syn> distribute, assign, set aside, designate
\<ant> withhold, hold back, deny

The new serum was *allocated* among the states by population.
새로운 혈청이 인구분포에 따라 각 주에 분배되었다.

amass
[əmǽs]

모으다, 축적하다

\<syn> collect, pile up, accumulate, gather, assemble, compile
\<ant> scatter, disperse, distribute, dispense

Through careful investment he had *amassed* a sizable fortune.
투자를 잘 해서 그는 상당한 재산을 모았다.

amplify
[ǽmpləfài]

확대하다, 확장하다, 증폭시키다

\<syn> enlarge, expand, increase, intensify
\<ant> reduce, decrease, cut down

Congressmen may *amplify* their remarks for appearance in the Record.
의원들은 자신들의 소견이 의사록에 실리도록 발표를 확대할 것이다.

append
[əpénd]

붙이다, 부가하다, 추가하다

\<syn> add, attach, affix, supplement
\<ant> remove, omit, leave out, detach

Exhibits should be *appended* to the report.
전시회가 보도에 추가되어야 한다.

assert
[əsə́:rt]

주장하다, 단언하다

\<syn> claim, state positively, maintain, insist
\<ant> deny, disavow, disclaim

He *asserted* his title to the property.
그는 그 재산에 대한 자신의 소유권을 주장하였다.

belittle
[bilítl]

축소하다, 얕잡아보다, 하찮게 보다

<syn> make smaller, make less important, disparage, scorn
<ant> overpraise, vaunt, elevate, boast about

He *belittled* the actress's talent by suggesting that her beauty, rather than her acting ability, was responsible for her success.
그는 그녀의 성공을 연기력보다는 예쁜 외모 덕분이라고 평가하여 그녀의 성공을 과소평가하였다.

cite
[sait]

인용하다

<syn> quote, refer to, mention, note
<ant> ignore, disregard, conceal

The lawyer *cited* a previous decision to support his point.
변호사는 자신의 관점을 뒷받침하기 위해 판례를 인용하였다.

collaborate
[kəlǽbərèit]

합작하다, 공동으로 일하다

<syn> work together, team up, cooperate

The friends decided to *collaborate* on a novel.
친구들은 소설을 합작하기로 결정하였다.

compel
[kəmpél]

강요하다, 억지로 시키다

<syn> force, drive, make, oblige
<ant> stop, deter, prevent

He was *compelled* by law to make restitution.
그는 배상할 것을 법원으로부터 명령받았다.

compensate
[kámpənsèit]

보상하다, 벌충하다

<syn> be equal to, make up for, make restitution, make compensation
<ant> add insult to injury, worsen, emphasize

Money could not *compensate* for his sufferings.
돈으로는 그의 고통을 보상할 수 없었다.

constrain
[kənstréin]

강제하다, 강요하다, 구속하다

<syn> restrain, compel, force, obligate
<ant> free, release

He felt *constrained* to make a full confession.
그는 완전한 자백을 하도록 강요받는 느낌이 들었다.

convene
[kənvíːn]

소집하다, 모으다, 회합하다

<syn> gather together, assemble, hold a session, bring together

The graduates will *convene* on the campus.
졸업생들이 캠퍼스에서 회합할 것이다.

debate
[dibéit]

토론하다

<syn> argue, dispute, discuss

The candidate challenged the incumbent to *debate* the issues on television.
그 후보는 당국자에 도전하여 텔레비전에서 이슈들을 토론하였다.

deceive
[disíːv]

속이다

<syn> trick, be false to, cheat, delude, mislead, swindle
<ant> enlighten, guide, tell the truth, be honest to

They *deceived* us by telling us that our donations would be used to provide food to the needy; in reality, the money was used to supply guns to the rebels.
그들은 우리가 내는 기부금이 가난한 사람들에게 식량을 제공하는 데 쓰일 거라고 말하며 우리를 속였다. 그런데, 실제로는 돈이 반역자들에게 총을 공급하는 데 사용되었다.

deduct
[didʌ́kt]

공제하다, 빼다

<syn> subtract, take away, remove, withdraw, decrease by
<ant> add, enlarge, amplify

Because the package was damaged, the seller *deducted* two dollars from the price.
포장이 파손되어서 판매원은 정가에서 2달러를 빼주었다.

degrade
[digréid]

격하시키다, 타락시키다

<syn> lower, demote, downgrade, debase
<ant> promote, lift in rank, dignigy

The celebrity refused interviews, feeling that it was *degrading* to have her personal life publicly discussed.
그 명사는 자신의 사생활이 대중 앞에 논의되는 것이 품격을 떨어뜨리는 것이라고 느껴 인터뷰를 거절하였다.

delete
[dilíːt]

삭제하다, 지우다

<syn> strike out, erase, remove, cut, cancel, take out
The proofreader *deleted* the superfluous word.
교정자가 불필요한 단어를 삭제하였다.

deplore
[diplɔ́ːr]

개탄하다, 애도하다, 유감으로 생각하다

<syn> lament, mourn, bemoan, grieve for, censure, condemn, disapprove strongly
Pacifists *deplore* violence even on behalf of a just cause.
평화주의자들은 정당한 이유에 의한 것이라 해도 폭력을 개탄한다.

designate
[dézignèit]

가리키다, 지명하다, 지정하다

<syn> name, appoint, indicate, choose, nominate, assign
We will rendezvous at the time and place *designated* on the sheet.
우리는 종이에 지정된 시간과 장소에서 만날 것이다.

devise
[diváiz]

궁리하다, 고안하다

<syn> contrive, invent, design, conceive
I will *devise* a plan of escape.
나는 탈출할 계획을 궁리할 것이다.

disdain
[disdéin]

경멸하다

<syn> look down upon, frown upon, reject as unworthy, despise, abhor
<ant> favor, admit, admire, regard, respect
Many beginners *disdain* a lowly job that might in time lead to the position they desire.
많은 초보자들이 머지않아 자신들이 바라는 자리까지 인도할지도 모르는 낮은 일자리를 멸시한다.

disjoin
[disdʒɔ́in]

떼다, 분리시키다

<syn> separate, disconnect, detach, split, divide
<ant> join, connect, attach
The links of the chain were *disjoined*.
체인의 연결이 분리되었다.

dispel
[dispél]

쫓아내다, 없애다

<syn> drive away, make disappear, expel, repel, eliminate, remove

The good-humored joke *dispelled* the tension in the room.
유머러스한 농담이 실내의 긴장을 해소하였다.

distract
[distrǽkt]

빗나가게 하다, 흩뜨리다, 미혹케 하다

<syn> divert, turn aside, disturb, trouble, perplex

The loud crash *distracted* the attention of the students.
시끄러운 충돌사고가 학생들의 주의를 흩뜨렸다.

effect
[ifékt]

v. (변화를) 가져오다, 초래하다; 실행하다

<syn> bring about, produce, make, cause, carry out
<ant> prevent, hinder, deter

New regulations have *effected* a shift in policy on applications.
새로운 규정들이 적용되면서 정책의 변화를 초래하였다.

n. 결과, 영향

<syn> result, consequence, outcome, influence
<ant> cause, occasion, inducement, incitement

The headache was an *effect* of sinus congestion.
두통은 누관의 충혈 때문이었다.

employ
[emplɔ́i]

사용하다, 고용하다

<syn> use, hire, utilize, make use of
<ant> discharge, dismiss, fire

The artist *employed* charcoal in many of her sketches.
그 화가는 자신의 많은 스케치에 목탄을 사용했다.

enforce
[enfɔ́ːrs]

집행하다, 강제하다

<syn> make forceful, impose by force, compel obedience to
<ant> ignore, disregard

Because of the holiday, parking restrictions are not being *enforced* today.
공휴일이라서 오늘은 주차단속이 집행되지 않고 있다.

erode
[iróud]

좀먹다, 부식하다, 침식하다

<syn> eat into, wear away, corrode, ravage, spoil
<ant> build up, strengthen, reinforce

The glaciers *eroded* the land, leaving deep valleys.
빙하가 육지를 침식시켜 깊은 계곡을 만들었다.

erupt
[irʌ́pt]

분출하다, 분화하다

<syn> break out, burst forth, explode, pour forth, gush
<ant> retain, contain, hold, be dormant, subside

The volcano *erupted* streams of lava.
화산이 용암 줄기를 분출하였다.

exceed
[iksíːd]

초과하다

<syn> go beyond, go over, surpass, excel, transcend
<ant> stay within, keep in

The business's profits for this year *exceeded* last year's profits by $16,000.
올해의 사업이익은 작년의 이익보다 16,000달러나 초과했다.

except
[iksépt]

빼다, 제외하다

<syn> exclude, exempt, excuse, omit, eliminate
<ant> include, reckon, count

He *excepted* the damaging remarks from his speech.
그는 자신의 연설에서 손해되는 부분을 제외시켰다.

exclude
[iksklúːd]

제외시키다, 배제하다

<syn> shut out, not permit, keep out, prohibit, except
<ant> invite, welcome, admit, include, accept

The children made a pact that all adults were to be *excluded* from the clubhouse.
어린이들은 모든 어른들이 클럽에서 배제되어야 한다는 협정을 맺었다.

exhibit
[igzíbit]

전시하다

<syn> show, display, put on view, make public
<ant> hide, conceal, suppress, secrets, bury

The paintings were *exhibited* in the municipal museum.
시립박물관에 회화작품들이 전시되었다.

expel
[ikspél]

쫓아내다, 물리치다

\<syn\> punish, force out, drive out, cast out, eject, discharge
\<ant\> take in, ingest, inhale, accept

When a balloon bursts, the air is *expelled* in a rush.
풍선이 터지자 공기가 분출되었다.

generate
[dʒénərèit]

발생시키다, 산출하다

\<syn\> beget, procreate, propagate, produce, create, originate, spawn
\<ant\> extinguish, end, terminate, annihilate

Every animal *generates* its own species.
모든 동물은 자신의 종족을 생산한다.

herald
[hérəld]

알리다, 포고하다

\<syn\> announce, proclaim, report, usher in, inform

Crocuses *herald* the advent of spring.
크로커스(식물)가 봄이 왔음을 알린다.

impel
[impél]

재촉하다, 추진시키다, 강제하다

\<syn\> drive forward, push, incite, force, compel, urge, spur
\<ant\> restraint, curb, check, inhibit, withhold

Although she was not personally involved, her sense of justice *impelled* her to speak out.
그녀가 개인적으로는 관련이 없지만, 정의감이 그녀로 하여금 말하게 하였다.

insure
[inʃúər]

보장하다, 보증하다, 보험을 계약하다 (n. insurance 보험)

\<syn\> make certain, guarantee, secure, underwrite
\<ant\> imperil, jeopardize

Bail is set to *insure* the defendant's appearance in court.
보석금은 피고가 법정에 나올 것을 보증하는 것이다.

intercept
[ìntərsépt]

가로채다, 차단하다

\<syn\> cut off, seize, get hold of, detain, stop
\<ant\> transmit, relay, hasten, expedite, permit

The missile was *intercepted* and destroyed before it reached its target.
미사일이 목표물에 도달하기 전에 요격되었다.

irritate
[írətèit]

화나게 하다, 초조하게 하다, 자극하다

<syn> annoy, vex, anger, inflame, make impatient, provoke
<ant> appease, mollify, pacify, please

The harsh cleansers used in the job can *irritate* the skin.
직장에서 사용되는 거친 세제는 피부를 자극할 수 있다.

mar
[mɑːr]

손상하다, 훼손하다

<syn> damage, spoil, taint, blemish, hurt
<ant> improve, enhance, restore

The floor had been *marred* by scratches and scuff marks.
마루바닥이 긁힌 자국과 신발 자국들로 훼손되었다.

miscalculate
[miskǽlkjəlèit]

계산을 잘못하다, 잘못짚다 (calculate erroneously)

He failed because of his *miscalculations*.
그는 계산착오로 실패하였다.

negotiate
[nigóuʃièit]

협상하다

<syn> bargain, confer with, discuss, arrange

As long as both sides are willing to *negotiate* in good faith, a strike can be avoided.
양측이 신뢰로 협상하고자 하는 한, 파업은 피할 수 있다.

perceive
[pərsíːv]

인지하다, 감지하다

<syn> feel, comprehend, note, understand, notice
<ant> overlook, ignore, miss, pass over

I *perceived* that the beast was harmless.
나는 그 짐승이 해를 끼치지 않음을 감지하였다.

persist
[pəːrsíst]

지속하다, 주장하다, 고집하다

<syn> continue, last, persevere, stand fast
<ant> falter, quit, give up, surrender, cease

Despite the rebuffs, he *persisted* in his efforts to befriend the disturbed youngster.
퇴짜를 맞으면서도 그는 정서 불안한 젊은이들과 친구 되려는 노력을 계속하였다.

presume
[prizúːm]

추정하다, 상상하다

<syn> assume, take for granted, believe, suppose

An accused person is *presumed* innocent until proved guilty.
기소된 사람은 유죄가 증명될 때까지 무죄로 추정된다.

I was furious that she had *presumed* to take the car without permission.
그녀가 허락도 없이 자동차를 탄 것으로 생각되어 나는 화가 났다.

proceed
[prousíːd]

앞으로 나가가다, 계속하다

<syn> go forward, continue, advance, progress
<ant> retreat, go backward, stop

Because of numerous interruptions, the work *proceeded* slowly.
방해가 많아서 작업이 느리게 나아갔다.

prolong
[proulɔ́ːŋ]

늘이다, 연장하다, 오래 끌다

<syn> lengthen, extend, draw out; hold back, delay, retard
<ant> curtail, shorten, abbreviate, lessen; expedite, hurry

The treatment *prolongs* life but cannot cure the disease, which is terminal.
그 치료는 생명을 연장하지만 질병을 치료할 수는 없으므로 치명적이다.

protract
[proutrǽkt]

연장하다, 오래 끌게 하다

<syn> prolong, extend, draw out, lengthen

The jury's deliberations were *protracted* by confusion over a point of law.
법률 취지에 대한 혼란으로 배심원의 협의가 연장되었다.

recollect
[rèkəlékt]

다시 모으다, 불러일으키다, 회상하다 (recall to memory, bring to mind)

<syn> recall, call to mind, remember, place

He could not *recollect* having made the appointment.
그는 약속을 한 사실을 기억할 수가 없었다.

recur
[rikə́ːr]

되돌아가다, 상기하다, 재발하다 (adj. recurrent 재발하는; 순환하는)

<syn> occur again, happen again, repeat, return, come back, return to mind

Unless social conditions are improved, the riots are bound to *recur*.
사회적 여건이 개선되지 않는 한, 폭동은 반드시 재발한다.

refrain
[rifréin]

그만두다, 삼가다 (keep from doing something, not do)

<syn> abstain, restrain oneself, keep oneself, hold off, forbear
<ant> indulge in, continue, persist, go ahead

Considerate parents *refrain* from criticizing their children in front of others.
사려 깊은 부모는 다른 사람들 앞에서 자식들을 꾸짖기를 삼간다.

retain
[ritéin]

보유하다, 유지하다, 보류하다

<syn> keep, detain, withhold, reserve, maintain, possess, hold
<ant> discard, lose, surrender, relinquish, abandon

Throughout the grueling day she had managed somehow to *retain* her sense of humor.
하루종일 벌을 받으면서도 어쩐 일인지 그녀는 유머감각을 유지하였다.

revive
[riváiv]

소생시키다, 회복시키다

<syn> restore to consciousness, come or bring back to life, reanimate, refresh

A cool drink and a bath *revived* her spirits.
시원한 음료와 목욕이 그녀의 정신을 회복시켰다.

simulate
[símjəlèit]

가장하다, 흉내내다 (give a false appearance of)

<syn> imitate, pretend, feign, put on, counterfeit, fake

Although she had guessed what the gift would be, she *simulated* surprise when she unwrapped the package.
선물이 무엇인지 추측했지만 그녀는 포장을 풀었을 때 놀라는 척하였다.

submit
[səbmít]

1. 복종하다, 굴복하다, 포기하다

<syn> give in, surrender, yield

Although the doctors were dubious of his full recovery, the patient refused to *submit* to despair.
의사들이 그의 완전한 회복에 회의적이었는데도, 그 환자는 절망하기를 거부하였다.

2. 제출하다

<syn> give, hand in

The couple *submitted* their application to the loan officer.
부부는 임대 담당자에게 지원서를 제출하였다.

supervise
[súːpərvàiz]

관리하다, 감독하다, 지휘하다

<syn> oversee, direct, superintend, look after, govern

A new employee must be carefully *supervised* to insure that he learns the routine correctly and thoroughly.
새로운 근로자는 작업과정을 바르고 철저히 배우는지를 확실히 하기 위해 잘 감독해야 한다.

terminate
[tə́ːrmənèit]

끝내다, 마무리하다

<syn> end, finish, complete, conclude, come to an end
<ant> begin, start, open, commence

She *terminated* the interview by standing up and thanking us for coming.
그녀가 자리에서 일어남으로써 면담을 마치고, 와줘서 고맙다고 우리에게 인사하였다.

transcribe
[trænskráib]

베끼다, 복사하다 (make a written copy of)

These almost illegible notes must be *transcribed* before anyone else will be able to use them.
거의 읽기 힘든 이 노트는 다른 누군가 그것들을 이용하기 전에 복사해야 한다.

translate
[trænsléit]

번역하다, 통역하다 (change from one medium to another, especially from one language or code to another)

The flight attendant *translated* the announcement into Spanish for the benefit of two of the passengers.
승무원은 승객들 가운데 두 사람의 편의를 위해 안내방송을 스페인어로 통역하였다.

vacate
[véikeit]

비우다, 떠나가다 (leave empty)

<syn> leave, withdraw, give up, depart from

The court ordered the demonstrators to *vacate* the premises.
법원은 시위자들에 구내를 떠날 것을 명령하였다.

warrant
[wɔ́(ː)rənt]

보장하다, 정당화하다, 허가하다

<syn> deserve, justify, permit ; affirm, certify, guarantee

The infraction was too minor to *warrant* a formal reprimand.
위반행위가 너무 경미해서 공식적인 징계를 허가할 수 없었다.

yearn
[jəːrn]

그리워하다, 동경하다, 갈망하다 (feel longing or desire)

<syn> crave, long, hanker
<ant> detest, despise, hate, loathe, abhor

The parents *yearned* for their recently deceased child.
그 부모는 최근에 죽은 자신들의 아이를 그리워하였다.

STEP 1 *Practice Test 1*

DIRECTIONS Select the word or phrase that means most nearly the same as the key word.

1 **abridge**
   (A) cross over   (B) shorten
   (C) extend   (D) circumvent

2 **accede**
   (A) proceed   (B) precede
   (C) prevent   (D) consent

3 **accept**
   (A) exclude   (B) admit
   (C) scrutinize   (D) anticipate

4 **abstain**
   (A) refrain from   (B) darken
   (C) remove   (D) abridge

5 **accelerate**
   (A) speed up   (B) climb
   (C) decline   (D) continue

6 **affix**
   (A) repair   (B) fasten
   (C) remove   (D) manipulate

7 **amplify**
   (A) expand   (B) amass
   (C) ambidextrous   (D) frighten

| ANSWER |

1. (A) 교차하다 (B) 줄이다
   (C) 확장하다
   (D) 앞지르다, 우회하다

2. (A) 나아가다 (B) 앞서다
   (C) 방지하다 (D) 동의하다

3. (A) 배제하다 (B) 인정하다
   (C) 자세히 검토하다 (D) 기대하다

4. (A) 삼가다 (B) 어둡게 하다
   (C) 제거하다 (D) 단축하다

5. (A) 속도를 내다 (B) 기어오르다
   (C) 기울다, 쇠퇴하다 (D) 지속하다

6. (A) 수리하다
   (B) 붙들어 매다, 붙이다
   (C) 제거하다 (D) 조작하다

7. (A) 확장하다
   (B) 모으다, 축적하다
   (C) 양손잡이인 (D) 겁주다

1. (B) 2. (D) 3. (B) 4. (A)
5. (A) 6. (B) 7. (A)

8 allocate
  (A) find (B) assign
  (C) discover (D) reprimand

9 amass
  (A) refuse (B) stupefy
  (C) affix (D) collect

10 assert
  (A) climb (B) push forward
  (C) state (D) denounce

11 collaborate
  (A) chain gang (B) work together
  (C) beat brutally (D) work overtime

12 compel
  (A) force (B) wheedle
  (C) invite (D) reject

13 compensate
  (A) make do (B) make up for
  (C) make up (D) make out

14 deduct
  (A) perquisite (B) bonus
  (C) subtract (D) multiply

15 convene
  (A) help (B) assemble
  (C) monitor (D) interpolate

16 deceive
  (A) send back (B) trick
  (C) forget (D) admonish

| ANSWER |

8. (A) 찾다 (B) 배당하다
   (C) 발견하다 (D) 징계하다
9. (A) 거절하다 (B) 마취시키다
   (C) 첨부하다 (D) 모으다, 수집하다
10. (A) 기어오르다 (C) 전진하다
    (C) 말하다, 주장하다 (D) 비난하다
11. (A) 같은 사슬에 매인 죄수
    (B) 협동하다 (C) 잔인하게 때리다
    (D) 잔업하다
12. (A) 강제하다 (B) 감언이설로 속이다
    (C) 초대하다 (D) 거절하다
13. (A) 임시 변통하다 (B) 보상하다
    (C) 만들다 (D) 이해하다
14. (A) 수당, 부수입 (B) 상여금
    (C) 빼다 (D) 곱하다
15. (A) 돕다 (B) 모으다
    (C) 감시하다 (D) 가필하다, 써넣다
16. (A) 되돌려 보내다 (B) 속이다
    (C) 잊다 (D) 훈계하다

8. (B) 9. (D) 10. (C) 11. (B) 12. (A)
13. (B) 14. (C) 15. (B) 16. (B)

17 delete
(A) please (B) pontificate
(C) alter (D) erase

18 dispel
(A) drive away (B) separate
(C) push back (D) drive forward

19 erode
(A) wear away (B) drive on
(C) push away (D) carry

20 herald
(A) announce departure (B) special delivery
(C) forecast (D) announce

21 impel
(A) drive forward (B) push out
(C) push down (D) drive away

22 insure
(A) guarantee (B) calm
(C) replace (D) secure

23 negotiate
(A) purchase (B) bargain
(C) sell (D) rent

24 simulate
(A) arouse (B) feign
(C) electrify (D) whimper

25 refrain
(A) avoid doing (B) sing
(C) paraphrase (D) accept openly

| ANSWER |

17. (A) 즐겁게 하다 (B) 거드름 피우다
    (C) 바꾸다 (D) 지우다

18. (A) 몰아내다 (B) 분리하다
    (C) 후퇴시키다 (D) 전진하다

19. (A) 침식하다 (B) 몰고가다
    (C) 밀어부치다 (D) 나르다

20. (A) 출발을 알리다 (B) 특별배달
    (C) 예보하다 (D) 알리다

21. (A) 추진하다 (B) 밀어내다, 내보내다
    (C) 밀어내리다 (D) 쫓아내다

22. (A) 보증하다 (B) 안정시키다
    (C) 제자리에 놓다 (D) 안전하게 하다

23. (A) 구매하다 (B) 협상하다, 흥정하다
    (C) 매매하다 (D) 임대하다

24. (A) 발생하다 (B) 가장하다
    (C) 감전시키다, 충전시키다
    (D) 훌쩍훌쩍 울다

25. (A) 삼가다 (B) 노래하다
    (C) 글을 다시 쓰다
    (D) 열린 마음으로 받아들이다

17. (D) 18. (A) 19. (A) 20. (D) 21. (A)
22. (A) 23. (B) 24. (B) 25. (A)

STEP 1

noun 명사

vocabulary 1000

ability
[əbíləti]

능력

\<syn\> capability, capacity, skill, power
\<ant\> inability, incapacity, incompetence

Her scores clearly indicated a remarkable *ability* for calculus.
그녀의 성적은 미적분에 놀라운 능력을 확실히 보여주었다.

access
[ǽkses]

입장, 통로

\<syn\> means of approach, admittance, entrance

Public libraries insure that people have *access* to vast stores of information.
공공도서관은 사람들이 거대한 정보의 창고로 입장하도록 해준다.

adversity
[ædvə́ːrsəti]

역경, 불운

\<syn\> misfortune, mishap, calamity, poverty
\<ant\> good fortune, success, blessings

Shakespeare praised the "sweet uses" of *adversity*.
셰익스피어는 역경을 슬기롭게 활용함을 찬양하였다.

aggression
[əgréʃən]

침략, 침범

\<syn\> unprovoked attack, invasion, raid
\<ant\> peace, pacification, submissiveness

The invasion of Afghanistan was denounced in the Western press as *aggression*.
아프가니스탄 침공은 서방 언론에서 침략으로 비난받았다.

alibi
[ǽləbài]

알리바이, 현장부재증명

<syn> a defensive excuse, explanation

His *alibi* was ironclad; he was in the hospital at the time of the murder.
그의 알리바이가 입증되었는데, 그는 살인이 일어난 시각에 병원에 있었다.

altitude
[ǽltətjùːd]

해발높이, 고도

<syn> height, above sea level

The plane had reached an *altitude* of four miles.
그 비행기는 해발 4마일에 다다랐다.

anarchy
[ǽnərki]

무정부, 무정부 상태

<syn> absence of government and law, disorder, lawless, chaos
<ant> order, discipline, government, authority

When the police union strikes, *anarchy* may soon follow.
경찰노조가 파업을 하면 곧바로 무정부 상태가 올 것이다.

assumption
[əsʌ́mpʃən]

가정, 추측

<syn> supposition, presumption, presupposition, premise

I prepared dinner on the *assumption* that they would be home by seven.
나는 그들이 7시까지 집에 올 것으로 가정하고 저녁식사를 준비하였다.

avocation
[ævoukéiʃən]

부업, 취미

<syn> sideline, secondary occupation, hobby, pastime
<ant> vocation, occupation, work, business

The person who can earn a living from his *avocation* is indeed fortunate.
자신의 취미로 생활비를 벌 수 있는 사람은 정말로 운이 좋다.

benediction
[bènədíkʃən]

축복, 감사기도

<syn> blessing, closing prayer
<ant> malediction, curse, imprecation

Many sought the *benediction* of their pastor during troubled times.
많은 사람들이 어려울 때 목사의 축복을 구했다.

breach
[briːtʃ]

파괴, 파열, 위반, 불화

<syn> opening, gap, break, failure to keep the terms, violation
<ant> closure, stoppage, adherence to, observance

When they failed to deliver the goods, they were guilty of a *breach* of contract.
그들이 상품을 배달하지 못할 때, 계약위반의 책임이 있었다.

brevity
[brévəti]

간결함, 요약

<syn> conciseness, terseness, briefness, shortness
<ant> long-windedness, prolixity, lengthiness

Brevity is the essence of journalistic writing.
간결함이 언론보도문의 본질이다.

capacity
[kəpǽsəti]

능력, 수용능력, 용량

<syn> ability, aptitude, capability
<ant> inability, incapacity

His prudent decisions proved his *capacity* for the top job.
그의 신중한 의사결정은 바로 최상의 업무를 위한 그의 능력을 입증하였다.

capitol
[kǽpitl]

국회의사당, 건물

<syn> a legislative building, statehouse, government house

The state Senate convened in the *capitol* today.
주 상원 회의가 오늘 의사당에서 열렸다.

censure
[sénʃər]

비난, 혹평, 불신임

<syn> blame, condemnation, reprimand
<ant> paise, approval, commendation

An act of *censure* may be enacted by the Senate.
불신임 결의안을 상원에서 제정할 수 있다.

chronology
[krənάlədʒi]

연대기

<syn> arrangement by time, list of events by date

The book included a *chronology* of the poets's life against the background of the major political events of his age.
그 책은 그 시대의 주요 정치적 사건들을 배경으로 시인들의 연보를 싣고 있었다.

cognition
[kɑgníʃən]

인식, 인지

<syn> perception, process of knowing

The mere *cognition* of a problem is only the first step toward a solution.
어떤 문제를 단순히 인식한다는 것은 해결을 향한 첫걸음일 따름이다.

cohesion
[kouhí:ʒən]

응집, 결속, 결합

<syn> sticking together, solidification

The *cohesion* of molecules creates surface tension.
분자의 응집력이 표면장력을 만든다.

concept
[kánsept]

개념, 생각

<syn> idea, general notion, theory, opinion

The *concept* that all individuals have inherent and inalienable rights is basic to our political philosophy.
모든 개인은 선천적이고도 양도할 수 없는 권리들을 가졌다는 개념은 우리 정치철학의 기본이다.

contract
[kántrækt]

계약

<syn> a written agreement, legal document, arrangement, compact

The company signed a *contract* to operate a bookstore on campus.
그 회사는 캠퍼스에 서점을 운영하는 계약에 서명하였다.

controversy
[kántrəvə:rsi]

논쟁, 말다툼

<syn> highly charged debate, conflict of opinion, argument, quarrel
<ant> agreement, unanimity accord

A *controversy* arose over whether to use the funds for highway improvement or for mass transit.
자금을 고속도로 개선을 위해 쓸 것인가, 아니면 대량수송수단에 쓸 것인가에 대해 논쟁이 일어났다.

demagogue
[déməgɔ:g]

선동정치가 (leader who uses mob passions)

Hitler was a *demagogue*.
히틀러는 선동정치가였다.

dilemma
[dilémə]

딜레마, 궁지, 진퇴양난

<syn> problem, plight, difficult choice, deadlock

Even a wrong decision may be preferable to remaining in a *dilemma*.
나쁜 결정이라도 딜레마에 빠져있는 것보다는 나을 수도 있다.

disputation
[dìspjutéiʃən]

논쟁, 토론, 논박, 반박

<syn> a controversy, debate, dispute

In his *disputation*, he defended the theories expressed in his paper.
논쟁에서 그는 자기 논문에 기술된 이론들을 방어하였다.

diversity
[divə́:rsəti]

다양성

<syn> variety, unlikeness, difference, divergence
<ant> likeness, similarity, sameness

A university should encourage a *diversity* of opinion among the faculty.
대학은 교수회의 다양한 의견을 격려해야 한다.

ecstasy
[ékstəsi]

무아경, 황홀 (extreme happiness)

The lovers were in *ecstasy* just in touching each other's hands.
연인들은 서로의 손만 만져도 황홀했다.

egotism
[í:goutìzəm]

자기중심주의, 자기본위

<syn> self-admiration, self-praise, bragging, boastfulness
<ant> modesty, humility, bashfulness, self-criticism

His *egotism* demanded that he always be the center of attention.
그의 자기중심주의는 언제나 자신이 관심의 중심일 것을 요구하였다.

epilogue
[épilɔ̀:g]

에필로그, 맺는 말

<syn> concluding addition, final section, afterword
<ant> preface, prologue, introduction

The *epilogue* is delivered at the conclusion of the drama.
에필로그는 드라마의 결말에 나온다.

evolution
[èvəlúːʃən]

진화, 발전

<syn> gradual change, growth, development,
<ant> deterioration, withering, contraction

Through the discovery of ancient bones and artifacts, anthropologists hope to chart the *evolution* of the human species.
고대인의 뼈와 유물들을 통해 인류학자들은 인종의 진화를 도표화하기를 바란다.

facility
[fəsíləti]

쉬움, 편의, 솜씨; 시설, 설비

<syn> ease, fluency, expertness, practicability; appliance, convenience, aid
<ant> ineptness, clumsiness, difficulty, hardship

Her *facility* in reading several languages made her ideal for the cataloguing job.
몇 개의 언어를 유창하게 읽는 그녀의 능력은 목록분류 일자리에 적격이었다.

foresight
[fɔ́ːrsàit]

선견지명, 예측

<syn> a looking ahead, power of foreseeing, prevision, prescience
<ant> aftersight, hindsight, retrospection

She had the *foresight* to realize that the restaurant would be busy, so she called ahead for reservations.
그녀는 식당이 붐빌 거라 예측을 하고 미리 예약을 하였다.

generalization
[dʒènərəlizéiʃən]

일반화, 보편화

<syn> induction, a general conclusion, speaking in generalities

Generalizations are apt to be as dangerous as they are tempting.
일반화의 유혹은 위험하기 십상이다.

homicide
[hάməsàid]

살인

<syn> murder, manslaughter, slaying, bloodshed

Killing in self-defense is considered justifiable *homicide*.
정당방위로 한 살인은 정당한 살인으로 간주된다.

ideology
[àidiάlədʒi]

관념, 이데올로기

<syn> set of beliefs, body of concepts, ideals, body of a social doctrine, dogma

The communist *ideology* holds the State important and the individual inconsequential.
공산주의 이데올로기는 국가가 중요하고 개인은 중요하지 않다고 주장한다.

inhibition
[ìnhəbíʃən]

금지, 억제

<syn> restraint, restriction, constraint, impediment

Inhibition is particularly important for emotional people.
억제는 감성적인 사람들에게 특히 중요하다.

innovation
[ìnouvéiʃən]

혁신, 쇄신

<syn> something new, a change

The celebration of the Mass in languages other than Latin is a major 20th-century *innovation* in the Roman Catholic Church.
라틴어 외에 다른 언어로 미사의 성찬을 올리는 것이 로마가톨릭교회의 20세기 중요한 혁신이다.

introvert
[íntrəvə:rt]

내향적인 사람 (a person whose thoughts are directed inward)

<syn> withdrawn person, inner-directed person, introspective person
<ant> extrovert, outgoing person

The *introvert* makes friends with difficulty; the extrovert makes friends with ease.
내성적인 사람은 친구를 어렵게 사귀는 반면, 외향적인 사람은 쉽게 친구를 사귄다.

irony
[áirəni]

아이러니, 풍자

[ex] He said he didn't like vacations because he liked school so much.
그는 공부를 너무 좋아해서 방학을 좋아하지 않는다고 말했다.

legislature
[lédʒislèitʃər]

입법부, 입법기관

<syn> lawmaking body; senate, parliament, congress, assembly, council, diet

The federal *legislature* of the United States, the Congress, has two houses.
미국의 연방 입법부인 의회는 양원을 가지고 있다.

longevity
[lɑndʒévəti]

수명, 장수

<syn> life span, long life, length of life

The Bible credits the first generations of men with a *longevity* unheard of today.
성경은 인류 최초의 세대가 오늘날에는 볼 수 없는 수명을 가진 것으로 믿고 있다.

morale
[mouræl]

(군대나 조직의) 사기

<syn> level of spirits, mental or emotional condition

After a landslide victory at the polls, *morale* in the party was at a peak.
여론조사에서 가파른 승리가 있은 다음, 그 정당의 사기가 최고조에 다다랐다.

nihilism
[náiəlìzəm]

허무주의

<syn> disbelief in anything, skepticism; anarchism

War fosters a spirit of *nihilism*, particularly among the defeated.
전쟁은 특히 패배자들 사이에 허무주의를 낳는다.

paradigm
[pærədim]

모범, 본보기

<syn> model, ideal, paragon, example, pattern to be copied

The teacher handed out a sample letter as a *paradigm* of the correct form.
그 선생님은 바른 형식의 모범으로 샘플 편지를 건네 주셨다.

paradox
[pærədàks]

역설, 패러독스 (internal contradiction, a statement that appears to contradict itself)

"This sentence is false." is an example of a *paradox*.
"이 문장은 틀렸다."는 패러독스의 한 예이다.

perception
[pərsépʃən]

지각, 인식, 인지

<syn> discernment, awareness, sense, apprehension, detection

Perception is that act of the mind whereby the mind becomes conscious of anything, including hunger, thirst, cold, or heat.
인식이란 배고픔, 갈증, 추위, 더위 등을 포함한 어떤 것을 마음이 의식하게 되는 바로 그런 마음의 행위이다.

precedent
[présədənt]

전례, 판례

<syn> example, pattern, model, standard, criterion

The lawyer's brief argued that the legal *precedents* cited by the opposition were not relevant because of subsequent changes in the law.
변호사의 설명은 상대가 인용한 판례들이 계속되는 법률의 개정 때문에 연관성이 없다는 주장이었다.

principle
[prínsəpl]

원칙, 법칙

<syn> rule, truth, law, fundamental rudiment

A man of *principle* never goes back on his word.
원칙주의자는 자기가 한 말을 결코 뒤집지 않는다.

query
[kwíəri]

질문하다, 묻다

<syn> ask, question, quiz, make inquiry, interrogate

He *queried* the witness about his alibi.
그는 증인에게 알리바이를 물었다.

quota
[kwóutə]

몫, 할당, 분담 (proportional share)

<syn> portion, share, proportion, allotment, distribution, allocation, percentage

The school had an unwritten *quota* system that set limits on the proportion of applicants from different geographical areas.
그 학교는 다양한 지역별로 지원자 할당을 제한하는 불문의 쿼터시스템을 가지고 있었다.

rapidity
[rəpídəti]

신속, 속도 (speed)

The *rapidity* with which her hands flew over the piano keys was too great to follow with the eye.
그녀의 손이 피아노 건반 위를 날아다니는 속도는 너무나 대단해서 눈으로 따라갈 수 없었다.

ratio
[réiʃou]

비율 (proportional or fixed relation of number or amount between two things)

<syn> proportion, interrelationship, equation

The *ratio* of women to men in middle-level positions in the firm is only one to seven.
회사의 중간 직위에서 여자 대 남자의 비율은 겨우 1대 7이다.

recipient
[risípiənt]

수령인, 수상자 (one who receives)

The *recipient* of the award had been chosen from among 200 candidates.
수상자는 200인 후보자 가운데서 뽑혔다.

successor
[səksésər]

상속자, 후계자 (one who follows another or one that succeeds, as to a throne, title, estate, or office)

Retiring from office, the mayor left a budget crisis and a transit strike to his *successor*.
퇴직한 시장은 후계자에게 예산위기와 운송파업을 남겼다.

symposium
[simpóuziəm]

심포지움, 향연, 토론회 (meeting for discussion of a subject)

\<syn\> conference, parley, panel discussion, round table, debate

They listened to a television *symposium* on the subject of better schools.
그들은 더 나은 학교라는 주제의 텔레비전 토론을 시청하였다.

synthesis
[sínθəsis]

통합, 합성 (combination of parts into a whole)

Photo*synthesis* is the process of making plant food from air and water, with the aid of sunlight.
광합성은 태양광선의 도움으로 공기와 물로 식물의 영양분을 만들어 가는 과정이다.

thesaurus
[θisɔ́ːrəs]

동의어 사전 (dictionary of synonyms)

A good *thesaurus* distinguishes the shades of meaning among words with similar definitions.
좋은 동의어사전은 비슷한 정의를 가진 단어들의 미묘한 차이점을 구분하고 있다.

thesis
[θíːsis]

논문; 명제

\<syn\> essay, paper, dissertation; proposition, proposal, argument

He completed his doctorial *thesis*.
그는 자신의 박사학위논문을 완성하였다.

transcript
[trǽnskript]

베낀 것, 사본 (written, printed, or typed copy)

The court reporter read from the *transcript* of the witness's testimony.
법원서기는 증인의 증언 사본을 읽었다.

verdict
[vɜ́ːrdikt]

(배심원의) 평결, 결정 (especially a legal judgement of guilt or innocence)

\<syn\> decision, judgement, determination, opinion

In our legal system, the *verdict* of a jury in convicting a defendant must be unanimous.
우리 법률체계상 피고에게 유죄를 선고하는 배심원의 평결은 만장일치라야 한다.

verity
[vérəti]

참, 진실 (the quality of being real or actual)

\<syn\> truthfulness, honesty, reality, veracity

The *verity* of the document could not be questioned.
문서의 진실성은 의문의 여지가 없었다.

vitality
[vaitǽləti]

생명력, 활력

\<syn\> life, life-force, strength, energy, liveliness, power to survive
\<ant\> lifelessness, lethargy, torpor, listlessness, apathy

She had been physically active all her life and at the age of eighty still possessed great *vitality*.
그녀는 평생 육체적으로 활동적이었으니 80세인데도 대단한 활력을 지니고 있다.

zeal
[zi:l]

열성, 열의, 열정

\<syn\> ardor, eagerness, fervor, enthusiasm, earnestness, zest
\<ant\> apathy, indifference, impassivity

He left a record for *zeal* that cannot fail to be an inspiration.
그는 감화 되기에 충분한, 열정의 기록을 남겼다.

zenith
[zí:niθ]

천정 (point in the sky directly overhead; twelve o'clock high)
정점 (peak, highest point, pinnacle, acme, summit, apex)

The sun reaches its *zenith* at noon.
태양이 정오에 천정에 있다.

STEP 1 Practice Test 2

DIRECTIONS Select the word or phrase that means most nearly the same as the key word.

1 access
   (A) approach   (B) openness
   (C) recess   (D) expect

2 alibi
   (A) foreigner   (B) excuse
   (C) restraint   (D) answer

3 altitude
   (A) descent   (B) height
   (C) haughtiness   (D) depth

4 breach
   (A) extenuate   (B) attenuate
   (C) gap   (D) bridge

5 capitol
   (A) wealth   (B) investment
   (C) headquarters (D) building

6 censure
   (A) retirement   (B) hundredth
   (C) affirmation   (D) blame

7 concept
   (A) idea   (B) belief
   (C) wish   (D) dream

ANSWER

1. (A) 접근 (B) 열림
   (C) 휴식 (D) 기대하다

2. (A) 외국인 (B) 변명
   (C) 금지, 억제 (D) 대답

3. (A) 하강, 내리막 (B) 높이
   (C) 오만함 (D) 깊이

4. (A) 경감하다
   (B) 묽게 하다, 엷게 하다
   (C) 틈새, 간격 (D) 다리

5. (A) 부 (B) 투자
   (C) 본부 (D) 건물

6. (A) 은퇴 (B) 100번째
   (C) 주장, 단언 (D) 비난

7. (A) 생각, 개념 (B) 신념
   (C) 소망 (D) 꿈

1. (B) 2. (B) 3. (B) 4. (C)
5. (D) 6. (D) 7. (A)

8 cognition
   (A) recollection   (B) memory
   (C) synthesis   (D) perception

9 demagogue
   (A) teacher   (B) manipulative leader
   (C) wily politician   (D) populist

10 dilemma
   (A) joke   (B) two-sided
   (C) problem   (D) half-baked

11 innovation
   (A) revolution   (B) retardation
   (C) expectation (D) change

12 irony
   (A) indurate   (B) opposite meaning
   (C) malleable (D) slow-wittedness

13 longevity
   (A) measurement of length
   (B) jollity
   (C) long life
   (D) far-sightedness

14 morale
   (A) standards of conduct (B) made of tin
   (C) customs   (D) level of spirits

15 paradigm
   (A) spasm   (B) model
   (C) confusion (D) matriarch

| ANSWER |

8. (A) 회상 (B) 기억
   (C) 합성 (D) 인지

9. (A) 교사 (B) 속임수의 지도자
   (C) 교활한 정치가 (D) 인민주의자

10. (A) 농담 (B) 양면의
    (C) 문제 (D) 반쯤 구운, 미완의

11. (A) 혁명 (B) 지연
    (C) 기대 (D) 변화

12. (A) 굳어진 (B) 반대의 의미
    (C) 늘일 수 있는, 연성의
    (D) 머리가 둔함

13. (A) 길이 측정 (B) 명랑
    (C) 장수 (D) 원시의, 먼 눈이 밝은

14. (A) 행동의 기준 (B) 양철로 만들어진
    (C) 관습 (D) 정신력의 단계

15. (A) 경련, 발작 (B) 모범
    (C) 혼돈 (D) 여성가장

8. (D) 9. (B) 10. (C) 11. (D)
12. (B) 13. (C) 14. (D) 15. (B)

16　perception
　　(A) tangent　　　　(B) sensory impression
　　(C) indoctrination　(D) sensation

17　nihilism
　　(A) disbelief　　　(B) death
　　(C) socialism　　　(D) conversation

18　precedent
　　(A) ancestor　　　(B) similar past event
　　(C) antebellum　　(D) standing before

19　ratio
　　(A) proportion　　(B) height
　　(C) duplicity　　　(D) division

20　synthesis
　　(A) phony
　　(B) collection
　　(C) combination of parts into whole
　　(D) splitting

21　query
　　(A) question　　　(B) quarrel
　　(C) quorum　　　 (D) quadrant

22　zeal
　　(A) freedom　　　(B) fear
　　(C) fervor　　　　(D) forgiveness

| ANSWER |

16. (A) 접촉하는 (B) 감각적 느낌
　　(C) 교육, 주입 (D) 감동, 흥분

17. (A) 불신 (B) 죽음
　　(C) 사회주의 (D) 대화

18. (A) 조상 (B) 유사한 과거 사건
　　(C) (미국) 남북전쟁 이전의
　　(D) 앞에 서 있는

19. (A) 비율 (B) 높이
　　(C) 표리부동 (D) 나누기

20. (A) 가짜의 (B) 수집
　　(C) 부분을 전체로 통합 (D) 분열

21. (A) 질문 (B) 싸움
　　(C) (의결에 필요한) 정족수
　　(D) 사분원(四分圓)

22. (A) 자유 (B) 공포
　　(C) 열정, 열의 (D) 용서

16. (B)　17. (A)　18. (B)　19. (A)
20. (C)　21. (A)　22. (C)

STEP 1
adjective & adverb
형용사 & 부사

adaptable
[ədǽptəbəl]

새로운 환경에 잘 적응하는

\<syn\> adjustable, applicable, flexible
\<ant\> inflexible, nonadjustable, fixed

Thanks to the intelligence that has made technology possible, humans are more *adaptable* to a variety of climates than any other species.
기술을 가능케 한 지능 덕분에, 인간은 다른 종보다 기후변화에 더 적응을 잘한다.

adequate
[ǽdikwit]

충분한

\<syn\> sufficient, enough, ample, satisfactory
\<ant\> inadequate, unsatisfactory, insufficient

Without *adequate* sunlight, many tropical plants will not bloom.
충분한 햇빛이 없으면 많은 열대식물들이 꽃을 피우지 못할 것이다.

adverse
[ædvə́ːrs]

반대의, 역의

\<syn\> opposing, contrary, unfavorable
\<ant\> favorable, helpful, supporting

Adverse winds are a hazard to sailing craft.
역풍은 돛배에는 하나의 위험요소이다.

amicable
[ǽmikəbəl]

우호적인, 친화적인

\<syn\> friendly, amiable, amenable, cordial
\<ant\> unfriendly, hostile, disagreeable

Courts often seek to settle civil suits in an *amicable* manner.
법원은 흔히 민사소송들을 우호적인 방식으로 해결하도록 모색한다.

annual
[ǽnjuəl]

일년의, 해마다의, 연례의

<syn> yearly, once a year
The company holds an *annual* picnic on the Fourth of July.
회사는 매년 7월 4일에 소풍을 간다.

anonymous
[ənánəməs]

익명의

<syn> bearing no name, unsigned, unidentified, nameless
<ant> named, signed, identified, known
Little credence should be given to an *anonymous* accusation.
신용이 없으면 익명의 고발을 받게 된다.

anterior
[æntíəriər]

전방의, 앞선

<syn> before in time, prior, toward the front
<ant> posterior, rear, back
The *anterior* section of the boy's brain was damaged in the accident.
소년의 뇌 앞부분이 사고로 손상되었다.

astral
[ǽstrəl]

별의, 별과 관련된

<syn> relating to the stars, starry
The number of *astral* bodies is beyond computation.
천체의 수는 헤아릴 수 없다.

aural
[ɔ́:rəl]

귀의, 청취의, 음향의

<syn> of the ear, acoustic
Since the sound system was not working properly, the *aural* aspect of the performance was a disappointment.
사운드시스템이 제대로 작동하지 않아서 공연의 음향부분은 실망이었다.

blithe
[blaið]

즐거운, 유쾌한

<syn> joyous, merry, cheerful, happy
<ant> sad, unhappy, gloomy, melancholy
Her *blithe* spirit provided an air of gaiety to the whole event.
그녀의 쾌활한 성격이 전체 행사에 활기를 주었다.

capital
[kǽpitl]

주요한 (n. 자본, 수도, 대문자)

<syn> adj. most significant, excellent, great
       n. wealth, funds, resource; chief city; large letter
That was a *capital* idea! An outlay of capital is necessary when starting a business.
그거 훌륭한 생각이로군! 사업을 시작할 때는 자본금이 필요해.

carnivorous
[kɑːrnívərəs]

육식의, 육식성의

<syn> flesh-eating, meat-eating
<ant> herbivorous, vegetarian

Tigers are among the *carnivorous* animals.
호랑이는 육식동물에 속한다.

coherent
[kouhíərənt]

조리 있는, 일관성 있는

<syn> logically connected, consistent, congruous
<ant> illogical, disconnected, rambling

They were too distraught to give a *coherent* account of the crash.
그들은 너무 괴로워서 그 사고에 대해 일관된 설명을 할 수 없었다.

comprehensible
[kàmprihénsəbəl]

이해할 수 있는 (able to be understood)

The episode was only *comprehensible* to those who knew the story thus far.
그 에피소드는 지금까지 그 이야기를 알고 있는 사람들에게는 이해가 되는 것이었다.

concise
[kənsáis]

간결한

<syn> belief, short, terse, to the point, abbreviated
<ant> rambling, discursive, wordy

A pr cis must be *concise* yet cover the topic.
개요는 간결하지만 주제를 담고 있어야 한다.

conscientious
[kànʃiénʃəs]

양심적인, 성실한

<syn> honest, faithful, scrupulous
<ant> unconscientious, unreliable, careless

He is *conscientious* in his work and so has won the trust of his employers.
그는 자기 일에 충실하고 그래서 고용주들의 신임을 얻고 있다.

cosmopolitan
[kàzməpálətən]

세계의, 세계적인

<syn> worldly, worldly-wise, international

New York is a *cosmopolitan* city, but many midwest cities are not.
뉴욕은 국제도시이지만, 많은 중서부 도시들은 그렇지 않다.

credible
[krédəbəl]

신뢰할 수 있는, 확실한

<syn> believable, plausible, reliable, trustworthy,
<ant> incredible, unbelievable, unreliable

The tale, though unusual, was entirely *credible*, considering the physical evidence.
그 이야기는 비록 생소했지만 물리적인 증거를 고려할 때 아주 확실하였다.

credulous
[krédʒələs]

쉽게 믿는, 속기 쉬운

<syn> inclined to believe, easily convinced, gullible, too trustful
<ant> uncredulous, unbelieving, suspicious, cynical

The *credulous* woman followed every instruction of the fortuneteller.
남의 말을 쉽게 믿는 그 여자는 점쟁이의 모든 말을 따랐다.

destitute
[déstətjùːt]

결핍한, 빈곤한

<syn> in extreme want, poor, needy, indigent, penniless
<ant> rich, affluent, opulent, wealthy

Even the most *destitute* person has hope for the future.
아무리 빈곤한 사람도 미래에 대한 희망을 가지고 있다.

discordant
[diskɔ́ːrdənt]

조화하지 않는, 각기 다른, 불협화음의

<syn> harsh, not harmonious, disputable, conflicting
<ant> harmonious, consonant, accord

The *discordant* cries of wild birds may make summer vacationers long for the familiar sounds of the city.
들새들의 조화롭지 않은 울음소리는 여름 여행객들로 하여금 도시의 익숙한 소리를 그리워하게 만들기도 한다.

dynamic
[dainǽmik]

역동적인

<syn> in motion, forceful, energetic, active, vigorous, vital

A *dynamic* leader can inspire followers with enthusiasm and confidence.
역동적인 지도자는 추종자들에게 열정과 자신감을 불어줄 수 있다.

egocentric
[ìːgouséntrik]

자기중심적인, 이기적인 (self-centered)

The *egocentric* individual has little regard for the feelings of others.
이기적인 사람은 다른 사람들의 감정을 거의 고려하지 않는다.

ethical
[éθikəl]

윤리적인, 도덕상의

\<syn\> moral, decent, virtuous
\<ant\> underhanded, shady, unfair, immoral, indecent

Although many members of his administration were corrupt, he adhered to strong *ethical* principles.
정부의 많은 구성원들이 부패했지만, 그는 강한 도덕적 원칙을 고수하였다.

fallible
[fæləbəl]

틀리기 쉬운, 속기 쉬운

\<syn\> capable of erring, being deceived in judgment, imperfect, frail
\<ant\> infallible, perfect, divine

All men are *fallible*.
모든 인간은 실수를 한다.

finite
[fáinait]

유한한, 한정된

\<syn\> having a limit, bounded, measurable, countable, confined
\<ant\> infinite, unlimited, unbounded, endless

There were only a *finite* number of men to be considered.
고려할 수 있는 사람은 한정된 몇 사람밖에 없었다.

flammable
[flǽməbəl]

가연성의, 불타기 쉬운

\<syn\> inflammable, combustible
\<ant\> nonflammable

They were careful to keep the material away from the sparks because it was *flammable*.
그들은 가연성인 그 물질을 불꽃에서 멀리하도록 주의하였다.

ignoble
[ignóubəl]

비천한, 천박한

\<syn\> dishonorable, shameful, mean
\<ant\> admirable, sublime, honorable

The *ignoble* purpose of his slander multiplied the crime.
그가 하는 비방의 천박한 목적은 범죄를 배가시켰다.

incessant
[insésənt]

끊임없는, 그칠 새 없는

\<syn\> unceasing, uninterrupted, continual, constant
\<ant\> intermittent, periodic, occasional, sporadic

The *incessant* rain kept the children indoors all day.
그치지 않는 비가 아이들을 하루 종일 집안에 있게 하였다.

integral
[íntigrəl]

완전한, 빠질 수 없는, 필수의

<syn> necessary to the whole, essential, indispensible, requisite
<ant> peripheral, unessential, unnecessary, unimportant

Alaska is an *integral* part of the United States.
알래스카는 미국의 빠질 수 없는 부분이다.

intensive
[inténsiv]

강화된, 집중적인, 철저한

<syn> concentrated, intense, powerful, strong
<ant> subdued, relaxed, easy, moderate

Intensive private tutoring is needed to take care of this student's reading problem.
그 학생의 독서 문제점을 보살피기 위해서는 철저한 개인지도가 필요하다.

inverse
[invə́:rs]

반대의, 역의

<syn> in reversed position, reversed, back to front, converse, backward
<ant> forward, direct

Double-check by reading the figures in *inverse* order.
역순으로 인물들을 읽음으로써 재확인하라.

judicial
[dʒu:díʃəl]

사법적인, 재판에 관련된

<syn> judiciary, jurisdictional, juristic, legal

Chief Justice of the Supreme Court is the highest *judicial* position in the United States.
대법원의 재판장은 미국에서 가장 높은 사법적 지위이다.

kindred
[kíndrid]

혈연의, 친족관계인; 유사한, 같은

<syn> alike, allied, closely related, similar
<ant> alien, unrelated, uncongenial, different

Though from diverse backgrounds, they were *kindred* spirits, alike in intellect and ambition.
다양한 배경 출신임에도 그들은 지식과 야망이 같은 친족 같은 사람들이다.

laudable
[lɔ́:dəbəl]

칭찬할 만한, 장한, 기특한

<syn> praiseworthy, estimable, admirable, commendable
<ant> contemptible, lowly, unworthy, ignoble

The girl listened to the old man's endless and repetitive stories with *laudable* patience.
소녀는 노인의 끝없이 반복되는 이야기를 기특한 인내심으로 들어주었다.

legible
[lédʒəbəl]

읽기 쉬운, 명료한

<syn> written clearly, able to be read, plain, visible, clear
<ant> illegible, unreadable, unclear, indistinct

Please print or type if your handwriting is not easily *legible*.
자네 손 글씨가 알아보기 어렵다면 인쇄나 타이프를 치게.

legitimate
[lidʒítəmit]

합법적인, 정당한

<syn> lawful, rightful, true, legal; genuine, justified, logical
<ant> unlawful, illegal, fraudulent, false; unjustified, unfair

The government of the country is *legitimate*.
그 나라의 정부는 합법적이다.

lucid
[lú:sid]

투명한, 명료한, 알기 쉬운, 두뇌가 명석한

<syn> clear, transparent, bright, easily understand, intelligible
<ant> dark, gloomy, obscure, vague, unclear

The directions were written in a style so *lucid* that a child could follow them.
어린이가 따라할 수 있도록 안내문이 아주 알기 쉽게 씌어졌다.

maximum
[mǽksəməm]

최대한의

<syn> most, greatest possible, greatest utmost, top, highest, maximal
<ant> minimum, minimal, least possible, least

In this course the *maximum* number of cuts allowed is six.
이 코스에서 허용되는 지름길의 최대의 수는 여섯 개이다.

median
[mí:diən]

중간의

<syn> middle, middle item in a series

In a series of seven items, the fourth is the *median*.
연속되는 일곱 개 가운데서 네 번째가 중간이다.

minute
[mainjúːt]

미세한, 정밀한; 상세한, 세심한

<syn> very small, tiny, very precise, imperceptible, diminutive, infinitesimal

The device records the presence of even minute amounts of radiation.
그 장치는 아주 미세한 양의 방사능까지도 기록한다.

The writer's *minute* attention to the refinements of style resulted in an elegantly worded essay.
문체를 다듬는 작가의 세심한 주의가 우아한 표현의 에세이를 낳았다.

negative
[négətiv]

부정적인, 소극적인

<syn> implying refusal, disapproving, rejecting, opposed
<ant> affirmative, positive, assenting

I received a *negative* answer to my request.
나는 나의 요청에 대한 부정적인 대답을 받았다.

neurotic
[njuərátik]

신경의, 신경증의

<syn> nervous, anxious, psychoneurotic, unstable, disturbed

Hysterical pain — physical discomfort without organic cause — is a common *neurotic* symptom.
히스테리성 질환은 유기적 원인이 없는 신체적 불안으로, 일반적인 신경증세이다.

objective
[əbdʒéktiv]

adj. 객관적인, 편견 없는

<syn> unbiased, impartial, unprejudiced, detached
<ant> subjective, personal, biased, prejudiced, unjust

It is extremely difficult to be *objective* about one's own weaknesses.
자신의 약점에 대하여 객관적이 되기란 아주 어렵다.

n. 목적, 목표, 객체

<syn> aim, goal, purpose, object, intent

Our *objective* is greater efficiency; we must study the possible means to that goal.
우리의 목표는 더 큰 효율성이다. 우리는 그 목적으로 가는 가능한 수단들을 연구해야 한다.

obscure
[əbskjúər]

어두운, 분명치 않은, 모호한

\<syn\> dim, murky, not easily understood, abstruse, unclear, vague
\<ant\> clear, lucid, plain, manifest

His message was *obscure*.
그의 메시지는 모호하였다.

occidental
[ùksədéntl]

서양의, 구미의

\<syn\> western
\<ant\> oriental, eastern

The finest gems come from *occidental* countries, according to some experts.
일부 전문가들에 따르면, 가장 멋진 보석들은 서양에서 온다.

optional
[ápʃənəl]

임의의, 선택적인

\<syn\> not required, open to choice, individually decided
\<ant\> mandatory, obligatory, required

Air conditioning is *optional*; its cost is not included in the sticker price.
에어컨은 선택사양이다. 그 비용이 가격표에 포함되지 않는다.

pacific
[pəsífik]

평온한

\<syn\> calm, tranquil, placid

The *Pacific* Ocean was so named by its discoverer because it was free from storms and tempests.
태평양이란 이름은 폭풍과 태풍이 없다는 이유로 발견자가 그렇게 붙였다.

panoramic
[pæ̀nərǽmik]

파노라마 같은 (offering a broad or unlimited view)

From the summit of the mountain one has a *panoramic* view of the whole range.
산 정상에서는 산 전체의 파노라마 같은 모습을 보게 된다.

partisan
[pɑ́ːrtəzən]

당파심이 강한 (n. 한동아리, 도당, 빨치산)

\<syn\> favoring one political party, predisposed toward one group

Partisan loyalty can no longer be taken for granted; voters are now attracted to individuals more than to parties.
당파적 충성심은 더 이상 당연한 것으로 수용될 수 없다. 유권자들은 이제 정당보다는 개인에 더 이끌린다.

patent
[pǽtənt]

adj. 특허권을 가진, 명백한, 빤한

<syn> obvious, easily seen, manifest, evident, trademarked, copyrighted

The promise of tax relief was a *patent* attempt to win last-minute support from the farmers.
감세 약속은 농부들로부터 막판 지원을 얻기 위한 빤한 시도였다.

n. 특허

<syn> exclusive right, registry, license, permit

The company's *patent* on the formula expires after a certain number of years.
그 제조법에 대한 회사의 특허는 몇 년이 지나면 소멸된다.

potential
[pouténʃəl]

잠재적인, 가능성이 있는

<syn> possible, conceivable, latent, concealed, not yet realized
<ant> actual, real, manifest

If she qualifies for the promotion, her *potential* earnings for the next year might be close to $20,000.
그녀가 진급할 자격이 되려면 그녀의 잠재적인 내년 수익이 20,000달러에 가까워야 할 것이다.

precise
[prisáis]

정확한, 정밀한

<syn> exact, specific, strict, accurate, incisive
<ant> inexact, implicit, vague, indistinct

The coroner determined the *precise* time of murder by examining the victim.
검시관은 희생자를 부검하여 정확한 살해시각을 결정하였다.

prejudiced
[prédʒədist]

편파적인, 편견을 가진

<syn> biased, slanted, one-sided, partial
<ant> unprejudiced, fair

Since I have never liked westerns, I was *prejudiced* against the film before I ever saw it.
나는 서구인들을 좋아하지 않았기 때문에, 보기 전까지는 그 영화에 대해 편견을 가지고 있었다.

principal
[prínsəpəl]

주요한, 제1의

<syn> main, most important, chief
<ant> least important, minor, secondary

The *principal* city economically is also the most populous in the state.
경제적으로 주요한 그 도시는 그 주에서 인구가 가장 많기도 하다.

psychic
[sáikik]

마음의, 심적인 (of the mind, acting outside of known physical laws)

<syn> of the mind, mental, psychological, cerebral, spiritual

He claimed special *psychic* powers, including the ability to foresee the future.
그는 미래를 내다보는 능력을 포함한 특별한 정신적인 능력을 주장하였다.

secure
[sikjúər]

adj. 확실한, 안전한, 안심하는

<syn> safe, reliable, free from fear or danger, protected
<ant> unsafe, endangered, threatened, unsure

Her *secure* job assured her of a steady income for as long as she chose to work.
확실한 직장은 그녀가 일을 하고자 하는 동안은 지속적인 수입을 보장해 주었다.

v. 안전하게 하다, 보증하다; 획득하다, 얻다

<syn> make safe, defend, free from harm; obtain, acquire
<ant> endanger, imperil, harm; lose, give up

I have *secured* two tickets for tonight's performance.
나는 오늘밤의 공연 티켓을 두 장 얻었다.

stoical
[stóuikəl]

스토아학파의, 금욕주의의, 냉철한, 자제력이 강한 (showing calm fortitude)

<syn> stoic, detached, impassive, unruffled
<ant> uncontrolled, undisciplined, excitable, emotional

He was *stoical* in the face of great misfortunes.
그는 대단히 불운한 얼굴의 냉철한 모습이었다.

ultimately
[ˈʌltəmitli]

궁극적으로, 결국, 드디어 (as a final result, at last)

Afflictions may *ultimately* prove to be blessings.
고생은 나중에 복이 될 수 있다.

unethical
[ənéθikəl]

비도덕적인 (without or not according to moral principles)

<syn> unprincipled, dishonorable, disputable

Although he did not break any law, the man's conduct in taking advantage of credulous clients was certainly *unethical*.
그 남자가 어떤 법률을 위반하지는 않았더라도 믿고 있는 고객들을 이용한 그의 행동은 확실히 비도덕적이다.

uniform
[júːnəfɔːrm]

한결같은, 균일한 (not varying in degree or rate, consistent at all times)

<syn> equal, unvarying, unchanging
<ant> uneven, unequal, variable

Most countries do not have a *uniform* temperature.
대부분의 나라들은 기온이 한결같지 않다.

vain
[vein]

헛된, 보람 없는

<syn> unsuccessful, futile, idle, worthless, ineffective
<ant> successful, useful, fruitful, effective

They tried *vainly* to win the game.
그들은 경기에 이기려고 헛되이 애를 썼다.

variable
[vέəriəbəl]

변하기 쉬운

<syn> changing, fluctuating, shifting
<ant> constant, unchanging, stable

The weather report stated that the winds would be *variable*.
바람이 변덕스럽게 불 것이라는 일기예보가 발표되었다.

STEP 1 Practice Test 3

DIRECTIONS Select the word or phrase that means most nearly the same as the key word.

1 adverse
(A) uncomfortable (B) contrary
(C) moving toward (D) lateral

2 amicable
(A) peace-loving (B) lively
(C) friendly (D) pensive

3 anonymous
(A) ubiquitous (B) unsigned
(C) affectionate (D) cryptic

4 anterior
(A) inside (B) outside
(C) lower parts (D) front

5 aural
(A) acoustic (B) golden
(C) spoken (D) astral

6 astral
(A) of the earth (B) of the sea
(C) of the sun (D) of the stars

7 blithe
(A) cheerful (B) thin
(C) addle-brained (D) stubborn

| ANSWER |

1. (A) 불편한 (B) 반대의
   (C) 전진하는 (D) 측면의

2. (A) 평화적인 (B) 발랄하게
   (C) 우호적인 (D) 생각에 잠긴

3. (A) 도처에 있는
   (B) 날인하지 않은
   (C) 다정한, 애정 깊은
   (D) 숨은, 비밀의

4. (A) 안의 (B) 밖의
   (C) 아래 부분 (D) 앞의

5. (A) 음향의 (B) 황금의
   (C) 구어의 (D) 별의

6. (A) 지구의 (B) 바다의
   (C) 태양의 (D) 별의

7. (A) 즐거운 (B) 얇은
   (C) 우둔한 (D) 고집 센

1. (B) 2. (C) 3. (B) 4. (D)
5. (A) 6. (D) 7. (A)

8 coherent
(A) connected (B) sticky
(C) attentive (D) absent

9 conscientious
(A) honest (B) pensive
(C) objectionable (D) mitigated

10 comprehensible
(A) tenable (B) understandable
(C) affable (D) defensible

11 concise
(A) biting (B) credible
(C) minute (D) brief

12 cosmopolitan
(A) worldly (B) urbane
(C) extraterrestrial (D) citizen

13 credible
(A) believable (B) dubious
(C) ingenuous (D) factual

14 credulous
(A) trustworthy (B) gullible
(C) believable (D) fatuous

15 dynamic
(A) theoretical (B) requiring electricity
(C) dormant (D) energetic

16 flammable
(A) fire-proof
(B) kiln-dried
(C) capable of being ignited
(D) igneous

| ANSWER |

8. (A) 연관된 (B) 집착하는
   (C) 주의 깊은 (D) 결석한

9. (A) 정직한 (B) 시름에 잠긴
   (C) 반대할 만한 (D) 완화시키다

10. (A) 견딜 수 있는 (B) 이해할 수 있는
    (C) 친절한 (D) 방어할 수 있는

11. (A) 날카로운, 신랄한 (B) 믿을 수 있는
    (C) 상세한 (D) 간결한

12. (A) 세계의 (B) 도시의
    (C) 외계의 (D) 시민의

13. (A) 믿을 수 있는 (B) 의심스러운
    (C) 솔직한, 성실한 (D) 사실의

14. (A) 믿을 수 있는 (B) 속기 쉬운
    (C) 믿을 수 있는 (D) 어리석은

15. (A) 이론적인 (B) 전기를 필요로 하는
    (C) 정지한 (D) 역동적인

16. (A) 방화의 (B) 인공 건조시킨
    (C) 불이 붙을 수 있는
    (D) 불의, 화성의

8. (A) 9. (A) 10. (B) 11. (D) 12. (A)
13. (A) 14. (B) 15. (D) 16. (C)

17 fallible
(A) capable of error
(B) false
(C) falling
(D) capable of crumbling

18 incessant
(A) continuous (B) concurrent
(C) calcified   (D) chattering

19 introvert
(A) turn inward (B) revolving
(C) turn away   (D) open-minded

20 inverse
(A) turn back   (B) implosion
(C) reversed   (D) difficult

21 integral
(A) unknowable (B) intense
(C) necessary   (D) wholesome

22 kindred
(A) related (B) one thousandth
(C) teased   (D) approximate

23 lucid
(A) ridiculous   (B) lightweight
(C) transparent (D) not bound

24 median
(A) middle
(B) maximum
(C) foreign
(D) poorly constructed

| ANSWER |

17. (A) 실수할 수 있는 (B) 틀린
    (C) 떨어지는 (D) 가루로 만들 수 있는

18. (A) 계속되는 (B) 동시발생의
    (C) 석회질화된 (D) 재잘거리는

19. (A) 내부로 향한 (B) 회전식의
    (C) 거절하다 (D) 열린 마음의

20. (A) 돌아가다 (B) 내파(내부파쇄요법)
    (C) 반대의 (D) 어려운

21. (A) 알 수 없는 (B) 강렬한
    (C) 필수의 (D) 전체의

22. (A) 관계된 (B) 1000번째
    (C) 괴롭히다 (D) 대략의

23. (A) 웃기는 (B) 가벼운
    (C) 투명한 (D) 얽매이지 않은

24. (A) 중간의 (B) 최대의
    (C) 외국의 (D) 부실하게 건설된

17. (A) 18. (A) 19. (A) 20. (C)
21. (C) 22. (A) 23. (C) 24. (A)

25 legitimate
 (A) readable (B) allowable
 (C) genuine (D) voted for

26 maximum
 (A) total (B) median
 (C) average (D) most

27 panoramic
 (A) multilingual (B) wheezy
 (C) goat-like (D) unlimited view

28 patent
 (A) shiny (B) obvious
 (C) hospitalized (D) relaxed

29 obscure
 (A) powerful (B) threatening
 (C) murky (D) preoccupied

30 partisan
 (A) devoted to a cause (B) many-colored
 (C) dubious (D) fragmented

31 principal
 (A) delegate (B) main
 (C) belief (D) potentate

32 stoical
 (A) frivolous (B) morbid
 (C) calmly strong (D) worried

33 variable
 (A) multiplied (B) many-parted
 (C) changing (D) stable

| ANSWER |

25. (A) 읽을 수 있는 (B) 허용되는
 (C) 진짜의, 진정한
 (D) …에게 투표하다

26. (A) 종합의 (B) 중간의
 (C) 평균의 (D) 최대의

27. (A) 다중언어의 (B) 헐떡거리는
 (C) 염소 같은, 호색인 (D) 끝없는 장면

28. (A) 빛나는 (B) 명백한
 (C) 입원한 (D) 이완된

29. (A) 강력한 (B) 위협적인
 (C) 어두운, 음울한 (D) 몰두한, 열중한

30. (A) 어떤 목적에 열중한
 (B) 다양한 색의
 (C) 의심스러운
 (D) 분해된, 파편이 된

31. (A) 대표하다, 위임하다 (B) 주된
 (C) 신념 (D) 권력가, 유력자

32. (A) 경솔한, 진지하지 못한
 (B) 병적인, 음침한
 (C) 조용히 강한 (D) 걱정하는

33. (A) 증식된, 증가된
 (B) 많은 조각으로 나뉜
 (C) 변화하는 (D) 정적인

25. (C) 26. (D) 27. (D) 28. (B) 29. (C)
30. (A) 31. (B) 32. (C) 33. (C)

Mastery Test 1

[Synonym Test]

DIRECTIONS Choose the word or phrase that means most nearly the same as the key word or the underlined word.

1. The word <u>diversity</u> means most nearly
   - (A) similarity
   - (B) value
   - (C) triviality
   - (D) variety

2. degraded
   - (A) unassorted
   - (B) declassified
   - (C) receded
   - (D) debased

3. coherent
   - (A) not clear
   - (B) courteous
   - (C) specific
   - (D) logically related

4. ideology
   - (A) subversive philosophy
   - (B) body of opinions
   - (C) science of thought processes
   - (D) belief in perfection

5. ignoble
   - (A) disowned
   - (B) mean
   - (C) disinherited
   - (D) unknowing

6. laudable
   - (A) arrogant
   - (B) clean
   - (C) boisterous
   - (D) praiseworthy

7. legible

(A) printed (B) allowed
(C) type   (D) readable

8. He was asked to pacify the visitor. The word pacify means most nearly

(A) escort   (B) interview
(C) calm   (D) detain

9. yearn

(A) crave   (B) gape
(C) feel sleepy (D) feel bored

10. supervise

(A) acquire (B) oppress
(C) oversee (D) restrain

11. uniformity

(A) costume (B) sameness
(C) custom   (D) boredom

12. He wishes to terminate the conversation. The word terminate means most nearly

(A) end   (B) postpone
(C) ignore (D) continue

13. A recurring problem is one that

(A) replaces a problem that existed previously
(B) is unexpected
(C) has long been overlooked
(D) comes up from time to time

] Antonym Test [

DIRECTIONS Choose the word or phrase that is most nearly opposite in meaning to the given word.

1. except
   - (A) receive
   - (B) anticipate
   - (C) admit
   - (D) deliver

2. finite
   - (A) regulated
   - (B) ending
   - (C) selfish
   - (D) limitless

3. objective
   - (A) biased
   - (B) personal
   - (C) aimless
   - (D) eastern

4. submission
   - (A) authorization
   - (B) defiance
   - (C) assignment
   - (D) defeat

Sentence Completion Test

DIRECTIONS Select the word or phrase that will best complete the meaning of the sentence as a whole.

1. Because Mayor Koch finished the speech in less than three minutes, those present applauded his _____.
   - (A) brevity
   - (B) allusions
   - (C) timeliness
   - (D) sense of humor

2. _____ cannot exist within a democracy, which is a structured form of government.
   (A) Anarchy   (B) Repression
   (C) Socialism   (D) Liberalism

3. Unfortunately these favorable influences can be expected to _____ or even disappear within the next few years.
   (A) multiply   (B) recur
   (C) abate   (D) vanish

4. Because the custom posed a danger to the children, the leaders of the community decided to _____ it.
   (A) implement   (B) abolish
   (C) fulfill   (D) continue

5. Because they offer a diversion from the more serious aspects of everyday life, stamp and coin collecting are _____.
   (A) avocations   (B) adulterous
   (C) adventurous   (D) enlightening

6. A great invention often occurs in a moment of insight, or _____.
   (A) recognition   (B) relativity
   (C) cognizance   (D) relevance

7. The _____ couple pleaded for help from holiday shoppers.
   (A) desultory   (B) destitute
   (C) maverick   (D) wealthy

8. The tendency to be totally absorbed with one's own mental life is called _____.
   (A) introspection   (B) acoustics
   (C) stimulation   (D) introversion

9. The Political Action Committee sought to _____ the right-wing demonstrators from the more liberal rally.
   (A) detain   (B) exclude
   (C) deny   (D) exacerbate

10. The old man had the _____ to save money during his teaching career so as not to be dependent on irregular Social Security checks after his retirement.
    (A) thrift   (B) stinginess
    (C) foresight   (D) foretelling ability

11. According to one school of scientific thought, man, slowly adapting to his changing environment, _____ from the same species as the ape.
    (A) evolved   (B) evoked
    (C) everted   (D) reverted

12. A seemingly contradictory statement that may nonetheless be true is called a _____.
    (A) paradigm   (B) parallax
    (C) paradox   (D) paramour

13. We can _____ the payments over a longer period of time.
    (A) deduct   (B) protract
    (C) perpetrate   (D) abolish

14. The young father's taking of a second job in order to pay for his child's schooling was a praiseworthy, or _____, action.
    (A) laudable   (B) scornful
    (C) tiring   (D) foolish

15. Because the sun regularly rises at the same time of day from year to year, its apparent action can be said to be _____.
    (A) recurrent   (B) rectilinear
    (C) rampant   (D) reactionary

STEP 1 • Mastery Test 1 | 61

ENGLISH FORUM

1000 essential words that often appear on the TOEFL
Step 2

STEP 2

verb 동사
vocabulary 1000

abase
[əbéis]

값을 내리다, 지위를 낮추다, 굴욕을 주다

\<syn\> reduce, degrade, cast down
\<ant\> elevate, raise, uplift

The French Revolution *abased* the proud nobility.
프랑스혁명은 거만한 귀족들의 지위를 땅에 떨어뜨렸다.

abbreviate
[əbríːvièit]

짧게 줄이다

\<syn\> shorten, abridge, curtail
\<ant\> lengthen, extend, enlarge

When he saw that the meeting was running late, he *abbreviated* his comments.
회의가 길어지는 것을 알고, 그는 자신의 코멘트를 짧게 줄였다.

abhor
[æbhɔ́ːr]

몹시 싫어하다, 혐오하다, 거부하다

\<syn\> detest, hate, loathe, regard with horror or loathing
\<ant\> love, adore, like

The pacifist *abhors* war.
평화주의자는 전쟁을 혐오한다.

abominate
[əbámənèit]

혐오하다

\<syn\> loathe, hate, abhor
\<ant\> love, like, affect

I *abominate* all laws that deprive people of their rights.
나는 국민들의 권리를 빼앗는 모든 법률을 혐오한다.

abut
[əbʌ́t]

인접하다, 경계를 접하다

<syn> meet end to end, adjoin, adjacent to, next to

When estates *abut*, borders must be defined properly.
부동산들이 인접할 때는, 그 경계가 적절히 규정되어야 한다.

acclaim
[əkléim]

환호하다, 갈채를 보내다

<syn> applaud, approve loudly, greet with praise
<ant> criticise, denounce, condemn, disapprove

The crowd in the square *acclaimed* their hero as the new president.
광장의 군중들은 그들의 영웅을 새 대통령으로 환호하였다.

accumulate
[əkjú:mjəlèit]

모으다, 축적하다

<syn> gather, pile up, heap up, assemble
<ant> scatter, disperse, distribute

Over the years she has *accumulated* a large collection of antique bric-a-brac.
수년 간 그녀는 많은 골동품을 모았다.

adhere
[ædhíər]

고수하다, 집착하다, 신봉하다

<syn> hold, stick to, cling
<ant> come loose, detach, break with, part from

Many persons *adhere* to their beliefs despite all arguments.
많은 사람들이 모든 문제에도 불구하고 자기들 신념을 고수한다.

agitate
[ǽdʒətèit]

동요시키다, 흔들다, 부추기다

<syn> stir up, disturb, shake
<ant> calm, compose, pacify, quiet

Rumors of change in the government *agitated* the population.
정부가 바뀔 거라는 소문이 사람들을 동요시켰다.

alienate
[éiljənèit]

멀리하다, 소원하게 하다, 소외시키다

<syn> make inimical or indifferent, estrange, separate, divorce, turn away
<ant> make friendly, reconcile, draw close, turn to

One purpose of the offer to the East was to *alienate* the Western nations.
동방에 제안한 한 가지는 서방 국가들을 멀리하게 하는 것이었다.

alleviate
[əlíːvièit]

줄이다, 완화하다, 해소하다

<syn> lessen, make easier, relieve, mitigate
<ant> increase, make worse, aggravate, intensify

The morphine helped to *alleviate* the pain.
모르핀은 통증을 해소하는 데 도움을 주었다.

annul
[ənʌ́l]

폐지하다, 취소하다, 무효화하다

<syn> wipe out, make void, nullify, invalidate, cancel
<ant> validate, enact, perform

The Supreme Court can *annul* a law which is unconstitutional.
대법원은 위헌법률을 무효화할 수 있다.

ascribe
[əskráib]

…의 탓으로 돌리다, …에 기인하다

<syn> attribute, assign, charge to, accredit
<ant> discredit, deny, discount, dissociate

His death was *ascribed* to poison.
그의 죽음은 독약에 의한 것이었다.

assure
[əʃúər]

보장하다, 확신을 시키다, 보증하다

<syn> make something certain, guarantee;
        promise with confidence, make sure
<ant> deny, refute, disavow, disclaim, be uncertain

The fact that they left their tickets *assures* that they will return.
그들이 티켓을 남겼다는 사실은 그들이 돌아올 거라는 확신을 준다.
I *assured* her that someone would be there to meet her.
나는 그녀에게 누군가 그녀를 만나려고 거기 있을 거라고 확신하였다.

avert
[əvə́ːrt]

돌리다, 비키다, 피하다

<syn> turn aside, turn away, ward off, prevent
<ant> hold steady, allow, permit

By acting quickly we *averted* disaster.
재빨리 조치를 취함으로써 우리는 재난을 피했다.

burnish
[bə́ːrniʃ]

닦다, 갈다, 광내다

<syn> polish by rubbing, buff, shine, rub up
<ant> abrade, scratch, mar

Burnished metal will gleam in the light.
광을 낸 금속은 빛을 받으면 번쩍인다.

cede
[siːd]

인도하다, 양도하다, 허용하다

<syn> yield, assign, transfer, deliver, grant
<ant> keep, retain, withhold, hold back

A bill of sale will *cede* title of the property.
매도증서는 소유권을 양도할 것이다.

chide
[tʃaid]

꾸짖다

<syn> rebuke, scold, reproach
<ant> praise, commend, laud

Parents should *chide* a disobedient child.
부모들은 말 안 듣는 아이는 야단을 쳐야 한다.

cleave
[kliːv]

1. 주장을 고수하다, 힘을 합치다 (adhere)

   Let us *cleave* together. 우리 힘을 합칩시다.

2. 쪼개지다, 분열하다 (split asunder)

   The blow *cleaved* the limb in two. 강풍이 가지를 둘로 쪼갰다.

commission
[kəmíʃən]

임무를 부여하다, 위임하다, 위탁하다

<syn> authorize, empower, assign, delegate
<ant> release, fire, let go

I have commissioned a neighbor to collect he mail while I'm away.
나는 이웃에게 내가 없는 동안 우편물을 모아달라고 부탁하였다.

comprise
[kəmpráiz]

포함하다; 형성하다

<syn> include, contain, made up of, consist of, constitute

The test will be *comprised* of the subject matter of the previous lessons.
그 시험은 이전에 배운 단원들의 주제들로 구성될 것이다.

condole
[kəndóul]

위로하다, 애도하다

<syn> express sympathy, console, comfort
<ant> congratulate

His friends gather to *condole* his loss.
친구들이 와서 그의 손실을 위로하였다.

contrive
[kəntráiv]

연구하다, 고안하다, 설계하다

<syn> devise, invent, design, scheme, plot, plan

They *contrived* a way to fix the unit using old parts.
그들은 오래된 부품들을 활용하여 장치를 고정시키는 방법을 고안하였다.

convoke
[kənvóuk]

(회의를) 소집하다 (n. convocation 회의소집)

<syn> summon, call together, convene

The conference was *convoked* to consider amending the constitution of the organization.
조직 구성의 개정을 논의하기 위한 회의가 소집되었다.

debase
[dibéis]

떨어뜨리다, 저하시키다

<syn> reduce in dignity, degrade, defile, deteriorate
<ant> enhance, elevate, uplift, improve, heighten

Do not *debase* yourself by answering him.
그에게 대꾸해서 당신의 가치를 떨어뜨리지 마라.

deduce
[didjúːs]

연역하다, 추론하다

<syn> derive by reasoning, conclude, reason, infer

From the facts presented, we *deduce* this conclusion.
열거된 사실들로부터 우리는 이 결론을 추론한다.

degenerate
[didʒénərèit]

나빠지다, 타락하다

<syn> decline, deteriorate

The discussion eventually *degenerated* into a shouting match.
토론은 결국 고성이 오가는 싸움으로 타락하였다.

delegate
[déligit]

대표로 파견하다, 위임하다

<syn> designate, appoint as a representative, entrust, assign, charge

Since I will be unable to attend the conference, I have *delegated* my assistant to represent me.
내가 회의에 참석할 수 없어서 나를 대신해 내 조수를 파견하였다.

demean
[dimíːn]

품위를 떨어뜨리다, 천박하게 하다

<syn> degrade, debase, lower, humble, humiliate, shame
<ant> dignify, honor, glorify, elevate

Could you *demean* yourself by joining in their crude pastimes?
너는 그들의 유치한 취미활동에 가입해서 자신의 품위를 떨어뜨릴 수 있나?

depreciate
[deprí:ʃièit]

가치가 떨어지다, 하락하다

<syn> lessen in value, belittle, disparage, downgrade, denigrate, scorn
<ant> appreciate, cherish, esteem, prize

Property will *depreciate* rapidly unless kept in good repair.
물건은 수리를 잘하며 보관하지 않으면 금방 가치가 떨어진다.

deride
[diráid]

조소하다, 비웃다 (a. derisive 조소하는)

<syn> mock, laugh at, ridicule, scorn

Many would *deride* the street-corner preacher.
많은 사람들이 길거리 전도사를 비웃을 것이다.

detract
[ditrǽkt]

줄이다, 손상시키다, 주의를 돌리다

<syn> take away a part, lessen, diminish, reduce, lower, subtract from
<ant> increase, heighten, enhance, add to

The old-fashioned engraving *detracted* from the value of the piece of jewelry.
구식의 조각술이 보석의 가치를 떨어뜨렸다.

deviate
[dí:vièit]

벗어나다, 빗나가다, 일탈시키다

<syn> stray, turn aside from, go astray
<ant> continue, remain, stick to

The honest man will never *deviate* from the path of rectitude.
정직한 사람은 결코 정도를 벗어나지 않는다.

digress
[daigrés]

옆으로 벗어나다, 이탈하다

<syn> depart from the subject, stray, deviate, wander
<ant> proceed, advance, continue

To *digress* from the main topic may lend interest to a theme, but at the cost of its unity.
주제에서 벗어나는 것은 어떤 테마로 관심을 돌리는 것이겠지만, 그 일관성을 잃게 된다.

disclaim
[diskléim]

포기하다, 기권하다, 거절하다

<syn> renounce, give up claim to, deny, repudiate, decline
<ant> claim, avow, affirm, accept, admit

In order to obtain United States citizenship, one must disclaim any title or rank of nobility from another nation.
미국시민권을 얻기 위해서는 다른 나라의 어떠한 고귀한 지위나 계급도 포기해야 한다.

dissuade
[diswéid]

(설득하여) 단념시키다

<syn> advise against, divert by persuasion, discourage, urge not to
<ant> persuade to, advise in favor of, urge to

His friends *dissuaded* him from that unwise plan of action.
친구들은 그를 설득하여 그 무모한 행동계획을 단념시켰다.

elicit
[ilísit]

이끌어내다, 꾀어내다, 유도해내다

<syn> draw out, evoke, extract, derive, fetch, educe
<ant> repress, discourage

Her direct question only *elicited* further evasions.
그녀의 단도직입적인 질문은 더욱 심한 핑계를 자아낼 뿐이었다.

embody
[embádi]

구현하다, 구체화하다

<syn> render concrete, incorporate, organize, express, realize

He tried to *embody* his ideas in the theme.
그는 그 주제 속에 자신의 아이디어를 구현하려고 하였다.

enact
[enǽkt]

제정하다, 안건을 통과시키다

<syn> put into law, do, act out, pass, legislate
<ant> reject, turn down, fail to pass, veto

A bill was *enacted* lowering the voting age to eighteen.
법안이 투표연령을 18세로 낮추기로 통과되었다.

engulf
[engʌ́lf]

삼키다

<syn> swallow up, envelop, bury, swamp

The rising waters *engulfed* the village.
해일이 마을을 삼켰다.

exploit
[éksplɔit]

개발하다, 활용하다, 착취하다, 이용하다

<syn> use to advantage, utilize, make use of; make selfish use of
<ant> pamper, coddle, spoil

Some employers *exploit* the labor of illegal immigrants, who are afraid to complain about long hours and substandard wages.
일부 고용주들은 장시간 노동과 수준 이하의 임금에 불평하기를 두려워하는 불법 이민자들의 노동을 착취한다.

extrude
[ikstrú:d]

밀어내다, 쫓아내다

<syn> expel, push out, protrude, press

The volcanic upheaval *extruded* molten lava over a vast area.
화산변동이 광범위한 지역에 용암을 밀어냈다.

facilitate
[fəsílətèit]

쉽게 하다, 돕다, 촉진하다

<syn> make easy, expediate, speed up, lesson the labor of
<ant> hinder, hamper, complicate

This piece of machinery will *facilitate* production.
이 기계가 생산을 도와줄 것이다.

indict
[indáit]

기소하다, 고발하다 (n. indictment 기소)

<syn> accuse formally, charge

The Grand Jury issues an *indictment*.
대배심은 기소를 결정했다.

indoctrinate
[indáktrənèit]

(교리나 원리를) 주입시키다, 가르치다

<syn> instruct, teach, inculcate, initiate, train

Children are sent to Sunday school to be *indoctrinated* in the basic tenets of a particular religion.
특정 종교의 교리를 가르치기 위해 어린이들을 주일학교에 보낸다.

induct
[indʌ́kt]

이끌어들이다, 안내하다

<syn> bring in, initiate a person

The Army *inducts* 100 men a week in New York.
육군은 뉴욕에서 일주일에 100명의 남자들을 끌어들인다.

integrate
[íntəgrèit]

통합하다

<syn> absorb into the organization, blend, mix, bring together, unite
<ant> disperse, scatter, separate, divide

Vertical *integration* results from the merger of companies that perform different operations in the manufacture of a product.
수직적 통합은 제품제작에서 서로 다른 역할을 하는 회사들을 합병한 결과이다.

irradiate
[iréidièit]

비추다, 밝히다

<syn> illuminate, enlighten, radiate, spread out heat by radiant energy

The heat from the fireplace *irradiated* the room, warming us all.
난로의 열이 방안을 밝히고, 우리 모두를 따듯하게 해주었다.

manifest
[mǽnəfèst]

명시하다, 나타나다, 발표하다

<syn> appear, make clear, show, exhibit, display
<ant> hide, conceal, cover up, obscure

He claims a greater devotion to that cause than his actions *manifest*.
그는 행동이 보여주는 것보다 그 목적에 더 큰 헌신을 요구하고 있다.

mitigate
[mítəgèit]

완화하다, 누그러뜨리다

<syn> lessen, make milder, relieve, moderate, alleviate
<ant> increase, augment, heighten, strengthen

He sought to *mitigate* the evil he had done.
그는 그가 행한 악행을 줄이려고 하였다.

neutralize
[njú:trəlàiz]

중립화하다, 중화시키다

<syn> render ineffective, counterbalance, nullify, negate

The sea was *neutralized* by the nations through a treaty.
그 바다는 국가들 간의 협정을 통해 중립화되었다.

obliterate
[əblítəréit]

지우다, 제거하다

<syn> demolish, annihilate, destroy, wipe out, erase
<ant> construct, create, write, add, keep

The building had been completely *obliterated*.
건물이 완전히 없어졌다.

obtrude
[əbtrú:d]

강요하다, 참견하다, 불쑥 내밀다

<syn> intrude, interfere, meddle

It was unfair to *obtrude* upon their privacy.
자신들의 프라이버시를 강요하는 것은 옳지 않다.

preclude
[priklú:d]

막다, 차단하다, 못하게 하다

<syn> make impossible, bar, prevent

Obeying the law would *preclude* my getting home in five minutes.
법을 지키다 보면 5분만에 집에 갈 수 없을 것이다.

prescribe
[priskráib]

규정하다, 지시하다; 처방하다(recommend, especially in a professional capacity)

For the headache the physician *prescribed* aspirin.
의사는 두통에 아스피린을 처방하였다.

proclaim
[proukléim]

공포하다, 선언하다

<syn> announce, declare, herald, make public
<ant> retract, recall, suppress, repress

When the victory was announced, a holiday was *proclaimed* and all work ground to a halt.
승리가 선언되자, 공휴일이 선포되고, 모든 직장이 휴무에 들어갔다.

procure
[proukjúər]

획득하다; 야기하다

<syn> get, obtain, acquire; cause to occur, effect, bring about, evoke

At the last minute the convict's attorney *procured* a stay of execution.
마지막 순간에 기결수의 변호인은 집행유예를 얻었다.

quote
[kwout]

인용하다 (cite a passage from some author)

He *quoted* the words of Woodrow Wilson in his speech.
그는 자신의 연설에 우드로 윌슨의 말을 인용하였다.

rebuke
[ribjú:k]

비난하다, 꾸짖다

<syn> reprimand sharply, criticize sharply, reprove, censure
<ant> laud, applaud, congratulate, commend

He *rebuked* the puppy in stern tones for chewing the carpet.
그는 카펫을 씹어놓은 강아지를 엄숙한 어조로 야단쳤다.

recede
[riːsíːd]

물러나다, 후퇴하다

\<syn\> go back or away, retreat, back up, regress
\<ant\> advance, proceed, move, forward

The waters *receded* and left the beach covered with seaweed.
바닷물이 해초로 뒤덮인 해변을 빠져나갔다.

reiterate
[riːítərèit]

되풀이하다, 반복하다 (repeat)

The instructions were *reiterated* before each new section of the test.
각각의 새로운 과정을 시험 치기 전에 강의가 되풀이되었다.

reprehend
[rèprihénd]

비난하다, 꾸짖다

\<syn\> censure, criticise, condemn, denounce, rebuke, reprimand, blame

He was *reprehended* for his rudeness and sent to his room.
그는 무례하게 굴어 야단맞고 자기 방으로 들여보내졌다.

reprove
[riprúːv]

꾸짖다, 훈계하다, 비난하다

\<syn\> censure, rebuke, find fault with, reprimand, admonish, reproach, chide, scold

The instructor *reproved* the student for failing to hand in the assignments on time.
강사는 제시간에 과제물을 제출하지 못한 학생을 꾸짖었다.

sanction
[sǽŋkʃən]

재가하다, 인가하다, 시인하다, 확정하다

\<syn\> endorse, accredit, certify, authorize, approve, legitimate, allow
\<ant\> disapprove, reject, ban, prohibit

The parent organization refused to *sanction* the illegal demonstration stated by the splinter group.
학부모 단체는 소수파가 주장한 불법시위의 인가를 거절하였다.

subdue
[səbdjúː]

정복하다, 억제하다, 가라앉히다 (render less intense or less harsh)

\<syn\> overcome, calm, vanquish, curb, moderate
\<ant\> awaken, quicken, arouse, vent, unleash

The understanding actions of the nurse helped to *subdue* the stubborn and unruly child.
간호사의 사려 깊은 행동이 고집 세고 제멋대로 인 아이를 차분하게 하는 데 도움이 되었다.

supersede/ supercede
[sùːpərsíːd]

(…의 지위를) 대신하다, 빼앗다, 면직시키다

<syn> take the place of, replace, displace, succeed

The administration appointed new department heads to *supersede* the old.
행정부는 오래된 부서장을 대신하여 새로운 부서장을 임명하였다.

supplicate
[sʌ́pləkèit]

탄원하다, 애원하다

<syn> beg, beseech, implore, entreat, plead

He *supplicated* for a pardon.
그는 용서해 줄 것을 애원하였다.

suspend
[səspénd]

1. 중지하다; 연기하다

<syn> stop, cease, halt; put off, postpone, delay

Service on the line was *suspended* while the tracks were being repaired.
철로가 보수될 동안 철도운행이 잠정 중단되었다.

2. 매달다, 걸다

<syn> hang, dangle, swing, append, sling

The light fixture was *suspended* from the beam by a chain.
가벼운 시설물은 쇠사슬로 대들보에 매달아 놓았다.

transmute
[trænsmjúːt]

변형시키다 (change from one form or substance to another)

Water power can be *transmuted* into electricity.
수력이 전기로 변형될 수 있다.

vanquish
[vǽŋkwiʃ]

이기다, 정복하다, 극복하다

<syn> conquer, overcome, overpower, defeat
<ant> lose, surrender, give up, submit

Napoleon *vanquished* the Austrian army.
나폴레옹은 오스트리아 군대를 물리쳤다.

verify
[vérəfài]

입증하다, 증명하다 (prove to be true, establish the proof of)

<syn> confirm, prove, certify
<ant> disprove, deny, dispute

The principal expected the student to *verify* his statements.
교장선생님은 학생이 자신의 진술을 입증하기를 기대하였다.

vilify
[víləfài]

비방하다, 욕하다, 헐뜯다 (attempt to degrade by slander)

<syn> defame, malign, calumniate, slander, libel, traduce

He was sued for attempting to *vilify* the physician.
그는 의사를 비방하려 했다는 이유로 기소를 당했다.

weld
[weld]

용접하다, 접착시키다 (join pieces of metal by compression and great heat)

Steel bars were *welded* to make a frame.
철강봉들이 골조를 만들기 위해 용접되었다.

STEP 2 Practice Test 4

DIRECTIONS Select the word or phrase that means most nearly the same as the key word.

1 abbreviate
(A) shorten   (B) cure
(C) complete   (D) mitigate

2 acclaim
(A) deny   (B) procure
(C) applaud   (D) denounce

3 accumulate
(A) gather   (B) compute
(C) expurgate   (D) release from prison

4 aggregate
(A) sum   (B) irritate
(C) breach   (D) division

5 abominate
(A) explode   (B) whiten
(C) loathe   (D) prevent

6 adhere
(A) listen   (B) cling
(C) slip away   (D) deceive

7 alienate
(A) accusation   (B) complement
(C) estrange   (D) unknown

| ANSWER |

1. (A) 줄이다 (B) 치료하다
   (C) 완성하다 (D) 완화시키다

2. (A) 부인하다 (B) 획득하다
   (C) 갈채를 보내다 (D) 비난하다

3. (A) 모으다 (B) 계산하다
   (C) 정화하다 (D) 석방하다

4. (A) 모으다, 합산하다 (B) 무효화하다
   (C) 위반 (D) 분리

5. (A) 폭발하다 (B) 표백하다
   (C) 혐오하다 (D) 방지하다

6. (A) 듣다 (B) 집착하다, 붙다
   (C) 가버리다 (D) 속이다

7. (A) 비난 (B) 보충
   (C) 멀리하다, 소원하게 하다
   (D) 모르는

1. (A) 2. (C) 3. (A) 4. (A)
5. (C) 6. (B) 7. (C)

8 alleviate
(A) lessen (B) warn
(C) dispose of (D) levitate

9 assure
(A) assuage (B) mollify
(C) guarantee (D) disclaim

10 ascribe
(A) attribute (B) scribble
(C) translate (D) erase

11 cede
(A) lease (B) acknowledge
(C) follow (D) yield

12 comprise
(A) compose (B) extract from
(C) consist of (D) develop

13 condole
(A) distribute (B) facilitate
(C) express sympathy (D) cajole

14 cleave
(A) heave (B) split
(C) simper (D) annihilate

15 contrive
(A) devise (B) distort
(C) oppose (D) adjoin

16 debase
(A) lower (B) remove
(C) reduce in dignity (D) lower in altitude

| ANSWER |

8. (A) 줄이다 (B) 경고하다
   (C) 처분하다 (D) 공중에 뜨게 하다

9. (A) 진정시키다 (B) 진정시키다
   (C) 보증하다 (D) 포기하다

10. (A) …의 탓으로 하다
    (B) 글씨를 갈겨쓰다
    (C) 번역하다 (D) 지우다

11. (A) 임대하다 (B) 인정하다
    (C) 따르다 (D) 양보하다

12. (A) 조립하다 (B) 추출하다
    (C) 포함하다 (D) 개발하다

13. (A) 분배하다 (B) 촉진시키다
    (C) 동정을 표하다
    (D) 감언으로 속이다

14. (A) 들어올리다 (B) 쪼개다
    (C) 선웃음치다 (D) 전멸시키다

15. (A) 고안하다 (B) 비틀다
    (C) 반대하다 (D) 인접하다

16. (A) 낮추다 (B) 제거하다
    (C) 위엄을 반감하다
    (D) 고도를 낮추다

8. (A) 9. (C) 10. (A) 11. (D) 12. (C)
13. (C) 14. (B) 15. (A) 16. (C)

17 delegate
   (A) annul   (B) slander
   (C) authorize to act for another   (D) usurp

18 demean
   (A) demote   (B) degrade
   (C) explain   (D) extirpate

19 convoke
   (A) rebuke   (B) recall
   (C) compose   (D) summon

20 deduce
   (A) lead away   (B) reason
   (C) topple   (D) confuse

21 degenerate
   (A) destitute   (B) decline
   (C) debilitate   (D) devolve

22 detract
   (A) lessen   (B) pull away
   (C) lower   (D) transform

23 digress
   (A) return   (B) parallel
   (C) wander   (D) do wrong

24 embody
   (A) bury   (B) engender
   (C) incorporate   (D) exhume

25 exploit
   (A) erupt   (B) use carefully
   (C) plunge   (D) use unfairly

| ANSWER |

17. (A) 무효화하다, 파기하다
    (B) 비방하다 (C) 위임하다
    (D) 빼앗다

18. (A) 계급을 떨어뜨리다, 강등시키다
    (B) 타락시키다, 명예를 떨어뜨리다
    (C) 설명하다 (D) 근절시키다

19. (A) 비난하다 (B) 상기하다
    (C) 구성하다 (D) 소환하다

20. (A) 데리고 가다 (B) 추론하다
    (C) 비틀거리다 (D) 혼동시키다

21. (A) 빈곤한 (B) 쇠퇴하다
    (C) 쇠약하게 하다
    (D) 위임하다, 양도하다

22. (A) 줄이다 (B) 나아가다
    (C) 낮추다, 떨어뜨리다
    (D) 변형시키다

23. (A) 돌아오다 (B) 평행하다
    (C) 방랑하다 (D) 잘못하다

24. (A) 파묻다 (B) 발생시키다
    (C) 통합하다 (D) 발굴하다

25. (A) (화산이) 분출하다
    (B) 주의해서 이용하다
    (C) 뛰어들다, 던지다 (D) 악용하다

17. (C) 18. (B) 19. (D) 20. (B) 21. (B)
22. (A) 23. (C) 24. (C) 25. (D)

26 extrude
(A) aggravate (B) include
(C) push out (D) pull in

27 indict
(A) speak freely (B) accuse formally
(C) exclaim (D) rebuke

28 induct
(A) channel (B) retire
(C) acquit (D) initiate

29 integrate
(A) necessary (B) of high standards
(C) ungrateful (D) absorb into

30 irradiate
(A) poison (B) contract
(C) spread out (D) exacerbate

31 indoctrinate
(A) care for (B) tether
(C) instruct (D) seduce

32 manifest
(A) make clear (B) holiday
(C) varied (D) make straight

33 obtrude
(A) insult (B) enter uninvited
(C) withdraw (D) deny

34 obliterate
(A) demolish (B) cloud
(C) forget (D) cover up

| ANSWER |

26. (A) 악화시키다 (B) 포함시키다
    (C)밀어내다 (D) 끌어들이다

27. (A) 자유로이 말하다
    (B) 정식으로 고소하다
    (C)외치다 (D) 비난하다

28. (A) 흘러보내다 (B) 물러나다
    (C)석방하다
    (D) 입문시키다, 시작하다

29. (A) 필요한 (B) 수준 높은
    (C)은혜를 모르는
    (D) 흡수하다, 병합시키다

30. (A) 독을 넣다 (B) 계약하다
    (C)발산하다 (D) 악화시키다

31. (A) 보호하다 (B) 매다, 속박하다
    (C)가르치다 (D) 유혹하다

32. (A) 명백히 하다 (B) 공휴일
    (C)가지각색의 (D) 바르게 펴다

33. (A) 모욕하다
    (B) 불쑥 들어가다, 참견하다
    (C)물러나다 (D) 부인하다

34. (A) 부수다, 폭파하다 (B) 구름
    (C)잊다 (D) 덮다

26. (C) 27. (B) 28. (D) 29. (D) 30. (C)
31. (C) 32. (A) 33. (B) 34. (A)

35 preclude
(A) postpone (B) foreclose
(C) anticipate (D) make impossible

36 procure
(A) heal (B) get
(C) worry (D) probe

37 rebuke
(A) clamor (B) reprimand
(C) compliment (D) question

38 recede
(A) push forward (B) turn aside
(C) drive ahead (D) go back

39 reiterate
(A) stutter (B) repeat
(C) query (D) tease

40 reprehend
(A) blame (B) remember
(C) grasp (D) eject

41 reprove
(A) invent (B) bolster
(C) censure (D) debate

42 supersede
(A) run ahead (B) contradict
(C) fly above (D) take the place of

43 supplicate
(A) beg (B) replace
(C) provide (D) bend gently

ANSWER

35. (A) 연기하다 (B) 따돌리다, 제외하다
    (C) 기대하다 (D) 불가능하게 하다

36. (A) 고치다, 낫게 하다 (B) 얻다
    (C) 걱정하다 (D) 탐사하다

37. (A) 떠들다 (B) 비난하다
    (C) 칭찬하다 (D) 질문하다

38. (A) 추진하다 (B) 가라앉히다
    (C) 전진하다 (D) 물러나다

39. (A) 말을 더듬다 (B) 반복하다
    (C) 질문하다
    (D) 괴롭히다, 지분거리다

40. (A) 비난하다 (B) 기억하다
    (C) 움켜잡다 (D) 분출하다, 추방하다

41. (A) 발명하다 (B) 덧대다, 받치다
    (C) 비난하다 (D) 토론하다

42. (A) 능가하다 (B) 반박하다
    (C) 높이 날다 (D) 자리를 대신하다

43. (A) 애원하다 (B) 교체하다
    (C) 제공하다
    (D) 상냥하게 머리를 숙이다

35. (D) 36. (B) 37. (B) 38. (D) 39. (B)
40. (A) 41. (C) 42. (D) 43. (A)

44 transmute
    (A) change direction   (B) change color
    (C) change form   (D) change money

45 vilify
    (A) spy out   (B) spear through
    (C) revitalize   (D) defame

| ANSWER |

44. (A) 방향을 바꾸다 (B) 색을 바꾸다
    (C) 형태를 바꾸다 (D) 환전하다

45. (A) 찾아내다 (B) 창으로 찌르다
    (C) 생기를 회복시키다 (D) 비방하다

44. (C) 45. (D)

STEP 2

noun 명사 — vocabulary 1000

affirmation
[æfərméiʃən]

단언, 주장, 확언

<syn> solemn avowal, strong assertion, declaration
<ant> denial, refutation, repudiation, renunciation

Quakers and others may testify in court on *affirmation*.
퀘이커교도들을 비롯한 여러 사람들이 법정에서 확정적인 증언을 할 것이다.

aggregate
[ǽgrigèit]

집성, 집합, 집계

<syn> gathering, accumulation, mass, collection, conglomeration, sum

The *aggregate* of uranium ores in the Colorado plateau amazed prospectors.
콜로라도 고원의 우라늄 광맥이 시굴자들을 놀라게 하였다.

amnesty
[ǽmnəsti]

사면

<syn> pardon for a large group, reprieve, immunity, forgiveness

The president granted *amnesty* to the rebels.
대통령은 반란자들에게 사면을 내렸다.

analogy
[ənǽlədʒi]

유사성, 유추

<syn> a similarity, partial likeness, resemblance
<ant> dissimilarity, difference

Countless poets have pointed out the *analogy* between youth and springtime.
수많은 시인들이 젊음과 봄의 유사성을 지적하였다.

animosity
[æ̀nəmásəti]

악의, 원한

<syn> ill will, resentment, antagonism, malice
<ant> good will, friendship, sympathy, congeniality

The *animosity* of the population of the occupied territories made the value of its labor doubtful to the conqueror.
점령지 주민들의 원한은 정복자에게 그들의 노동 가치를 의심스럽게 만들었다.

antipathy
[æntípəθi]

반감

<syn> dislike, aversion, distaste
<ant> affinity, sympathy, affection

She had an *antipathy* toward men.
그녀는 남자들에게 반감을 가지고 있다.

artifice
[ɑ́ːrtəfis]

술책, 교묘한 솜씨, 책략

<syn> trickery, clever device, contrivance
<ant> frankness, candor, artlessness, sincerity

He used every *artifice* to win the contract.
그는 계약을 성사시키기 위해 모든 술책을 이용하였다.

beneficiary
[bènəfíʃièri]

(보험, 연금 등의) 수혜자, 수령인

<syn> inheritor, legatee, heir, receiver, recipient

The man named his wife as the *beneficiary* of the insurance policy.
그 남자는 보험의 수령인으로 아내를 지정했다.

bibliography
[bìbliágrəfi]

도서목록, 인용문헌 (list of sources of information on a particular subject)

She assembled a *bibliography* of major works on American history published since 1960.
그녀는 1960년 이후 출간된 미국사에 관한 주요 저서들의 목록을 모았다.

candor
[kǽndər]

공정, 정직, 솔직

<syn> frankness, impartiality, sincerity, honesty, truthfulness
<ant> diplomacy, flattery, subtlety, deceit

Candor and innocence often go hand-in-hand.
정직과 순수는 흔히 나란히 간다.

carnal
[káːrnl]

육체의, 육욕의

<syn> of the body, of flesh
<ant> chaste, modest, virginal, pure

The *carnal* pleasures of Babylon were deplored by the ancients.
바빌론의 육체적인 쾌락은 고대인들도 개탄하였다.

citation
[saitéiʃən]

1. 인용, 인증 (quotation, excerpt, illustration, example)

The Oxford English Dictionary contains *citations* of the written language to illustrate how words have been used.
옥스퍼드 영어사전은 단어의 용례를 밝히기 위해 문어의 인용들을 포함하고 있다.

2. 소환, 소환장 (summons to appear in court)

Caught for speeding, I received a *citation*.
속도위반으로 걸려서 소환장을 받았다.

3. 표창 (an official praise, as for bravery)

Three firefighters received *citations* for the heroic rescue effort.
세 명의 소방관들이 영웅적인 구조노력으로 표창을 받았다.

4. 전례, 관례 (reference to legal precedent or authority)

The attorney asked the clerk to check the *citations* to cases in the Supreme Court.
변호사가 서기에게 대법원에 오른 사건들의 판례들을 확인하도록 시켰다.

coalition
[kòuəlíʃən]

연합, 합동

<syn> union, alliance, partnership, league, federation, association

Various environmentalist groups formed a *coalition* to work for the candidate most sympathetic to their cause.
여러 환경단체들이 자신들의 주장에 가장 동조하는 후보를 위해 일하려고 연합체를 형성하였다.

conception
[kənsépʃən]

생각, 구상, 시작

<syn> beginning, original idea, mental image, formation, creating
<ant> completion, finish, ending, outcome, result

The *conception* of the plan was originally his.
그 기획의 구상은 본래 그의 것이었다.

conformity
[kənfɔ́:rməti]

적합, 일치

<syn> harmony, agreement, accord, compliance, observance
<ant> disagreement, disharmony, discord, opposition

In *conformity* with the rule, the meeting was adjourned.
규정에 따라 회의가 휴회되었다.

consonance
[kánsənəns]

조화, 공명, 협화

<syn> agreement, harmony, pleasant sounds together

Their *consonance* of opinion in all matters made for a peaceful household.
모든 문제에서 의견의 일치가 평화로운 가정을 만들었다.

correlation
[kɔ̀:rəléiʃən]

상호관계, 상관관계

<syn> mutual relation, connectedness

The doctor explained the *correlation* between smoking and lung disease.
의사는 흡연과 폐암의 상관관계를 설명하였다.

credence
[krí:dəns]

신용, 신뢰

<syn> faith, belief, trustworthiness

One could have little *credence* in the word of a known swindler.
유명한 사기꾼의 말에는 신뢰를 가질 수 없다.

distortion
[distɔ́:rʃən]

왜곡, 비틀어짐

<syn> twisting out of shape, misstatement of facts, deformation

The *distortions* of the historians left little of the man's true character for posterity.
역사가들이 왜곡되어 그 사람의 진정한 인품을 후세들에게 거의 남기지 않았다.

ecology
[i:kálədʒi]

생태학 (science of the relation of life to its environment)

Persons concerned about *ecology* are worried about the pollution of the earth's environment and the effect this will have on life.
생태학에 관심 있는 사람들은 지구의 환경오염과 이것이 생명에 미치게 될 영향에 대해 걱정하고 있다.

enmity
[énməti]

증오, 적의

<syn> state of being an enemy, hostility, hatred, animosity

The *enmity* between China and Vietnam is traditional and unabated.
중국과 베트남 사이의 적의는 전통적이고 누그러들지 않는다.

expertise
[èkspərtíːz]

전문기술, 전문지식

<syn> special skill, technical knowledge, know-how, expertness, specialization

The *expertise* with which he handled the animal delighted the spectators.
동물을 다루는 그의 기술이 관중들을 즐겁게 하였다.

genealogy
[dʒìːniǽlədʒi]

가계, 혈통

<syn> history of family descent, a family tree, ancestry, lineage

They were able to trace their *genealogy* back four generations to a small village in Sicily.
그들은 시칠리아의 작은 마을에서 4대까지 그들의 가계를 추적할 수 있었다.

gratuity
[grətjúːəti]

선물, 팁, 보상

<syn> tip, gift

He left a *gratuity* for the chambermaid.
그는 객실담당에게 팁을 남겼다.

helix
[híːliks]

나선

<syn> spiral line, coil of wire

The wire was wound into a *helix*.
와이어가 나선형으로 감겼다.

holograph
[hάləgræf]

자필문서 (personally handwritten document)

A *holograph* attached to a will needs no witnesses.
유언장에 있는 자필문서는 증인을 필요로 하지 않는다.

humanities
[hjuːmǽnətiz]

인문학, 고전문학

The essence of the *humanities* is a concern with human nature, experience, and relationships.
인문학의 본질은 인간의 본성과 경험, 관계에 대한 관심이다.

incision
[insíʒən]

(칼로) 베기, 절개 (cut)

The surgeon made an *incision* above the navel.
외과의사는 배꼽 위를 절개하였다.

infraction
[infrǽkʃən]

위반 행위, 침해

<syn> violation, breaking of a law, infringement, breach

The building inspector noted several *infractions* of the health and safety codes.
건물 검열관은 보건과 안전 규정의 위반사항 몇 가지를 적었다.

initiation
[iniʃiéiʃən]

시작, 착수, 입회, 입문

<syn> beginning, introduction, induction, entrance, opening
<ant> expulsion, rejection, exit, end, finish

The *initiation* of new members into the fraternity will be held soon and the old members can hardly wait.
남학생클럽 신입회원의 입회식이 곧 열릴 텐데 기존 회원들은 거의 기다릴 수 없다.

inquest
[ínkwest]

(배심원의) 심리, 검토

<syn> judicial investigation, official inquiry or examination

The state held an *inquest* to examine the cause of the disaster and determine whether charges should be brought against any parties.
국가는 재난의 원인을 규명하고 어느 정당에 대해 책임을 물을 것인지를 결정하기 위해 심리를 열었다.

jollity
[dʒáləti]

명랑, 즐거움, 환락

<syn> noisy mirth, gaiety, merriment

The *jollity* of the occasion will always be remembered.
그 행사의 즐거움은 언제나 기억될 것이다.

laxity
[lǽksəti]

느슨함, 이완, 소홀

<syn> looseness, lack of strictness

In summer, when business was slow, the manager allowed the employees some *laxity* in their hours.
사업이 느슨한 여름철에 부장은 직원들이 자기시간의 여유를 갖도록 허용하였다.

legacy
[légəsi]

유산

<syn> something inherited, bequest, devise, estate

He acquired the house as a *legacy* from his grandmother.
그는 할머니로부터 유산으로 집을 얻었다.

liaison
[líːəzɑ̀n]

연락, 접촉; 연락관

<syn> connection, linking, contact; mediator, go-between

He had served as a *liaison* between the Allied command and the local government.
그는 연합군사령부와 현지 정부 간의 연락관으로 일하였다.

magnitude
[mǽgnətjùːd]

크기, 양, 중대성

<syn> size, extent, expanse, dimensions, proportions, mass, bulk
<ant> smallness, diminutiveness, meanness

The apparent *magnitude* of the moon is greater near the horizon than at the zenith.
달의 외견상의 크기는 천정에서보다 지평선 가까운데서 더 커 보인다.

mandate
[mǽndeit]

명령, 지령, 위임

<syn> a specific order, decree, command, dictate, authorization

Some islands are still ruled by League of Nations or U.N. *mandate*.
일부 섬들이 아직 국제연맹이나 국제연합의 통치를 받고 있다.

matriarch
[méitriɑːrk]

여성 가장 (mother who rules a family or clan)

<syn> female head, female chieftain, female, ruler, female leader

All important decisions were referred to the *matriarch* of the tribe.
모든 중요한 결정은 부족의 여 추장에게 맡겨졌다.

misappropriation
[mìsəpróupriéiʃən]

남용, 악용, 횡령, 착복

<syn> using for a wrong purpose, misuse, embezzling, stealing

The *misappropriation* of the funds caused much misery.
자금의 남용이 많은 불행을 가져왔다.

miscellany
[mísəlèini]

잡다한 것의 혼합, 잡동사니

<syn> collection of various or unlike things, mixture, medley, hodgepodge

The old steamer trunk contained a *miscellany* of papers, clothes, and assorted junk.
구식 증기기차의 화물칸은 종이와 옷가지, 잡다한 쓰레기들을 실었다.

morass
[mərǽs]

소택지, 늪; 곤경, 혼란상태

<syn> swamp, mire, bog, messy or troublesome state

The application became mired in a *morass* of paperwork; there was no response for several weeks.
지원서류가 문서 더미에 묻혀 있었다. 몇 주일 간 응답이 없었다.

novice
[návis]

초심자, 신참자

<syn> beginner, tyro, apprentice, newcomer, amateur
<ant> master, old hand, professional

A *novice* in the job, she needed more time than an experienced worker to complete the same tasks.
초심자인 그녀는 같은 임무를 완수하는 데 경험자보다 더 많은 시간을 필요로 하였다.

paraphrase
[pǽrəfrèiz]

문장 바꿔 쓰기, 바꿔 말하기

<syn> rewording, restating, stating in other words, recapitulating

To *paraphrase* someone's work without acknowledging the source of one's information is a form of plagiarism.
정보의 출처도 알지 못하면서 남의 작품을 바꿔 쓰는 것은 표절의 한 유형이다.

parity
[pǽrəti]

등위, 등가, 형평, 패리티(농산물 가격과 생필품 가격의 비율)

<syn> comparative equality, equivalence

Congress aims to keep farm prices at 80 percent of a *parity* with prices of manufactured goods.
의회는 농산물 가격을 공산품 가격의 80% 비율에 유지하려고 한다.

patron
[péitrən]

후원자, 보호자

<syn> supporter, defender, sponsor, backer, benefactor, promoter
<ant> protégé

For donating her time and energy to the museum, she was honored as a *patron* of the arts.
시간과 정열을 박물관에 바친 공로로 그녀는 예술의 후원자라는 명예를 얻었다.

percussion
[pəːrkʌ́ʃən]

충돌, 진동, 타악기의 연주

<syn> violent striking, sharp blow, impact

The drum is a *percussion* instrument.
드럼은 타악기이다.

posterity
[pɑstérəti]

자손, 후세

<syn> succeeding generations, future generations, offspring, descendants

Many things we build today are for *posterity*.
우리가 오늘날 건설하는 많은 것들은 후세를 위한 것이다.

predecessor
[prédisèsər]

전임자, 선배

In his inaugural address the new president of the association praised the work done by his *predecessor*.
그의 취임식에서 협회의 새 회장은 전임자가 이룬 업적을 칭송하였다.

prototype
[próutoutàip]

원형, 표준, 모범

<syn> original model, first example, archetype

Homer's Iliad became the *prototype* for much of the later epic poetry of Europe.
호머의 일리아드는 후세 유럽의 수많은 서사시의 원형이 되었다.

punctuality
[pʌ̀ŋktʃuǽləti]

시간엄수, 정확함, 꼼꼼함 (being on time)

The train had an excellent record for *punctuality*; it almost always arrived precisely at 8:15.
그 열차는 시간을 잘 지키기로 우수한 기록을 가지고 있었으니, 거의 언제나 8시 15분에 정확하게 도착하였다.

radiation
[rèidiéiʃən]

방사, 복사, 방사형 (divergence in all directions from a point)

Solar radiation is the *radiation* of the sun as estimated by the amount of energy that reaches the earth.
태양복사는 지구까지 도달하는 에너지의 양으로 측정되는 태양의 방사이다.

reprimand
[réprəmæ̀nd]

질책, 징계, 비난 (severe criticism, especially a formal rebuke by someone in authority)

<syn> sharp reproval, rebuke, reproach, admonition
<ant> commendation, compliment, applause, approval

Since it was a first offense, the judge let the teenager off with a *reprimand*.
초범이었기 때문에 판사는 그 청소년을 훈방하였다.

solicitude
[səlísətjùːd]

걱정, 염려 (uneasiness of mind occasioned by the fear of evil or the desire for good)

<syn> concern, anxiety

The teacher had a great *solicitude* for the welfare of her students.
선생님은 학생들의 복지를 위해 많은 염려를 하였다.

tardiness
[táːrdinis]

느림, 더딤, 지각 (lateness)

His *tardiness* was habitual; he was late getting to class most mornings.
그의 지각은 습관적이었으니, 그는 거의 아침마다 수업에 지각하였다.

Practice Test 5

DIRECTIONS Select the word or phrase that means most nearly the same as the key word.

1. affirmation
   - (A) avowal
   - (B) confirmation
   - (C) denial
   - (D) strengthening

2. amnesty
   - (A) reward
   - (B) forgetfulness
   - (C) retribution
   - (D) pardon

3. artifice
   - (A) work of art
   - (B) wealth
   - (C) trickery
   - (D) ingenuousness

4. candor
   - (A) rudeness
   - (B) rancor
   - (C) frankness
   - (D) stealth

5. coalition
   - (A) heat
   - (B) annulment
   - (C) sympathy
   - (D) temporary union

6. consonance
   - (A) harshness
   - (B) harmony
   - (C) condolence
   - (D) cacophony

7. correlation
   - (A) adherence
   - (B) collusion
   - (C) connectedness
   - (D) genealogy

| ANSWER |

1. (A) 공언 (B) 확정
   (C) 부인 (D) 강화

2. (A) 보상 (B) 건망증
   (C) 응징, 보복 (D) 용서

3. (A) 예술작품 (B) 부
   (C) 술책 (D) 솔직함

4. (A) 무례함 (B) 원한, 악의
   (C) 솔직함 (D) 몰래 하기, 기밀

5. (A) 열 (B) 폐지
   (C) 동정 (D) 일시적 연합

6. (A) 거칠음 (B) 조화
   (C) 애도 (D) 불협화음

7. (A) 고수, 집착 (B) 공모
   (C) 상관관계 (D) 혈통

1. (A) 2. (D) 3. (C) 4. (C)
5. (D) 6. (B) 7. (C)

8 credence
　　(A) harmony　　(B) religion
　　(C) orthodoxy　　(D) belief

9 expertise
　　(A) ideology　　(B) skill
　　(C) snobbery　　(D) wishfulness

10 genealogy
　　(A) family tree　　(B) cousins
　　(C) care of the aged　　(D) study of genetics

11 helix
　　(A) long road　　(B) rare bird
　　(C) spiral　　(D) star

12 legacy
　　(A) summons　　(B) inheritance
　　(C) written document　　(D) affidavit

13 miscellany
　　(A) annotations　　(B) itinerary
　　(C) collection of unlike things　　(D) foolishness

14 morass
　　(A) field　　(B) mountain range
　　(C) inundation　　(D) swamp

15 liaison
　　(A) linking　　(B) courtesan
　　(C) laziness　　(D) lassitude

16 magnitude
　　(A) loudness　　(B) weight
　　(C) color　　(D) size

| ANSWER |

8. (A) 조화 (B) 종교
　(C) 정교, 정통 (D) 믿음

9. (A) 이데올로기 (B) 기술
　(C) 속물근성 (D) 바램

10. (A) 가계 (B) 사촌
　(C) 노인보호 (D) 유전학

11. (A) 장도 (B) 희귀조
　(C) 나선 (D) 별

12. (A) 소환 (B) 유산
　(C) 문서 (D) 선서문

13. (A) 주석, 주해 (B) 여정, 여행계획
　(C) 잡동사니 (D) 어리석음

14. (A) 필드 (B) 산맥 (C) 범람 (D) 늪

15. (A) 연결 (B) 고급 창녀
　(C) 게으름 (D) 권태, 나른함

16. (A) 시끄러움 (B) 무게
　(C) 색 (D) 규격

8. (D)　9. (B)　10. (A)　11. (C)　12. (B)
13. (C)　14. (D)　15. (A)　16. (D)

17 matriarch
  (A) conjunction   (B) female ruler
  (C) female politician   (D) old woman

18 novice
  (A) nine-year old   (B) inexperienced person
  (C) immigrant   (D) clumsy person

19 parity
  (A) mockery   (B) entertainment
  (C) destitution   (D) equality

20 paraphrase
  (A) quote   (B) joke
  (C) rewording   (D) attribution

21 posterity
  (A) rear guard   (B) retrogression
  (C) afterthought   (D) future generations

| ANSWER |

17. (A) 연결 (B) 여성지배자
    (C) 여성정치인 (D) 늙은 여자

18. (A) 9세의 (B) 경험이 없는 사람
    (C) 이주민
    (D) 솜씨 없는, 세련되지 않은

19. (A) 조롱 (B) 연회 (C) 결핍 (D) 형평

20. (A) 인용하다 (B) 농담하다
    (C) 바꿔 말하기 (D) 귀속, 속성

21. (A) (군대의) 후위, 후진
    (B) 후퇴, 역행
    (C) 때늦은 생각, 되짚어 봄
    (D) 미래 세대

17. (B) 18. (B) 19. (D)
20. (C) 21. (D)

STEP 2
adjective & adverb 형용사 & 부사

abject
[ǽbdʒekt]

비참한

\<syn\> miserable, wretched, hopeless
\<ant\> hopeful, dignified

Many Asians live in a state of *abject* poverty.
많은 아시아인들이 비참하도록 가난하게 살고 있다.

adept
[ədépt]

숙련된, 정통한

\<syn\> skilled, well-versed, adroit, dextrous
\<ant\> beginning, inept, unskilled, clumsy

A journalist is *adept* at the use of words.
언론인은 언어의 구사에 숙달되어 있다.

adroit
[ədrɔ́it]

능숙한, 솜씨 좋은, 기민한

\<syn\> skillful, dextrous, deft
\<ant\> clumsy, awkward, unhandy

The *adroit* juggler held the attention of the crowd.
능숙한 요술쟁이가 군중의 주목을 끈다.

affluent
[ǽflu(:)ənt]

풍부한, 부유한, 많은

\<syn\> abundant, rich, wealthy, well-off
\<ant\> poor, impoverished, impecunious, destitute

The United States is an *affluent* nation.
미국은 부유한 나라이다.

aloof
[əlúːf]

멀리 떨어진, 무관심한, 냉담한

<syn> distant, reserved, cold in manner, indifferent
<ant> warm, friendly, familiar

Her elegant appearance and formal politeness made her seem *aloof*, though in reality she was only shy.
실제로 그녀는 단지 수줍기만 했는데, 그녀의 우아한 외모와 형식적인 친절은 거리감을 느끼게 하였다.

apathetic
[æpəθétik]

냉담한, 무관심한

<syn> without feeling, indifferent, unconcerned
<ant> concerned, interested, responsive

The *apathetic* attitude of voters enables a minority to control the election.
유권자들의 무관심한 태도는 소수파가 선거를 좌우하게 한다.

apprehensive
[æprihénsiv]

염려하는, 걱정하는

<syn> fearing some coming event, anxious, worried, concerned
<ant> confident, assured, at ease, unafraid

She was *apprehensive* about the examination.
그녀는 시험을 걱정하고 있었다.

archaic
[ɑːrkéiik]

고풍의, 고어의, 낡은

<syn> out of use, out-of-date, antiquated, ancient
<ant> modern, current, up-to-date

Some words like "thou" are *archaic*.
"thou" 같은 일부 단어들은 고어들이다.

baneful
[béinfəl]

파괴적인, 치명적인, 해로운

<syn> actively evil, disastrous, poisonous, venomous
<ant> blessing, prized, joyful, comfortable

The ex-convict exerted a *baneful* influence on the other members of the group.
그 전과자는 집단의 다른 구성원들에게 악영향을 미쳤다.

biennial
[baiéniəl]

2년마다의, 2년에 한 번씩 (happening every two years)

Many state legislatures convene on a *biennial* basis.
여러 주의 입법기관들이 2년 단위로 회합한다.

capacious
[kəpéiʃəs]

널찍한, 넓은

<syn> spacious, wide

The *capacious* railroad terminals offer a bright welcome to tourists.
널찍한 철도 터미널이 여행객들을 환하게 맞는다.

celestial
[siléstʃəl]

하늘의, 천체의

<syn> heavenly, divine
<ant> earthly, terrestrial

Planets are *celestial* bodies.
행성은 천체이다.

colloquial
[kəlóukwiəl]

구어체의, 회화체의

<syn> of speech, informal, conversational, ordinary, plain
<ant> formal, sophisticated, literary

Having only studied formal French, she was unable to understand many of her host's *colloquial* expressions.
그녀는 격식 있는 불어만 배웠기에 주인의 구어적인 표현들을 많이 이해하지 못했다.

compulsory
[kəmpʌ́lsəri]

강제적인, 의무적인, 필수의

<syn> required, forced, mandatory, obligatory
<ant> voluntary, optional, discretionary

Attendance is *compulsory* unless one has a medical excuse.
아프지 않은 다음에야 참석은 의무적이다.

contentious
[kənténʃəs]

논쟁적인, 다투기 좋아하는

<syn> quarrelsome

One *contentious* student can ruin a debate.
다투기 좋아하는 한 학생이 토론을 망칠 수 있다.

covert
[kʌ́vəːrt]

숨은, 은밀한

<syn> hidden, secret, concealed, disguised
<ant> overt, known, open, public

To avoid a public outcry, the president ordered a *covert* military action and publicly denied that he was sending combat troops.
대중의 항의를 피하기 위해 대통령은 은밀한 군사작전을 지시하였고, 전투부대의 파병을 공식적으로는 부인하였다.

discreet
[diskríːt]

분별 있는, 신중한

<syn> prudent, diplomatic, careful, tactful
<ant> rash, heedless, careless, imprudent

She countered the rude question with a soft-spoken and *discreet* denial.
그녀는 부드러운 말로 신중하게 부인하며 무례한 질문을 받아쳤다.

disinterested
[disíntəristid]

사욕이 없는, 청렴한, 치우치지 않은

<syn> not involved in, unprejudiced, impartial, unbiased, neutral
<ant> partial, biased, prejudiced, selfish,

A *disinterested* witness is one who has no personal involvement in the outcome of the matter under dispute.
치우치지 않은 증인이란 분쟁중인 문제의 결과에 개인적인 관련이 없는 사람이다.

docile
[dásəl]

유순한, 가르치기 쉬운, 다루기 쉬운

<syn> easily led, manageable, compliant, tame, obedient, tractable
<ant> unruly, wild, disobedient, ungovernable

The child was *docile* until he discovered his mother was gone.
어머니가 사라졌다는 것을 알기 전까지 아이는 유순했다.

dogmatic
[dɔ(ː)gmǽtik]

독단적인, 독자적인, 임의의, 교리에 얽매인

<syn> arbitrary, opinionated, biased, prejudiced
<ant> diffident, vacillating, uncertain

His *dogmatic* statements were not supported by evidence.
그의 독단적인 진술은 증거가 뒷받침되지 못했다.

dubious
[djúːbiəs]

의심스러운, 미심쩍은

<syn> in doubt, doubtful, uncertain, skeptical, unconvinced, suspicious
<ant> sure, positive, certain, reliable, dependable, trustworthy

He had the *dubious* distinction of being the best liar at the school.
그는 학교에서 가장 거짓말쟁이라는 믿을 수 없는 명성을 가지고 있다.

enlightened
[enláitnd]

계몽된

<syn> free from prejudice or ignorance, advanced, illuminated, civilized
<ant> mystified, perplexed, bewildered, mislead

No *enlightened* society could condone the exploitation of children as it was once practiced in American industry.
한때 미국 산업에 있었던 아동착취는 어떤 문명사회도 용서할 수 없다.

ethnic
[éθnik]

인종의, 민족의

<syn> native, national, indigenous, racial

Of all the *ethnic* foods available in this city, Italian pizza and Middle Eastern falafel are the most important
이 도시에서 애용되고 있는 모든 민족 음식 가운데, 이탈리아 피자와 중동의 팔라펠이 가장 중요하다.

exempt
[igzémpt]

면제된

<syn> excused, not subject to, immune, excepted, relieved, freed
<ant> liable, subject, responsible, chargeable

Having broken his leg, the child was *exempt* from gym for the rest of the term.
그 아이는 다리가 부러져서 남은 학기를 체육에서 면제되었다.

fallacious
[fəléiʃəs]

불합리한, 틀린

<syn> untrue, misleading, deceptive

His arguments were transparently *fallacious*.
그녀의 논지는 분명히 틀렸다.

feasible
[fíːzəbəl]

실행할 수 있는, 가능한

<syn> practicable, possible, conceivable, workable, achievable
<ant> unfeasible, unworkable, unachievable

It is *feasible* to complete the project by July.
7월까지 그 프로젝트를 완성하는 것은 가능하다.

garrulous
[gǽrjələs]

수다스러운, 말 많은

<syn> talkative, loquacious, wordy, chattery
<ant> reticent, taciturn, quiet, reserved

She was so *garrulous* that she said everything at least three times.
그녀는 너무 수다스러워서 모든 것을 최소한 세 번은 말했다.

genial
[dʒíːnjəl]

온화한, 다정한

<syn> pleasant, friendly, cheerful, kindly, affable, congenial, cordial

The president's rotund and *genial* face made him the perfect Santa Claus.
대통령의 둥글고 온화한 얼굴은 그를 완벽한 산타클로스로 만들었다.

habitable
[hǽbətəbəl]

거주할 수 있는, 살기 적당한

<syn> capable of being inhabited or dwelt in, capable of sustaining human beings

The climate of the North Pole makes it scarcely *habitable*.
북극의 기후는 거의 사람이 살 수 없게 한다.

illegible
[ilédʒəbəl]

읽기 어려운, 판독하기 어려운

<syn> impossible to read, obscured

The letter was so water stained that the handwriting was *illegible*.
글자가 물로 얼룩이 져서 글을 읽을 수 없었다.

impotent
[ímpətənt]

무력한, 허약한

<syn> lacking power, weak, disabled, helpless
<ant> potent, powerful, forceful

The disease left him *impotent* even to walk across the room.
질병이 실내를 걷기도 힘들 정도로 그를 허약하게 만들었다.

indolent

[índələnt]

나태한, 게으른

<syn> lazy, habitually idle, sluggish
<ant> industrious, busy, diligent

An *indolent* lad never learns much.
게으른 놈은 결코 많이 배우지 못한다.

indubitable

[indjú:bətəbəl]

의심의 여지가 없는, 확실한

<syn> undeniably true, unquestionable

That 2 x 2 = 4 is *indubitable*.
2 X 2 = 4는 확실하다.

inept

[inépt]

서투른, 바보 같은

<syn> incompetent, clumsy, inefficient, unapt
<ant> efficient, skillful, apt

The basketball team's center is tall and powerful but so physically *inept* that he frequently loses the ball.
그 농구팀의 센터는 키가 크고 힘은 좋은데 몸이 너무 둔해서 자주 공을 놓친다.

insolvent

[insálvənt]

파산한, 지불불능의, 돈을 다 써버린

<syn> unable to meet debts, penniless, destitute, ruined
<ant> solvent, wealthy, flourishing

The corporation was *insolvent* after the loss of the ship.
선박을 잃고 회사는 파산상태가 되었다.

intangible

[intǽndʒəbəl]

만져서 알 수 없는, 무형의

<syn> untouchable, imperceptible, abstract, insubstantial, impalpable
<ant> tangible, palpable, perceptible, concrete

The company's goodwill among its customers is a genuine but *intangible* asset.
고객들 사이의 그 회사에 대한 호의는 무형의 자산이지만 진정한 것이다.

intrepid

[intrépəd]

용맹스러운, 대담한

<syn> brave, fearless, bold, valiant, courageous
<ant> cowardly, timid, fearful

The *intrepid* explorers stepped out onto the lunar surface.
용감한 탐험가들이 달 표면에 착륙하였다.

intrinsic
[intrínsik]

본질적인, 고유의

<syn> belonging naturally, essential, innate, inherent, basic
<ant> extrinsic, accidental, incidental, added

The *intrinsic* value of diamonds lies in their hardness.
다이아몬드 고유의 가치는 경도에 있다.

invidious
[invídiəs]

비위에 거슬리는, 불쾌한

<syn> insulting, causing hard feelings, inciting ill will, offensive
<ant> fair, just, placating, flattering

His tactlessness was *invidious*.
그의 분별 없음이 비위에 거슬렸다.

judicious
[dʒuːdíʃəs]

사려분별이 있는, 현명한

<syn> prudent, sensible, wise, sagacious, sage, discerning
<ant> injudicious, imprudent, thoughtless, unreasonable

His policy was *judicious* and the results effective.
그의 정책은 현명하였고 결과는 효과적이었다.

kinetic
[kinétik]

운동의, 운동에 의한 (of or caused by motion)

Kinetic energy is produced by a stream turning a water wheel.
수차를 돌리는 물줄기에 의해 운동에너지가 생산된다.

latent
[léitənt]

숨어있는, 잠재적인

<syn> hidden from ordinary observation, dormant, quiescent, potential
<ant> activated, developed, apparent, expressed

He could see the *latent* possibilities of the situation.
그는 그 상황의 잠재적인 가능성들을 볼 수 있었다.

liable
[láiəbəl]

...에 노출된, ...당하기 쉬운

<syn> exposed, open to, vulnerable, subject, inclined
<ant> exempt, immune

A physician is *liable* to contagion.
의사는 전염병에 걸리기 쉽다.

longitudinal
[làndʒətjú:dinəl]

경도의, 날줄의, 세로의

\<syn\> pertaining to length, extending lengthwise
\<ant\> latitudinal

They measured the *longitudinal* distance carefully.
그들은 경도의 거리를 주의 깊게 측정하였다.

malignant
[məlígnənt]

악의적인, 악성의, 유해한

\<syn\> very malicious, injurious, malign, vicious, malevolent
\<ant\> benignant, benevolent, benign

A *malignant* person is dangerous, even as a friend.
악의적인 사람은 친구로서 위험하다

negligible
[néglidʒəbəl]

하찮은, 사소한, 무시해도 좋은

\<syn\> too small, insignificant, unimportant, trifling, trivial

The difference in their ages is *negligible*.
나이 차이는 사소한 것이다.

obsolete
[àbsəlí:t]

못쓰게 된, 폐물이 된

\<syn\> outmoded, out of use, out of date

Since several offices have been relocated, the old directory is *obsolete*.
여러 사무실이 이사를 해서 옛날 전화번호부는 못쓰게 되었다.

orbicular
[ɔːrbíkjələr]

공(고리) 모양의, 원형의

\<syn\> circular, orb-shaped

The boomerang made an *orbicular* path back to the sender.
부메랑은 보낸 사람에게로 원형을 그리며 되돌아왔다.

permeable
[pə́ːrmiəbəl]

침투성 있는, 투과할 수 있는 (capable of having fluids pass through)

Most clay dishes are *permeable*.
대부분의 지점토 접시는 액체를 투과시킨다.

placid
[plǽsid]

평온한, 조용한

<syn> calm, quiet, tranquil, peaceful, undisturbed, serene
<ant> turbulent, agitated, rough, excited

The drug had relieved her anxiety, leaving her in a *placid* and jovial mood.
그 약은 분노를 제거하여 그녀를 평온하고 유쾌한 분위기에 있게 하였다.

precarious
[prikɛ́əriəs]

불안정한, 불확실한

<syn> insecure, uncertain, dubious; hazardous, perilous, unsafe
<ant> certain, sure, secure, safe

His position on the ledge was *precarious*.
바위 턱에 앉은 그의 위치는 불안하였다.

quadrennial
[kwɑdréniəl]

4년 간의, 4년마다의 (lasting four years, occurring once in four years)

The *quadrennial* games were anticipated eagerly.
4년마다 열리는 경기가 학수고대되었다.

recessive
[risésiv]

퇴행의, 역행의 (tending to recede or not make itself felt)

The characteristic encoded in a *recessive* gene may be passed on to an individual's offspring even though it is not apparent in the individual.
한 개인의 퇴행유전자 속에 암호화된 성격은 비록 그에게 나타나지는 않지만 그 자식에게로 전달될 수 있다.

sardonic
[sɑːrdɑ́nik]

조소적인, 냉소적인, 빈정대는

<syn> ironical, satiric, sarcastic, cynical, sneering, mocking, scornful

His *sardonic* smile irritated the guests.
그의 냉소적인 웃음이 손님들을 화나게 하였다.

secular
[sékjələr]

세속의, 비종교적인 (not religious)

The *secular* authorities often have differences with the church in Italy.
세속의 기관들은 이탈리아의 교회와 다르다.

simultaneous
[sàiməltéiniəs]

동시의, 동시에 일어나거나 존재하는 (occurring or existing at the same time)

<syn> concurrent, coincident, synchronous, contemporary

There were *simultaneous* broadcasts of the game on local television and radio stations.
지역 텔레비전과 라디오 방송에서 경기중계를 동시에 방송하였다.

subversive
[səbvə́:rsiv]

전복하는, 파괴적인 (tending to undermine or destroy secretly)

<syn> destructive

The editor was accused of disseminating propaganda *subversive* to the national security.
편집자는 국가안보를 전복하는 선전을 유포한 혐의로 고발을 당하였다.

superfluous
[su:pərfluəs]

남는, 여분의, 불필요한 (beyond what is necessary)

<syn> extra, surplus, spare

It was clear from the scene what had happened; his lengthy explanations were *superfluous*.
무슨 일이 있었는지는 그 광경이 명백하게 보여주었기에 그의 긴 설명은 불필요하였다.

tangible
[tǽndʒəbəl]

만져서 알 수 있는, 확실한, 실질적인 (capable of being touched, having objective reality and value)

<syn> palpable, touchable, material, physical; concrete, real, actual

The new position offered an opportunity for creativity as well as the more *tangible* reward of a higher salary.
새로운 지위는 더 많은 봉급이라는 실질적인 보상뿐 아니라 창작의 기회를 제공하였다.

tedious
[tí:diəs]

지루한, 따분한

<syn> boring, tiring, tiresome, dull, wearisome, irksome
<ant> exciting, interesting, amusing

The film was so *tedious* that we walked out in disgust before it was half over.
영화가 너무 지루해서 절반도 지나기 전에 우리는 싫어져서 밖으로 나왔다.

terse
[tə:rs]

간결한, 생동감 있는

\<syn\> concise, brief and to the point, using few words
\<ant\> rambling, circuitous, roundabout, diffuse

The official's *terse* replies to our questions indicated that he did not welcome being interrupted.
우리 질문에 대한 그 관리의 간결한 답변은 그가 방해받기를 좋아하지 않음을 나타내 주었다.

transverse
[trænzvə́:rs]

가로의, 횡단하는 (lying across)

They placed the ties *transversely* on the tracks and waited for the train to crash.
그들은 끈을 철로 위에 가로로 걸쳐놓고 열차가 돌진하기를 기다렸다.

unprecedented
[ʌnprésədèntid]

전례 없는, 미증유의 (never before done, without precedent)

\<syn\> unexampled, extraordinary, exceptional
\<ant\> familiar, usual, regular

Sputnik I accomplished *unprecedented* feats.
내가 완성한 스퓨트닉은 미증유의 공적이다.

urbane
[ə:rbéin]

도회풍의, 세련된, 점잖은 (polished in manner)

\<syn\> smoothly polite, suave, elegant
\<ant\> crude, coarse, rough, rude

He travels in *urbane* circles and is as suave as any of his friends.
그는 도회지를 여행하여 자기 친구들 누구보다도 세련되었다.

Practice Test 6

DIRECTIONS Select the word or phrase that means most nearly the same as the key word.

1 affluent
  (A) gaseous   (B) well-spoken
  (C) wealthy   (D) esoteric

2 abject
  (A) complaint   (B) hidden
  (C) wretched   (D) soporific

3 archaic
  (A) atypical   (B) no longer used
  (C) geriatric   (D) no longer needed

4 aloof
  (A) congenial   (B) risible
  (C) moribund   (D) distant

5 baneful
  (A) unhappy   (B) morose
  (C) evil   (D) obstreperous

6 capacious
  (A) skillful   (B) concealing
  (C) greedy   (D) spacious

7 carnal
  (A) of the body   (B) of the heart
  (C) of the spirit (D) of the mind

| ANSWER |

1. (A) 가스의 (B) 말씨가 세련된
   (C) 부유한 (D) 비밀의

2. (A) 불평 (B) 숨겨진
   (C) 가엾은, 비참한 (D) 최면의

3. (A) 파격적인
   (B) 더 이상 사용되지 않은
   (C) 노인병의 (D) 더 이상 필요 없는

4. (A) 같은 성질의 (B) 웃을 수 있는
   (C) 죽어 가는 (D) 멀리 떨어진

5. (A) 불행한 (B) 까다로운
   (C) 해로운, 악의 (B) 시끄럽게 날뛰는

6. (A) 능숙한 (B) 숨김
   (C) 탐욕스런 (D) 넓은

7. (A) 육체의 (B) 가슴의
   (C) 정신의 (D) 마음의

1. (C) 2. (C) 3. (B) 4. (D)
5. (C) 6. (D) 7. (A)

8 colloquial
(A) conversational (B) loquacious
(C) garrulous (D) terse

9 compulsory
(A) of the heart (B) vacillating
(C) occasional (D) required

10 covert
(A) heated (B) absconded
(C) secret (D) retired

11 contentious
(A) honest (B) adjoining
(C) catchy (D) quarrelsome

12 disinterested
(A) unprejudiced (B) bored
(C) ignorant (D) unavailable

13 dubious
(A) talented (B) doubtful
(C) forceful (D) malicious

14 feasible
(A) practicable (B) sumptuous
(C) grandiose (D) implemented

15 illegible
(A) unlawful (B) handwritten
(C) unreadable (D) unwarranted

16 impotent
(A) imbued (B) significant
(C) powerless (D) brash

| ANSWER |

8. (A) 대화의, 대화체의 (B) 수다스러운
   (C) 수다스러운 (D) 간결한

9. (A) 마음의 (B) 망설이는
   (C) 이따금씩의 (D) 필수의

10. (A) 뜨거워진 (B) 도망한
    (C) 비밀의 (D) 은퇴한

11. (A) 정직한 (B) 인접하는
    (C) 걸리기 쉬운 (D) 싸우기 좋아하는

12. (A) 편견 없는 (B) 지루한
    (C) 모르는 (D) 이용할 수 없는

13. (A) 재능 있는 (B) 의심스러운
    (C) 강제적인 (D) 악의적인

14. (A) 실행할 수 있는 (B) 호화로운
    (C) 웅장한 (D) 도구가 된

15. (A) 불법의 (B) 손으로 글씨 쓴
    (C) 읽기 어려운 (D) 공인되지 않은

16. (A) 감염된, 고취된 (B) 중요한
    (C) 무력한 (D) 건방진

8. (A) 9. (D) 10. (C) 11. (D) 12. (A)
13. (B) 14. (A) 15. (C) 16. (C)

17 inept
    (A) unavailable   (B) clumsy
    (C) hard-to-reach   (D) expert

18 intangible
    (A) cut cleanly   (B) undefinable
    (C) affixed   (D) unreachable

19 intrepid
    (A) trembling   (B) unconscious
    (C) fearless   (D) fleet

20 intrinsic
    (A) sinister   (B) holding fast
    (C) wound tightly   (D) belonging naturally

21 invidious
    (A) whiny   (B) gracious
    (C) bringing joy   (D) arousing resentment

22 liable
    (A) summons   (B) owned by
    (C) prone   (D) exposed to

23 kinetic
    (A) electrical   (B) pertaining to motion
    (C) spinal   (D) pertaining to heat

24 negligible
    (A) insignificant   (B) transparent
    (C) overlooked   (D) shunned

25 neutralized
    (A) sexless   (B) harbinger
    (C) recharged   (D) indifferent

| ANSWER |

17. (A) 입수되지 않은 (B) 서투른
    (C) 도달하기 어려운 (D) 노련한

18. (A) 깨끗이 자르다
    (B) 정의 내릴 수 없는, 알 수 없는
    (C) 첨부한 (D) 도달할 수 없는

19. (A) 전율하는 (B) 무의식의
    (C) 용맹한 (D) 순식간의

20. (A) 불길한, 재난의 (B) 굳게 지속되는
    (C) 단단히 감긴 (D) 본질에 속하는

21. (A) 흐느껴 우는 (B) 인자한
    (C) 즐거움을 가져오는
    (D) 반감을 일으키는

22. (A) 소환 (B) …소유의
    (C) …하는 경향이 있는
    (D) 노출된, …하게 되기 쉬운

23. (A) 전기의 (B) 운동에 관련된
    (C) 척추의 (D) 열에 관련된

24. (A) 중요하지 않은 (B) 투명한
    (C) 간과한 (D) 회피한

25. (A) 성별이 없는 (B) 선구자
    (C) 재충전하다
    (D) 무관심한, 치우지지 않는

17. (B) 18. (B) 19. (C) 20. (D) 21. (D)
22. (D) 23. (B) 24. (A) 25. (D)

26 obsolete
(A) current (B) off-color
(C) bound   (D) outmoded

27 orbicular
(A) of the age (B) of the feet
(C) circular   (D) rectangular

28 permeable
(A) penetrable by fluids (B) transferrable
(C) translucent   (D) impervious

29 placid
(A) peaceful (B) flabby
(C) swollen   (D) agitated

30 precarious
(A) insecure (B) wealthy
(C) deceitful (D) precipitous

31 secular
(A) not religious   (B) naval
(C) sanctimonious   (D) unorthodox

32 simultaneous
(A) chronological   (B) temporal
(C) at the same time (D) permanent

33 terse
(A) loquacious   (B) mumbled
(C) to the point (D) harmonious

34 transverse
(A) carried (B) broken into parts
(C) obtuse   (D) lying across

| ANSWER |

26. (A) 흐르는, 시사적인
    (B) 기분이 꺼림칙한 (C) 속박된
    (D) 구식의

27. (A) 나이의 (B) 발의
    (C) 원형의 (D) 직사각형의

28. (A) 액체가 통과할 수 있는
    (B) 옮길 수 있는, 양도할 수 있는
    (C) 반투명의 (D) 투과하지 않는

29. (A) 평화로운
    (B) (신체가) 무기력한, 맥없는
    (C) 부어오른 (D) 흥분한, 동요된

30. (A) 불안정안 (B) 부유한
    (C) 속이는, 거짓의
    (D) (절벽이) 가파른, 험한

31. (A) 종교적이 아닌 (B) 해군의
    (C) 신앙 깊은 체하는 (D) 비정통적인

32. (A) 연대기적인 (B) 임시의
    (C) 동시의 (D) 영원한

33. (A) 말 많은, 수다스런
    (B) 중얼거린 (C) 간결한, 요점의
    (D) 조화로운

34. (A) 운반된; 넋을 잃은, 황홀한
    (B) 산산이 부서지다
    (C) 둔한, 무딘 (D) 가로로 놓인

26. (D) 27. (C) 28. (A) 29. (A) 30. (A)
31. (A) 32. (C) 33. (C) 34. (D)

35 unprecedented
    (A) not planned   (B) never done before
    (C) without warning   (D) totally forgotten

36 superfluous
    (A) rapidly flowing   (B) very bright
    (C) extra   (D) necessary

37 tedious
    (A) boring   (B) minute
    (C) child-like   (D) melodious

38 urbane
    (A) from the city   (B) sneaky
    (C) smoothly polite   (D) rough-edged

39 quadrennial
    (A) every four years   (B) quarterly
    (C) four-eyed   (D) four-legged

| ANSWER |

35. (A) 계획되지 않은 (B) 전에 없는
    (C) 경고도 없이 (D) 완전히 잊혀진

36. (A) 급속히 흐르는 (B) 아주 똑똑한
    (C) 여분의 (D) 필요한

37. (A) 지루한 (B) 상세한
    (C) 유치한 (D) 선율이 아름다운

38. (A) 도시로부터의 (B) 남몰래 하는
    (C) 점잖은 (D) 무딘

39. (A) 4년마다의 (B) 분기별로, 연 4회의
    (C) 눈이 넷인 (D) 다리가 넷인

35. (B) 36. (C) 37. (A) 38. (C) 39. (A)

STEP 2 Mastery Test 2

[Synonym Test]

DIRECTIONS Choose the word or phrase that means most nearly the same as the key word.

1. analogous
   - (A) alike
   - (B) hidden
   - (C) metallic
   - (D) unreasonable

2. adroit
   - (A) clever
   - (B) moist
   - (C) aimless
   - (D) artistic

3. abhor
   - (A) convene
   - (B) deter
   - (C) applaud
   - (D) loathe

4. dogmatic
   - (A) manual
   - (B) doctrinaire
   - (C) canine
   - (D) unprincipled

5. garrulous
   - (A) fretful
   - (B) artistic
   - (C) murderous
   - (D) talkative

6. fallacious
   - (A) faltering
   - (B) stumbling
   - (C) deceptive
   - (D) foolish

7. indolence
   - (A) audacity
   - (B) arrogance
   - (C) laziness
   - (D) poverty

8. mitigate
   - (A) lessen
   - (B) incite
   - (C) measure
   - (D) prosecute

9. reprimand
   - (A) renege
   - (B) reorder
   - (C) rebuke
   - (D) retroactive

10. subversive
    - (A) secret
    - (B) foreign
    - (C) evasive
    - (D) destructive

11. subdue
    - (A) underground
    - (B) underweight
    - (C) vanquish
    - (D) overdue

] Antonym Test [

DIRECTIONS Choose the word or phrase that is most nearly opposite in meaning to the given word.

1. apathy
   - (A) sleep
   - (B) temptation
   - (C) zeal
   - (D) hospitality

2. agitate
   - (A) irritate
   - (B) placate
   - (C) pacify
   - (D) demonstrate

3. apprehensive
   - (A) appreciative
   - (B) aggressive
   - (C) estranged
   - (D) secure

4. avert
   - (A) hide
   - (B) cause
   - (C) excuse
   - (D) deny

5. animosity
   - (A) thoughtfulness
   - (B) friendliness
   - (C) reliability
   - (D) anxiety

6. apathetic
   - (A) alert
   - (B) sad
   - (C) infected
   - (D) harrowing

7. derisive
   - (A) dividing
   - (B) furnishing
   - (C) reflecting
   - (D) laudatory

8. deride
   - (A) fly
   - (B) praise
   - (C) amend
   - (D) admit

9. latent
   - (A) obvious
   - (B) invented
   - (C) troubled
   - (D) unique

10. recessive
    - (A) giving
    - (B) gouged
    - (C) slow-healing
    - (D) dominant

11. tangible
    - (A) required
    - (B) untouchable
    - (C) presentable
    - (D) illegal

Sentence Completion Test

DIRECTIONS Select the word or phrase that will best complete the meaning of the sentence as a whole.

1. He was the chief _____ of his uncle's will. After taxes he was left with an inheritance worth close to twenty thousand dollars.
   (A) executor
   (B) pensioner
   (C) beneficiary
   (D) contestant

2. A(n) _____ assistant is a great help to any employer.
   (A) sleepy
   (B) adept
   (C) absent
   (D) left-handed

3. One who _____ another is laughing at him, not with him.
   (A) derides
   (B) defiles
   (C) lambastes
   (D) defers

4. The otherwise beautiful music sounded tinny, because it was _____ by the strong wind in the open-air theater.
   (A) broken
   (B) distorted
   (C) dislocated
   (D) distracted

5. Because it is a creature of the wild, the timber wolf is not a _____ animal.
   (A) feline
   (B) lovable
   (C) docile
   (D) pleasing

6. She was a woman of _____ integrity; no one questioned her standards.
   (A) vague
   (B) indubitable
   (C) suspected
   (D) mysterious

7. The _____ mediator in the labor talks was known for his record of fairness in similar cases.
   (A) lucrative   (B) judicious
   (C) serendipitous (D) ludicrous

8. The druggist will fill any order your doctor _____.
   (A) prescribes (B) forbids
   (C) schedules   (D) proscribes

9. The heavy snowfall _____ my driving to work.
   (A) placated   (B) prejudiced
   (C) precluded (D) preoccupied

10. A news reporter, committed to printing only that which is true, always _____ a story before deadline.
    (A) verbifies   (B) verifies
    (C) ascertains (D) violates

11. Matters pertaining to daily life are referred to as _____ as opposed to religious.
    (A) sectarian (B) secluded
    (C) secular   (D) secondary

12. In some communist countries, residents are jailed as _____ when authorities feel that they are trying to overthrow the government.
    (A) incurables   (B) incorrigibles
    (C) perversives (D) subversives

ENGLISH FORUM

1000 essential words that often appear on the TOEFL
Step 3

| STEP 3 |

verb 동사

vocabulary 1000

abdicate
[ǽbdikèit]

포기하다, 버리다

<syn> give up, resign, abandon
<ant> claim, possess, keep

The father *abdicated* his responsibility by not setting a good example for the boy.
아버지는 자식에게 모범을 보이지 못함으로써 자기 책임을 포기하였다.

abet
[əbét]

부추기다, 선동하다

<syn> encourage, support, sustain, incite
<ant> discourage, dissuade, deter

Aiding and *abetting* an enemy of the country constitutes treason.
국가의 적을 돕고 선동하는 것은 반역죄에 해당한다.

abjure
[əbdʒúər]

포기하다, 철회하다

<syn> renounce, forswear, recant

A new citizen must *abjure* allegiance to his former country.
새로 시민이 되는 자는 이전 국가에 대한 의무를 포기해야 한다.

abscond
[æbskánd]

도망하다, 도피하다

<syn> steal off, flee, fly, run away

The teller *absconded* with the bank's funds.
은행 출납원이 은행자금을 가지고 달아났다.

STEP 3 · 동사 | 123

acquit
[əkwít]

석방하다, 고소를 취하하다

<syn> set free, declare not guilty, exonerate, release
<ant> charge, indict, convict, declare guilty

The jury *acquitted* the defendant.
배심원은 피고를 석방하였다.

actuate
[ǽktʃuèit]

작동시키다, 자극하다, 격려하다

<syn> put into action, incite, motivate, stimulate
<ant> check, curb, restrain, hinder

The machine was *actuated* by an electric starter.
기계는 전동기에 의해 작동되었다.

adjourn
[ədʒə́:rn]

휴회하다, 산회하다, 연기하다

<syn> suspend proceedings, recess, postpone, put off
<ant> convene, be in session, continue, reopen

Since it is now five o'clock, I move that we *adjourn* until tomorrow morning.
이제 5시가 되었으므로 저는 내일 아침까지 휴회할 것을 동의합니다.

admonish
[ædmάniʃ]

경고하다, 충고하다, 주의를 주다

<syn> warn, caution, advise
<ant> praise, compliment, commend

The child was *admonished* not to run into the roadway.
그 아이는 도로에 뛰어들지 않도록 주의를 받았다.

advocate
[ǽdvəkit]

주장하다, 촉구하다, 변호하다

<syn> plead for, urge, propose
<ant> oppose, combat, attack

Socialists *advocate* public ownership of utilities.
사회주의자들은 공공설비의 공공소유를 주장한다.

allay
[əléi]

가라앉히다, 누그러뜨리다, 완화시키다

<syn> pacify, calm, relieve, ease
<ant> arouse, excite, make worse

Therapy will often *allay* the fears of the neurotic.
치료법이 신경증 환자의 두려움을 누그러뜨려 주기도 할 것이다.

allude
[əlúːd]

언급하다, 넌지시 비추다, 암시하다

<syn> refer indirectly, hint, mention, speak of
<ant> keep secret, keep quiet about

The report *alludes* to a later document.
보도는 나중의 기록에 대해 언급하고 있다.

amalgamate
[əmǽlgəmèit]

합병하다, 융합하다, 혼합하다

<syn> combine, blend, merge, fuse, join together
<ant> separate, part, divide, disunite

We will have to *amalgamate* all our groups in order to be strong.
강해지기 위해 우리는 모든 조직을 통합해야 할 것이다.

annotate
[ǽnətèit]

주를 달다, 주석하다

<syn> provide explanatory notes, explicate, commentate, remark

Annotations are sometimes the most interesting part of a text, but they are often overlooked.
주석은 때로 텍스트의 가장 재미있는 부분이 되기도 하는데, 흔히 간과된다.

apprise
[əpráiz]

알리다, 통지하다

<syn> give notice, inform, notify, tell
<ant> keep secret, keep quiet about

He was captured because none could *apprise* him of the enemy advance.
아무도 적의 진격을 알려주지 못해 그는 포로로 잡혔다.

ascertain
[æ̀sərtéin]

확인하다, 조사하다, 알아내다

<syn> find out, establish, determine, learn, discover, detect

Because the woman's story was so confused, we have been unable to *ascertain* whether a crime was committed or not.
그 여자의 이야기는 너무 혼동되어서 우리는 범죄가 저질러졌는지 아닌지 알아낼 수가 없었다.

attenuate
[əténjuèit]

묽게 하다, 엷게 하다, 줄이다

<syn> make thin, dilute, weaken, reduce
<ant> make thick, enlarge, expand, increase

His mumbling delivery and hesitant manner *attenuated* the force of his remarks.
그의 중얼거리는 연설과 망설이는 태도는 자기 소견의 설득력을 반감시켰다.

beguile
[bigáil]

현혹시키다, 미혹시키다, 사기치다

\<syn\> mislead, deceive, delude, lure
\<ant\> enlighten, disabuse, alert

Where he found himself weak, he would *beguile* the opposition into applauding his propositions.
자신이 약하다는 사실을 알게 되면, 그는 상대를 현혹시켜 자신의 제안에 성원하도록 할 것이다.

capitulate
[kəpítʃəlèit]

항복하다, 조건부로 항복하다

\<syn\> surrender, give up, yield, lay down one's arms
\<ant\> defeat, win over, be victorious

The city *capitulated* to the victors.
그 도시는 정복자들에게 항복하였다.

coincide
[kòuinsáid]

일치하다, 동시에 발생하다, 겹치다

\<syn\> be concurrent, be alike, occur at the same time
\<ant\> disagree, be unlike, be inconsistent

This year Thanksgiving *coincides* with her birthday.
올해는 추수감사절이 그녀의 생일과 일치한다.

concede
[kənsí:d]

인정하다, 시인하다

\<syn\> admit, acquiesce, accept, yield, give up
\<ant\> deny, refute, reject

When the candidate realized she could not win, she *conceded* gracefully.
그 후보는 자신이 이길 수 없음을 깨닫고 깨끗이 인정했다.

condone
[kəndóun]

용서하다, 관용을 베풀다

\<syn\> pardon, overlook an offense, forgive, let pass
\<ant\> condemn, denounce, censure, disapprove

The law will not *condone* an act on the plea that the culprit was intoxicated.
피의자가 중독되었다는 핑계에도 어떤 행동을 법률은 용서하지 않을 것이다.

confute
[kənfjú:t]

논박하다, 논박하여 꼼짝못하게 하다 (overwhelm by argument)

His logical rebuttal *confuted* the reasoning of the opposition.
그의 논리적인 반증이 반대파의 이의를 잠재웠다.

construe
[kənstrúː]

해석하다, 추론하다

<syn> interpret, analyze, comprehend, understand, figure out

His attitude was *construed* as one of opposition to the proposal.
그의 태도는 그 제안에 대한 반대로 해석되었다.

converge
[kənvə́ːrdʒ]

한 데 모이다, 집중하다, 수렴하다

<syn> move nearer together, head for one point, come together

The flock *converged* on the seeded field.
새떼가 파종한 밭에 모여들었다.

countermand
[kàuntərmǽnd]

명령을 철회하다, 주문을 취소하다 (revoke an order or command)

The wise executive will not hesitate to *countermand* an unwise order.
현명한 관리자는 현명하지 못한 명령을 철회하는 데 주저하지 않는다.

curtail
[kəːrtéil]

줄이다, 생략하다, 삭감하다

<syn> reduce, shorten, cut, pare down, abridge
<ant> lengthen, extend, prolong, expand

Classes were reduced to *curtail* teaching costs.
교육비를 줄이기 위해 학급들이 줄어들었다.

decry
[dikrái]

비방하다, 중상하다

<syn> clamor against, criticize, denounce, condemn, disparage, censure
<ant> extol, acclaim, laud, commend, praise

Critics *decry* the lack of emotion on the stage.
비평가들은 무대에서 감정이 결핍되어 있다고 비난한다.

defile
[difáil]

더럽히다, 모독하다

<syn> befoul, make profane, dishonor, debase
<ant> hallow, consecrate, sanctify

A man is not allowed to wear shoes in a mosque, lest he *defile* it.
이슬람사원에서 남자는 사원을 더럽히지 않도록 신발을 신는 것이 허용되지 않는다.

denigrate
[dénigrèit]

더럽히다, 모독하다, 훼손하다

<syn> blacken, defame, cast aspersions on

The lawyer tried to *denigrate* the character of the witness by implying that he was a liar.
변호사는 증인이 거짓말쟁이라고 암시함으로써 그의 인격을 훼손하려고 애썼다.

deplete
[diplíːt]

고갈시키다, 빼앗다

<syn> empty, use up, exhaust, drain, lessen, reduce, decrease
<ant> increase, augment

At the present rates of consumption, the known reserves will be *depleted* before the end of the century.
현재의 소비 속도로 볼 때, 알려진 매장량은 세기말이 되기 전에 고갈될 것이다.

dilate
[dailéit]

팽창시키다, 넓히다

<syn> expand, swell, enlarge, distend, inflate, broaden
<ant> constrict, contract, shrink, compress, narrow

Some drugs will cause the pupil of the eye to *dilate*.
어떤 약은 눈동자의 동공을 팽창시키기도 한다.

disparage
[dispǽridʒ]

얕보다, 비방하다, 나쁘게 말하다

<syn> speak slightingly of, belittle, discredit, denigrate
<ant> applaud, praise, laud, acclaim, commend, compliment

A teacher who *disparages* the efforts of beginners in her subject is not helping them.
초보자들이 자기 과목에서 보여주는 노력을 깔보는 교사는 그들을 돕는 게 아니다.

diverge
[divə́ːrdʒ]

갈라지다

<syn> separate, deviate, split off, deflect
<ant> converge, agree, concur

The map showed a main lode with thin veins *diverging* in all directions.
지도는 모든 방향으로 갈라지는 얇은 선으로 간선도로를 보여주었다.

divulge
[divʌ́ldʒ]

누설하다, 폭로하다

<syn> reveal, make public, disclose, impart, make known, communicate
<ant> conceal, hide, keep secret

Newspapermen have long fought the courts for the right not to *divulge* their sources of information.
신문기자들은 자신들의 취재원을 누설하지 않을 권리를 위해 법원과 오래 싸웠다.

edify
[édəfài]

교화하다, 계몽하다 (instruct)

Some teachers *edify*; others merely try.
어떤 교사는 품성을 고양시키는데, 어떤 교사는 시도만 한다.

enervate
[énərvèit]

약화시키다, 기력을 빼앗다

\<syn\> weaken, enfeeble, exhaust, weary
\<ant\> energize, invigorate, strengthen, vitalize

A poor diet will *enervate* a person.
어설픈 다이어트는 사람의 기력을 빼앗는다.

engender
[endʒéndər]

발생시키다, 야기하다

\<syn\> produce, cause, beget, give rise to, bring about, generate
\<ant\> kill, end, crush

Angry words may *engender* strife.
성낸 말은 다툼을 일으킬 수 있다.

engross
[engróus]

마음을 빼앗다, 몰두시키다

\<syn\> fully absorb, occupy, involve, monopolize
\<ant\> bore, tire, weary, vex

He was so *engrossed* in his hobbies that he neglected his studies.
그는 자기 취미에 너무 빠져서 자기 공부를 소홀히 하였다.

exhort
[igzɔ́:rt]

권고하다, 충고하다

\<syn\> incite by words, advice, encourage, spur
\<ant\> dissuade, discourage, forbid

He *exhorted* the mob to attack the station.
그는 군중들에게 역을 공격할 것을 권고하였다.

extenuate
[iksténjuèit]

정상을 참작하다, 변명하다, 약화시키다

\<syn\> partially excuse, justify, mitigate, attenuate, seem to lessen
\<ant\> unjustify, aggravate, intensify

His abrupt rudeness was *extenuated* by his distraught state of mind; no one could blame him for it.
그의 퉁명스런 무례함은 그의 혼란한 마음상태로 참작되어서 아무도 그것을 비난할 수 없었다.

fluctuate
[flʌ́ktʃuèit]

오르내리다, 변동하다

\<syn\> change continually, rise and fall, vary irregularly, shift
\<ant\> hold fast, persist, stand firm

Fluctuations in stock market prices create many paper losses and profits.
주식시황의 많은 변동은 많은 증권의 손실과 이익을 창출한다.

illuminate
[ilú:mənèit]

밝히다, 비추다, 설명하다

<syn> throw light on, explain, irradiate, clarify
<ant> darken, obliterate, obscure

The editor's notes *illuminated* the more obscure passages in the text.
편집자의 주는 텍스트의 매우 불확실한 단락들을 설명해 주고 있었다.

impede
[impí:d]

방해하다

<syn> hinder, obstruct, block, deter, interrupt
<ant> assist, promote, advance, help, aid

The flying shrapnel *impeded* the progress of the troops.
날아다니는 포탄파편이 부대의 전진을 방해하였다.

impute
[impjú:t]

...의 탓으로 돌리다, 고소하다

<syn> attribute, ascribe, charge, refer

The difficulties were *imputed* to his negligence.
어려움은 그의 부주의 탓으로 돌아갔다.

incur
[inkə́:r]

손해를 입다, 빚을 지다

<syn> contract, bring into being, assume, bring on, acquire

The debts *incurred* in the legal proceedings were to be paid off in monthly installments.
법률적 과정에서 진 빚은 월부로 갚기로 되어 있었다.

intercede
[ìntərsí:d]

중재하다, 조정하다

<syn> interpose, intervene, arbitrate, mediate, play intermediary
<ant> withdraw, remain aloof, remain neutral

He asked his preacher to *intercede* with the judge.
그는 자기 전도사에게 판사와 중재할 것을 부탁하였다.

inundate
[ínəndèit]

범람시키다, 넘치게 하다

<syn> flood, engulf, overflow, fill with water
<ant> drain dry, reclaim, desiccate

When the craze was at its height, the police were *inundated* with daily reports of UFO sightings.
열광이 최고조에 달하자 UFO 목격보고가 매일 경찰서에 넘쳐 났다.

knead
[niːd]

반죽하다, 혼합하다, 빚어 만들다

<syn> mix, squeeze, and press with the hands, massage

She *kneaded* the dough before shaping it into four loaves for baking.
그녀는 밀가루를 반죽하여 빵으로 굽기 위해 네 덩어리로 만들었다.

militate
[mílitèit]

작용하다, 영향을 미치다

<syn> operate against, work against

A poor appearance at the interview will *militate* against your being hired.
인터뷰에서의 어설픈 모습이 네가 고용되는 것에 영향을 줄 것이다.

mollify
[málifài]

진정시키다, 달래다

<syn> soothe, placate, appease, calm, moderate, ease
<ant> exasperate, agitate, stir, increase

The irate customer was *mollified* by the manager's prompt action and apology.
화난 고객이 지배인의 즉각적인 조치와 사과로 진정되었다.

mutilate
[mjúːtəlèit]

절단하다, 손상을 입히다

<syn> cut up, damage severely, butcher, maim, lacerate

The computer cannot read a mutilated card.
컴퓨터는 손상된 카드를 읽지 못한다.

negate
[nigéit]

부인하다, 취소하다, 무효화하다

<syn> make nothing, undo, make ineffective
<ant> affirm, confirm, ratify

The witness's full confession *negated* the need for further questions.
증인의 완전한 자백이 더 이상의 질문이 필요 없게 하였다.

nullify
[nʌ́ləfài]

무효화하다, 폐기시키다

<syn> make void, repeal, cancel, abolish, set aside
<ant> enact, decree, legislate, ratify, confirm

The new contract *nullifies* their previous agreement.
새로운 계약이 그들의 이전의 합의를 무효화시켰다.

obsess
[əbsés]

(귀신이나 망상이) 들리다, 붙다, 괴롭히다

<syn> beset, possess, dominate, haunt the mind

He was *obsessed* with the idea he was important.
그는 자기가 중요하다는 생각에 사로잡혔다.

obviate
[ábvièit]

방지하다, 제거하다, 회피하다

<syn> prevent, avert, forestall, preclude, do away with
<ant> require, necessitate, make essential

Obviate the necessity for earning money, and all your time is your own.
돈벌이의 필요성을 없애라. 그러면 모든 시간은 당신 자신의 것이다.

oscillate
[ásəlèit]

진동하다, 왔다갔다하다 (swing in a regular motion)

The pendulum continued to *oscillate*, but the clock hands did not move.
진자는 계속해서 왔다갔다하였으나 시계바늘은 움직이지 않았다.

palliate
[pǽlièit]

(잘못을) 가볍게 하다, 완화하다, 변명하다

<syn> ease a disease without curing, cover by excuse and apologies

He attempted to *palliate* his error by explaining the extenuating circumstances.
그는 정상참작의 상황을 설명하여 자신의 실수를 변명하려고 하였다.

perpetrate
[pə́:rpətrèit]

(나쁜 짓을) 행하다, 저지르다, 범하다

<syn> do something evil, commit a crime

The committee *perpetrated* the hoax in an attempt to defame the rival candidate.
위원회는 경쟁후보를 비난하려는 시도로 날조를 하였다.

placate
[pléikeit]

달래다, 화해시키다, 회유하다

<syn> soothe, pacify, calm, mollify, assuage, appease, conciliate

A quick temper is often easily *placated*.
급한 성격이 흔히 쉽게 화해된다.

reconcile
[rékənsàil]

화해시키다, 조화시키다 (bring to agreement)

<syn> conciliate, conform, accommodate, harmonize, coordinate, settle

After hours of recalculating the incorrect figures, we were able to *reconcile* the two accounts.
잘못된 총액을 몇 시간 동안 다시 계산한 뒤에야 우리는 두 고객을 화해시킬 수 있었다.

redeem
[ridí:m]

되찾다, 회복하다, 벌충하다

<syn> save, ransom, free by buying back, recover, compensate for
<ant> lose, forfeit, yield, give up, break

Though the film is boring in parts, it is *redeemed* by a gripping finale.
영화가 일부 따분하지만 주의를 끄는 결말로 벌충한다.

remit
[rimít]

송금하다, 지급하다

<syn> pay, send payment, reimburse, compensate

The invoice was *remitted* by check; you should be receiving it shortly.
매입송장이 수표로 송금되었으니 곧 수령하게 될 것입니다.

renounce
[rináuns]

포기하다, 부인하다, 단념하다 (give up or disown, usually by formal statement)

<syn> give up, refuse, resign, abdicate, relinquish
<ant> avow, assert, proclaim, maintain, uphold

The nation was urged to *renounce* its dependence on imports and to buy more American cars.
그 나라는 독자적인 수입을 포기하고 미국 자동차를 더 구매할 것을 촉구받았다.

repress
[riprés]

억압하다, 저지하다 (keep from expression or consciousness)

<syn> subdue, hold back, keep down, keep in check, curb, restrain
<ant> let out, release, express, encourage, incite

We could not *repress* a certain nervousness as the plane bumped along the runway.
비행기가 활주로를 덜컥거리며 지나갈 때 우리는 어떤 신경과민증세를 억제할 수가 없었다.

repudiate
[ripjú:dièit]

거부하다, 받아들이지 않다 (refuse to accept)

<syn> reject, deny, disown, disavow, cast off, discard
<ant> accept, approve, adopt

The candidate *repudiated* the endorsement of the Communist party.
그 후보자는 공산당을 승인하기를 거부하였다.

rescind
{risínd}

폐지하다, 취소하다, 무효로 하다 (cancel formally or take back)

<syn> revoke, reverse, retract, recall, repeal
<ant> uphold, support, validate

They *rescinded* their offer of aid when they became disillusioned with the project.
그들은 프로젝트에 환멸을 느끼게 되어 돕겠다던 자신들의 제안을 취소하였다.

retrogress
{rétrəgrès}

후퇴하다, 퇴화하다, 역행하다 (go backward, lose ground)

Because of the devastation of the recent earthquakes, living conditions in the region have *retrogressed*.
최근의 지진의 참사로 그 지역의 생활조건이 후퇴하였다.

suffuse
{səfjúːz}

뒤덮다, 확 퍼지다, 채우다 (spread over or through in the manner of a fluid or light)

<syn> overspread, infuse, imbue, ingrain

The floor was *suffused* with a disinfectant wax.
바닥이 소독용 왁스로 뒤덮였다.

temporize
{témpəràiz}

임시 변통하다, 시간을 끌다 (delay immediate action in order to gain time)

He *temporized* until he knew what they wanted from him.
그는 그들이 자기에게서 원하는 것이 무엇인지 알게 될 때까지 시간을 끌었다.

upbraid
{ʌpbréid}

꾸짖다, 나무라다 (charge with something disgraceful, reprove with severity)

<syn> reproach, criticize, scold severly, reprove, rebuke, reprimand
<ant> praise, laud, compliment, command, applaud

The husband *upbraided* his wife for her extravagances.
남편은 아내의 사치를 나무랐다.

vindicate
{víndəkèit}

입증하다; 주장하다

<syn> uphold, support, advocate, maintain, assert, justify

The judgement of the author was *vindicated* by the phenomenal sale of the text.
저자에 대한 판단은 텍스트의 놀라운 판매로 입증되었다.

STEP 3 Practice Test 7

DIRECTIONS Select the word or phrase that means most nearly the same as the key word.

1. **abjure**
   - (A) swear
   - (B) remember
   - (C) legislate
   - (D) renounce

2. **abscond**
   - (A) forgive
   - (B) abstain
   - (C) cut and slash
   - (D) steal and flee

3. **acquit**
   - (A) walk out
   - (B) condemn
   - (C) set free
   - (D) apply for

4. **advocate**
   - (A) speak to
   - (B) warn
   - (C) plead for
   - (D) scold

5. **actuate**
   - (A) conceive
   - (B) promulgate
   - (C) deny
   - (D) incite

6. **allude**
   - (A) escape
   - (B) stick out
   - (C) suggest
   - (D) prevent

7. **amalgamate**
   - (A) allocate
   - (B) dispersal
   - (C) bring together
   - (D) decorate

| ANSWER |

1. (A) 맹세하다 (B) 기억하다
   (C) 법규를 제정하다
   (D) 포기하다, 단념하다

2. (A) 용서하다 (B) 삼가다, 금하다
   (C) 삭감하다 (D) 훔쳐 달아나다

3. (A) 외출하다 (B) 비난하다
   (C) 석방하다 (D) 지원하다

4. (A) 언급하다 (B) 경고하다
   (C) 변호하다 (D) 꾸짖다

5. (A) 상상하다 (B) 공포하다
   (C) 부인하다 (D) 부추기다

6. (A) 탈출하다 (B) 튀어나오다
   (C) 제안하다, 언급하다 (D) 방지하다

7. (A) 분배하다 (B) 분산
   (C) 모으다 (D) 장식하다

1. (D) 2. (D) 3. (C) 4. (C)
5. (D) 6. (C) 7. (C)

8 ascertain
   (A) uncover   (B) sweeten
   (C) ponder   (D) prove

9 allay
   (A) mixture   (B) a greeting
   (C) tuck in   (D) calm

10 annotate
   (A) tear   (B) protect by law
   (C) provide explanation (D) truncate

11 apprise
   (A) startle   (B) revenge
   (C) give notice (D) close

12 beguile
   (A) deceive   (B) wander
   (C) fling   (D) harass

13 capitulate
   (A) surrender   (B) decapitate
   (C) invest   (D) demand

14 construe
   (A) hurl   (B) intercept
   (C) interpret   (D) spread

15 converge
   (A) plummet
   (B) climb
   (C) move closer together
   (D) whisper

| ANSWER |

8. (A) 드러내다 (B) 달콤하게 하다
   (C) 깊이 생각하다 (D) 입증하다

9. (A) 혼합하다 (B) 인사
   (C) 밀어 넣다 (D) 가라앉히다

10. (A) 눈물을 흘리다
    (B) 법률로 보호하다
    (C) 설명하다 (D) 끝을 자르다

11. (A) 놀라게 하다 (B) 복수하다
    (C) 통지하다 (D) 닫다

12. (A) 속이다 (B) 방랑하다
    (C) 던지다 (D) 괴롭히다

13. (A) 항복하다 (B) 목을 베다
    (C) 투자하다 (D) 요구하다

14. (A) 집어던지다 (B) 가로막다
    (C) 해석하다 (D) 펼치다

15. (A) 수직으로 떨어지다
    (B) 기어오르다 (C) 함께 모이다
    (D) 속삭이다

8. (D) 9. (D) 10. (C) 11. (C)
12. (A) 13. (A) 14. (C) 15. (C)

16 curtail
(A) remove (B) repeal
(C) reduce (D) remorse

17 defile
(A) befoul (B) misplace
(C) disown (D) adulterate

18 countermand
(A) invoke (B) revoke an order
(C) slap (D) retired

19 denigrate
(A) defame (B) assign
(C) deny (D) renounce

20 deplete
(A) disperse (B) empty
(C) devalue (D) erase

21 divulge
(A) expansive actions (B) increase
(C) engorge (D) reveal

22 engross
(A) increase (B) monopolize
(C) amass (D) resume

23 exhort
(A) warm (B) incite by advice
(C) report (D) deceive

24 fluctuate
(A) erupt (B) guess
(C) worry (D) vary

| ANSWER |

16. (A) 제거하다 (B) 무효화하다
    (C) 줄이다 (D) 후회, 양심의 가책

17. (A) (명예를) 더럽히다
    (B) (자리를) 잘못 두다
    (C) 소유를 부인하다
    (D) 타락시키다

18. (A) 기원하다, 빌다
    (B) 명령을 철회하다
    (C) 손바닥으로 한번 때림
    (D) 퇴직한

19. (A) 명예를 훼손하다 (B) 위임하다
    (C) 부인하다 (D) 포기하다

20. (A) 흩뜨리다 (B) 비우다, 고갈시키다
    (C) 가치를 내리다 (D) 지우다

21. (A) 거리낌없는 행동 (B) 증가하다
    (C) 포식하다 (D) 누설하다

22. (A) 증가시키다 (B) 독점하다
    (C) 축적하다 (D) 회복하다

23. (A) 따뜻하게 하다
    (B) 충고로 자극하다
    (C) 보고하다 (D) 속이다

24. (A) 분출하다 (B) 추측하다
    (C) 걱정하다 (D) 변화하다

16. (C) 17. (A) 18. (B) 19. (A) 20. (B)
21. (D) 22. (B) 23. (B) 24. (D)

25 incur
(A) acquire through actions (B) do again
(C) flowing beneath (D) make black

26 intercede
(A) interpose (B) interfere
(C) intercept (D) intermural

27 inundate
(A) interrupt (B) flood
(C) cancel (D) empty

28 militate
(A) work against (B) arm
(C) attack (D) debate

29 negate
(A) mock (B) make ineffective
(C) transmute (D) weigh down

30 mutilate
(A) damage severely (B) grind
(C) masticate (D) return unopened

31 oscillate
(A) swallow (B) swim
(C) hammer (D) swing

32 palliate
(A) spear (B) lessen
(C) ride across (D) spread

33 remit
(A) allow to return (B) send away
(C) welcome (D) send payment

| ANSWER |

25. (A) 행위를 통해 얻게 되다
    (B) 다시 하다
    (C) 아래로 흐르다 (D) 검게 하다

26. (A) 삽입하다, 중재하다 (B) 간섭하다
    (C) 가로채다 (D) 도시 간의

27. (A) 중단시키다 (B) 범람하다
    (C) 취소하다 (D) 비우다

28. (A) 반대하다, (나쁘게) 작용하다
    (B) 무장하다 (C) 공격하다
    (D) 토론하다

29. (A) 비웃다 (B) 무효화하다
    (C) 변형시키다
    (D) 힘주어 내리누르다

30. (A) 심하게 손상을 입히다
    (B) 갈다, 가루로 만들다
    (C) (음식물을) 씹다, 분쇄하다
    (D) 포장된 채 돌아오다

31. (A) 삼키다 (B) 수영하다
    (C) 망치질하다
    (D) 왔다갔다하다, 흔들거리다

32. (A) 창으로 찌르다 (B) 줄이다
    (C) 타고 건너다 (D) 퍼지다

33. (A) 반환을 허락하다 (B) 멀리 보내다
    (C) 환영하다 (D) 송금하다

25. (A) 26. (A) 27. (B) 28. (A) 29. (B)
30. (A) 31. (D) 32. (B) 33. (D)

34 repress
(A) iron again   (B) subdue
(C) prod   (D) encourage

35 repudiate
(A) go on foot   (B) become ill
(C) accept as legitimate (D) refuse to accept

36 reconcile
(A) bring to agreement (B) reconsider
(C) ponder   (D) bring to fruition

37 rescind
(A) cancel (B) burn
(C) raise   (D) return

38 retrogress
(A) lose ground (B) return
(C) diminish   (D) spiral

39 suffuse
(A) overspread (B) inject
(C) suppress   (D) welter

40 temporize
(A) count (B) delay
(C) order (D) select

| ANSWER |

34. (A) 다시 다림질하다 (B) 억압하다
    (C) 찌르다, 자극하다 (D) 격려하다

35. (A) 걸어가다 (B) 발병하다
    (C) 옳다고 받아들이다
    (D) 수용을 거부하다

36. (A) 합의에 이르다 (B) 재고하다
    (C) 생각하다 (D) 결실을 맺다

37. (A) 취소하다 (B) 불태우다
    (C) 일으키다 (D) 돌려보내다

38. (A) 물러가다, 패퇴하다
    (B) 되돌려주다 (C) 줄이다
    (D) 나선형의

39. (A) 만연하다, 널리 퍼지다
    (B) 주입하다 (C) 억압하다
    (D) 소요, 동요

40. (A) 수를 세다 (B) 시간을 늦추다
    (C) 주문하다 (D) 고르다

34. (B) 35. (D) 36. (A)
37. (A) 38. (A) 39. (A) 40. (B)

STEP 3

noun 명사

vocabulary 1000

acumen
[əkjúːmən]

예민함, 총명

<syn> sharpness, keenness, acuteness
<ant> obtuseness, dullness, ignorance

The *acumen* of many early industrialists accounts for their success.
수많은 영리한 초기 산업가들이 성공을 거두었다.

affiliation
[əfìliéiʃən]

가입, 결연, 제휴

<syn> connection, association, relationship, alliance, union

His *affiliation* with the club has been of long standing; he has been a member for over ten years.
그가 그 클럽에 가입한 것은 오래되었으니, 10년이 넘도록 회원이다.

annals
[ǽnəlz]

연대기, 연보

<syn> chronological/yearly records, chronicles, historical rolls

The *annals* of the scientific societies reflect the advance of our era.
과학 학회들의 연보는 우리 시대의 진보를 반영하고 있다.

antecedent
[æ̀ntəsíːdənt]

선례, 전례, 이전 일

<syn> something preceding, precedent, precursor
<ant> successor, consequence, result

All history is a repetition of *antecedents*.
모든 역사는 전례의 반복이다.

antithesis
[æntíθəsis]

정반대

<syn> direct opposite, reverse, contrast, converse
Black is the *antithesis* of white.
흑은 백의 정반대이다.

archetype
[ά:rkitàip]

원형

<syn> prime example, original model, prototype
Solomon is the *archetype* of the wise man.
솔로몬은 현인의 원형이다.

bastion
[bǽstʃən]

요새, 방어거점

<syn> fortress, fortification, bulwark, stronghold
The *bastion* projects outward from the main enclosure.
그 요새는 본부병영으로부터 밖으로 불쑥 나와 있었다.

biped
[báiped]

두 발 동물 (a two-footed animal)

Man and birds are listed among the *bipeds*.
인간과 조류가 두 발 동물에 속한다.

calligraphy
[kəlígrəfi]

서예

<syn> penmanship
The *calligraphy* of the monks is the basis of many printing typefaces today.
수사들의 서예는 오늘날 수많은 인쇄용 서체들의 기본이다.

carnage
[ká:rnidʒ]

살육, 대량학살

<syn> destruction of life, slaughter, mass killing, massacre
The *carnage* of modern warfare is frightful to consider.
현대전의 대량살상은 생각만 해도 끔찍하다.

catalyst
[kǽtəlist]

촉매, 기폭제

Platinum is a *catalyst* in many processes; it speeds chemical changes without being affected itself.
수많은 화학공정의 촉매로 쓰이는 백금은 화학적 변화를 촉진시키면서도 스스로는 아무런 영향을 받지 않는다.

circumlocution
[sə̀ːrkəmloukjúːʃən]

완곡한 표현, 장황한 표현

<syn> roundabout expression, meandering
<ant> directness, brevity

The audience was restive as the speaker's *circumlocution* went on and on without making a point.
연설자의 완곡한 표현이 핵심을 잡지 못하고 계속 나가자 관중들이 술렁거렸다.

colloquy
[kάləkwi]

대화, 토의, 회의

<syn> conversation, conference

The faculty held a *colloquy* on grading methods.
교수회는 등급 방식에 관한 토의를 가졌다.

complement
[kάmpləmənt]

1. 보충, 보완

<syn> completion, supplement

An expensive wardrobe is the *complement* to his impeccable grooming.
비싼 옷장은 그의 완벽한 치장에 보완이다.

2. 정원, 정족수

<syn> full amount, full number, total

A *complement* of twelve citizens make up the jury.
시민 12명의 정족수로 배심원단을 채웠다.

complicity
[kəmplísəti]

공모, 연루

<syn> partnership in wrongdoing, accomplice

By withholding evidence she became guilty of *complicity* in the crime.
증거를 고지하지 않음으로써 그녀는 범죄의 공범이 되었다.

dictum
[díktəm]

공식견해, 단정

<syn> an authoritative statement, pronouncement, decree, saying

The professor's *dictum* ended the debate.
교수님의 견해가 토론을 끝냈다.

diffidence
[dífidəns]

자신 없음, 망설임, 사양

<syn> timidity, humility, shyness, reserve
<ant> boldness, audaciousness, confidence

His *diffidence* caused him to miss many opportunities.
자신감 부족이 그로 하여금 많은 기회를 놓치게 하였다.

disparity
[dispǽrəti]

같지 않음, 불일치, 불균형

<syn> inequality, difference in degree

A *disparity* in age need not mean an incompatible marriage.
나이가 다르다고 해서 어울리지 않는 결혼이라 생각할 필요는 없다.

duplicity
[dju:plísəti]

이중성, 표리부동, 사기, 불성실

<syn> hypocrisy, double-dealing, deceit, fraud, dishonesty
<ant> straightforwardness, candor, forthrightness

The *duplicity* of the marketplace may shock the naive.
시장의 이중성은 순진한 사람들에게 충격을 줄 수 있다.

edict
[í:dikt]

칙령, 포고

<syn> public notice, decree, proclamation, pronouncement, dictum

The *edict* issued by the junta dissolved the government.
의회에서 발표된 포고문은 행정부를 해체시켰다.

equanimity
[ì:kwəníməti]

평정, 침착

<syn> calm temper, evenness of mind, composure self-possession
<ant> panic, hysteria, disquiet, agitation, discomposure

Adversity could not disturb his *equanimity*.
역경도 그의 평정을 흔들지 못했다.

eulogy
[jú:lədʒi]

찬사, 송덕문 (v. eulogize 칭송하다)

<syn> oration of praise, praise of the dead, encomium, panegyric, tribute
<ant> condemnation, criticism, vilification

He asked that no *eulogy* be delivered at his funeral.
그는 자신의 장례식에 어떤 송덕문도 발표하지 말 것을 주문하였다.

euphemism
[jú:fəmìzəm]

완곡어법

<syn> mild expression, restrained expression, delicate term

Like many other people, he used "gone" and "passed away" as *euphemisms* for "dead".
다른 많은 사람들처럼, 그는 "죽었다"는 말 대신에 "갔다"와 "떠났다"는 말을 사용했다.

euthanasia
[jùːθənéiʒiə]

안락사

<syn> easy death, mercy killing

Euthanasia is not legal.
안락사는 불법이다.

evasion
[ivéiʒən]

회피, 둘러댐

<syn> equivocal statement, avoiding, dodging, eluding, circumventing
<ant> confronting, facing up to, frankness, candor

His indirect answers were an attempt at *evasion*.
그의 간접적인 대답은 회피하려는 시도였다.

expulsion
[ikspʌ́lʃən]

추방, 배제

<syn> expelling, ejection, ousting, removal, act of driving out
<ant> acceptance, entering

The *expulsion* of the students from the university was unfair.
대학에서 학생들을 추방하는 것은 옳지 않았다.

hindsight
[háindsàit]

뒤 가늠자, 때늦은 지혜

<syn> a looking backward, aftersight, retrospection
<ant> a looking ahead, power of foreseeing, prevision,

With *hindsight* I realize that everything she said to me was true, though I could not accept it at the time.
그녀가 내게 말한 모든 것을 당시에는 받아들일 수 없었지만 때늦은 지혜로, 사실임을 깨닫는다.

holocaust
[háləkɔ̀ːst]

대학살; 큰불

<syn> a great destruction of living beings by fire

As the fire raged out of control, thousands of lives were lost in the *holocaust*.
통제할 수 없는 큰 화재로 수천 명이 목숨을 잃었다.

hypertension
[háipərtènʃən]

고혈압 (high blood pressure)

Hypertension is often a cause of serious diseases.
고혈압은 흔히 심각한 질병의 원인이다.

hypothesis
[haipáθəsis]

가설 (as unproved explanation)

She started with the *hypothesis* that the earth was spheroid and concluded it would be possible to go east by sailing west.
그녀는 지구가 회전타원체라는 가설로 시작하여 서쪽으로 항해하면 동쪽으로 갈 수 있을 것이라는 결론을 내렸다.

ideologue
[áidiəlɔ̀(:)g]

이론가, 공상가 (one who believes in and propagates a social doctrine)

The communist *ideologue* argued that the state was more important than any individual.
그 공산주의 이론가는 국가가 어떤 개인보다 더 중요하다고 주장하였다.

inception
[insépʃən]

처음, 발단

<syn> beginning, start, commencement, birth
<ant> termination, end, completion, finish

The scheme was hare-brained from its *inception*; it was no surprise when it was abandoned.
설계가 처음부터 무모한 것이었기에, 그것이 폐기되는 것이 놀라울 일도 아니었다.

interdict
[ìntərdíkt]

금지, 금지령 (official order prohibiting)

He issued an *interdict* on carrying arms.
그는 무기휴대 금지령을 내렸다.

lassitude
[lǽsitjùːd]

나른함, 권태, 피로

<syn> weariness, fatigue, languor, languidness
<ant> vigor, freshness, verve, spirit, vitality

The heat created a *lassitude* among the tourists that caused them to postpone their sightseeing.
더위가 여행객들을 피곤하게 하여 관광을 취소하게 만들었다.

levity
[lévəti]

경솔함, 경거망동, 경박함

<syn> lightness of spirit, frivolity, playfulness, whimsy, hilarity
<ant> gravity, seriousness, sobriety, earnestness, dignity

The party toys and silly costumes epitomized the *levity* of the occasion.
파티 장난감과 바보 같은 의상들이 그 행사의 경박함을 요약해 보여주었다.

magnate
[mǽgneit]

(경제분야의) 실력자, 거물

<syn> important business person, dominant person, VIP
<slang> bigwig, big shot, big wheel, big gun, tycoon

The steel *magnate* refused to approve the consolidation.
철강왕은 합병승인을 거절하였다.

matrix
[méitriks]

모형, 컴퓨터의 입출력 회로망, 매트릭스 (something which gives form; e.g., a mold)

The linotype machine is equipped with a brass *matrix* for each letter so that a line can be assembled and cast in lead.
라이노타이프(자동주조 식자기)는 라인이 납으로 조립되어 주조될 수 있도록 각각의 글자가 황동 모형으로 입혀져 있다.

mores
[mɔ́ːriːz]

관습, 사회적 관행

<syn> habits, manners, customs, principles of conduct of a culture

The *mores* of any group are enforced by indoctrination and social pressure to conform.
어떤 집단의 관행이든 교육과 사회적 압력에 의해 따르도록 강요받는다.

mutation
[mjuːtéiʃən]

변화, 변천

<syn> change, alteration, permutation, variation

He deplored the *mutations* of fortune.
그는 운명의 변화를 개탄하였다.

obeisance
[oubéisəns]

경례, 경의, 복종

<syn> gesture of respect, bowing, curtsy, kneeling, loyalty, fidelity
<ant> disrespect, disregard, dishonor

They made an *obeisance* to the king.
그들은 임금에게 경의를 표했다.

pantheism
[pǽnθiːzəm]

범신론, 다신교 (any religion that identifies the universe with God)

Monism is an essential element of *pantheism*.
일원론은 범신론의 필수요소이다.

peccadillo
[pèkədílou]

가벼운 죄나 과오, 작은 결점

<syn> small fault, slight offence

He insisted on cavilling over *peccadillos*.
그는 계속해서 작은 결점들을 트집잡았다.

precursor
[priːkə́ːrsər]

선구자, 선각자

<syn> predecessor, forerunner, vanguard

The Continental Congress was the *precursor* of our bicameral Congress of today.
대륙의회는 오늘날 우리 양원의회의 선구였다.

probity
[próubəti]

정직, 성실

<syn> complete honesty, trustworthiness, uprightness

The *probity* of the witness was placed in doubt.
증인의 정직성이 의심을 받게 되었다.

protagonist
[proutǽgənist]

소설이나 드라마의 주인공 (leading character)

Mike Hammer is the *protagonist* of a whole series of detective stories.
마이크 해머는 탐정소설 전 시리즈의 주인공이다.

protocol
[próutəkɔ̀l]

외교의전; 의정서, 프로토콜

<syn> diplomatic or court etiquette, proprieties

Protocol demands that we introduce the ambassador before the special envoy; to fail to do so would be interpreted as an affront.
외교의전은 우리가 특사보다 먼저 대사를 소개할 것을 요구하고 있다. 그렇게 하지 못하면 무례로 해석될 것이다.

provocation
[prɑ̀vəkéiʃən]

성나게 함, 약올림, 도발

<syn> incitement, vexation, irritation, annoyance

The attack, coming with *provocation*, took them by surprise.
그들은 도발과 함께 기습공격을 받았다.

proximity
[prɑksíməti]

근접, 가까움 (nearness)

The *proximity* of the shopping mall is a great advantage to those residents who do not drive.
쇼핑몰이 가까이 있다는 것은 운전을 하지 않는 주민들에게 큰 이점이다.

quandary
[kwɑ́ndəri]

곤혹, 당혹, 궁지, 곤경 (a state of difficulty or perplexity)

<syn> dilemma, difficulty, doubt, uncertainty, predicament, impasse

He was in a *quandary* because the problem was so complex.
그는 문제가 너무 복잡하여 곤경에 처했다.

schism
[sízəm]

(단체의) 분리, 분열, 분파 (a formal division in or separation from a religious body)

<syn> division, split, break-up, discord, dissension

The Great *Schism* created two Christian churches, the Eastern and the Western.
대분열은 기독교회를 동서로 나누었다.

surfeit
[sə́:rfit]

과다, 과음과식, 포만

<syn> excess, superabundance

There was a *surfeit* of food at the table, and no one could finish the meal.
식탁에 음식이 넘쳤으므로 아무도 식사를 끝낼 수 없었다.

tenacity
[tənǽsəti]

고집, 끈기, 불굴의 의지 (persistence, quality of holding firmly)

His *tenacity* as an investigator earned him the nickname "Bulldog."
심사관으로서 그의 의지는 "불독"이라는 별명을 붙여주었다.

transgression
[trænsgréʃən]

위반, 일탈, 죄 (the breaking of a law or commandment)

<syn> offense, sin, misdeed, iniquity, wrongdoing
<ant> virtue, morality, probity, good deed, righteousness

We ask God to forgive our *transgressions*.
우리는 신께 우리의 죄를 용서해 줄 것을 구한다.

trepidation
[trèpidéiʃən]

공포, 전율 (an involuntary trembling, particularly from fear or terror)

The stories they had heard caused them much *trepidation*.
그들이 들은 이야기들은 그들에게 많은 공포심을 일으켰다.

tribulation
[trìbjəléiʃən]

고난, 시련 (great trouble)

<syn> trial, affliction, cross, ordeal, suffering
<ant> happiness, joy, delight, ease, comfort

The Pilgrims faced many *tribulations* before the first colonies were firmly established.
청교단은 첫 식민지가 굳건히 건설될 때까지 많은 고난에 직면하였다.

vertex
[vɔ́ːrteks]

정점, 절정

<syn> top, highest point, apex, summit

The view was breathtaking from the *vertex* of the hill.
언덕 꼭대기에서의 전망이 아슬아슬하였다.

vestige
[véstidʒ]

자취, 흔적

<syn> remnant, remainder, trace, sign, relic

The artifacts were the last *vestiges* of an earlier civilization.
그 인공물은 초기 문명의 마지막 흔적이었다.

volition
[voulíʃən]

의지, 결의, 의욕

<syn> deliberate will, conscious choice, decision, resolution
<ant> coercion, compulsion, duress

He performed the act of his own *volition*.
그는 자신의 결의를 행동으로 옮겼다.

yowl
[jaul]

울부짖는 소리, 신음소리 (a protracted, wailing cry)

<syn> howl, wail, yelp, cry, roar

The dog's *yowls* went on all night.
개의 울부짖는 소리가 밤새도록 계속되었다.

STEP 3 Practice Test 8

DIRECTIONS Select the word or phrase that means most nearly the same as the key word.

1 autocrat
(A) prime example (B) despot
(C) self-starter (D) self-conscious

2 complement
(A) flattery
(B) that which praises
(C) that which completes
(D) wholesomeness

3 complicity
(A) partnership in wrongdoing
(B) naivete
(C) difficulty
(D) impediment

4 euphemism
(A) pleasant-sounding
(B) polite circumlocution
(C) painless
(D) complement

5 hindsight
(A) prescience (B) overseeing
(C) foreboding (D) looking backwards

| ANSWER |

1. (A) 모범사례 (B) 독재자
   (C) 자동시동장치 (D) 자의식의

2. (A) 아첨 (B) 칭찬하는 것
   (C) 완성하는 것 (D) 유익한 것

3. (A) 나쁜 일의 파트너 (B) 천진난만한
   (C) 어려움 (D) 신체장애

4. (A) 듣기 좋은 (B) 완곡한 어법
   (C) 무통증의 (D) 보충

5. (A) 선견지명 (B) 내려다보기
   (C) 예감 (D) 뒤돌아보기

1. (B) 2. (C) 3. (A) 4. (B) 5. (D)

6 holocaust
(A) highly acidic   (B) indigestion
(C) destruction by fire   (D) destruction by flood

7 hypothesis
(A) unproved explanation
(B) low pressure
(C) theory
(D) proposition

8 magnate
(A) attractive
(B) great-hearted
(C) begger
(D) important business person

9 matrix
(A) queen   (B) survivor
(C) mold   (D) highway

10 mores
(A) plenitude   (B) customs
(C) surplus   (D) morale

11 mutation
(A) silence   (B) purification
(C) flux   (D) change

12 obeisance
(A) compliance   (B) overweight
(C) sickliness   (D) gesture of respect

13 precursor
(A) kindred   (B) forerunner
(C) accuser   (D) pedagogue

| ANSWER |

6. (A) 높은 산성의 (B) 소화불량
   (C) 화재로 인한 파괴
   (D) 홍수로 인한 파괴

7. (A) 증명되지 않은 설명 (B) 저압
   (C) 이론 (D) 제안

8. (A) 매력적인 (B) 위대한
   (C) 거지 (D) 경제계의 거물

9. (A) 여왕 (B) 생존자
   (C) 모형 (D) 고속도로

10. (A) 충분함, 풍부 (B) 관습
    (C) 잉여 (D) (조직의) 사기

11. (A) 침묵 (B) 정화
    (C) 흐름 (D) 변화

12. (A) 승낙, 순종 (B) 과체중
    (C) 병약함 (D) 경례

13. (A) 친족 (B) 선구자
    (C) 고소인, 고발인 (D) 교육자

6. (C) 7. (A) 8. (D) 9. (C) 10. (B)
11. (D) 12. (D) 13. (B)

14 probity
    (A) litigation   (B) thoughtfulness
    (C) peccadillo   (D) trustworthiness

15 schism
    (A) hard rock   (B) aperture
    (C) ice   (D) split

16 tribulation
    (A) acclaim   (B) great trouble
    (C) great reward   (D) branching out

17 vertex
    (A) dizziness   (B) nadir
    (C) apex   (D) median

18 transgression
    (A) breaking the law (B) greeting
    (C) extending   (D) willfulness

19 trepidation
    (A) trembling   (B) fortitude
    (C) stumbling   (D) hazard

20 vestige
    (A) clothing   (B) poverty
    (C) wordiness   (D) remnant

21 quandary
    (A) four-legged   (B) perplexity
    (C) explanation   (D) solution

| ANSWER |

14. (A) 소송, 기소 (B) 사려 깊음
    (C) 가벼운 과오, 결점 (D) 성실

15. (A) 하드록 (B) 벌어진 틈
    (C) 얼음 (D) 분리, 쪼개짐

16. (A) 갈채, 환호 (B) 큰 문제
    (C) 큰 보상 (D) 가지를 뻗다

17. (A) 현기증 (B) 최저점, 최하점
    (C) 정상, 정점 (D) 중간

18. (A) 법률위반 (B) 인사
    (C) 확장 (D) 고집, 제멋대로 임

19. (A) 전율 (B) 용기, 불굴의 정신
    (C) 비틀거림 (D) 위험

20. (A) 의복 (B) 가난
    (C) 말이 많음 (D) 나머지, 자취

21. (A) 다리가 넷인 (B) 당혹
    (C) 성명 (D) 해법

14. (D) 15. (D) 16. (B) 17. (C) 18. (A)
19. (A) 20. (D) 21. (B)

STEP 3
adjective & adverb 형용사 & 부사

abortive
[əbɔ́ːrtiv]

무모한, 실패하는

\<syn\> ineffectual, unsuccessful
\<ant\> effective, successful

The rebels made an *abortive* attempt to capture the radio station.
폭도들은 라디오방송국을 접수하려는 무모한 시도를 하였다.

abstruse
[əbstrúːs]

이해하기 어려운, 난해한

\<syn\> deep, obscure in meaning, incomprehensible
\<ant\> simple, easy, clear obvious

The concepts of Albert Einstein were *abstruse* even to physicists.
아인슈타인의 개념들은 물리학자들에게 조차도 난해하였다.

acoustic
[əkúːstik]

음향의, 청각의

\<syn\> pertaining to hearing

The *acoustic* qualities of a room may be improved by insulation.
실내 음향의 질은 방음으로 향상될 수 있다.

aesthetic/esthetic
[esθétik]

미(학)적인, 예술적인

\<syn\> appreciative of beauty, appealing to artistic taste, artistic
\<ant\> unaesthetic, upappreciative

Modern design seeks to produce machines which have *aesthetic* as well as functional appeal.
현대의 디자인은 기능뿐 아니라 예술적인 면까지 갖춘 기계의 생산을 추구한다.

affable
[ǽfəbəl]

상냥한, 친근한, 붙임성 있는

<syn> amiable, easy to talk to, congenial, cordial, friendly, pleasant
<ant> unfriendly, unsociable, unpleasant

The smiling face and *affable* manner of the agent put the child at ease.
대리인의 웃는 얼굴과 친근한 태도는 아이를 편안하게 해주었다.

ambiguous
[æmbígjuəs]

애매한, 여러 가지 뜻의

<syn> equivocal, vague, unclear, having a double meaning
<ant> explicit, definite, clear

The *ambiguous* nature of many legislative acts requires clarification by the courts.
많은 법률 조항들의 애매한 성질은 법정에서 명확히 밝힐 필요가 있다.

ambivalent
[æmbívələnt]

반대감정이 병존하는 (having conflicting feelings)

I am *ambivalent* about the job; although the atmosphere is pleasant, the work itself is boring.
나는 그 일이 분위기는 좋지만 일 자체는 따분하다는 생각을 가지고 있다.

atypical
[eitípikəl]

틀에 박히지 않은, 격식을 벗어난, 불규칙한

<syn> nor normal, unusual, nontypical, abnormal, irregular
<ant> typical, representative, common, familiar, usual

The usually clam man's burst of temper was *atypical*.
보통 말없는 남자가 성질을 폭발하는 일은 흔하지 않다.

autocratic
[ɔ̀:təkrǽtik]

독재적인, 독재 정치의

<syn> having absolute power, dictatorial, despotic, tyrannical
<ant> limited, constitutional, democratic

The *autocratic* attitude of the Russian ruling class elicited resentment from the people.
러시아 지배계급의 독재적인 태도는 국민들로부터 분노를 자아냈다.

benign
[bináin]

자비로운, 친절한, 온화한

<syn> kindly, tender, gentle, gracious, benevolent
<ant> unkindly, harsh, malicious, malevolent, malign

His *benign* influence helped to alleviate the suffering of the poor.
그의 자비가 불쌍한 사람들의 고통을 덜어주었다.

capricious
[kəpríʃəs]

변덕스러운, 변하기 쉬운, 일시적인

<syn> changing suddenly, wilful, fickle, erratic
<ant> consistent, unchangeable, firm, fixed

The lady is *capricious*; today she likes me, tomorrow she likes someone else.
여자는 변덕스러워서, 오늘은 나를 좋다했다가 내일은 다른 사람을 좋아한다.

caustic
[kɔ́:stik]

부식성의, 인화성의, 신랄한

<syn> biting, burning, stinging, corrosive
<ant> bland, mild, healing

The surface of the wood had been marred by some *caustic* substance.
나무의 표면은 어떤 부식성의 물질에 손상을 입었다.

chronic
[kránik]

만성적인, 상습적인

<syn> long-lasting, recurring, habitual, persisting
<ant> temporary, infrequent, once-in-a-lifetime

His *chronic* asthma flares up at certain times of the year.
그의 만성 천식은 1년에 몇 차례씩 재발된다.

circuitous
[sə:rkjú:itəs]

완곡한, 돌아가는, 우회의

<syn> roundabout, indirect, devious
<ant> direct, straight, undeviating

Sometimes a *circuitous* route is the fastest way to reach your destination.
가끔은 우회로가 목적지에 도착하기 위한 가장 빠른 길이기도 하다.

cognizant
[kágnəzənt]

인식하고 있는

<syn> having knowledge, aware, informed, acquainted
<ant> unaware, uninformed, ignorant

He was *cognizant* of all the facts before he made a decision.
그는 결정을 내리기 전에 모든 사실들을 인식하고 있었다.

concurrent
[kənkə́:rənt]

동시에 발생하는, 동반하는, 협력하는

<syn> running together, happening at the same time, coinciding, harmonious
<ant> in disagreement, different

Concurrent action by the police and welfare authorities reduced juvenile crime.
경찰과 복지당국의 협력이 청소년 범죄를 줄였다.

congenital
[kəndʒénətl]

타고난, 선천적인

<syn> inherent, dating from birth, innate, hereditary, inherited, natural
<ant> acquired, assumed, learned

The patient's tendency to schizophrenia is *congenital*.
그 환자의 정신분열증 성향은 선천적이다.

congruent
[káŋgruənt]

일치하는, 어울리는

<syn> congruous, in agreement, in harmony

Congruent figures coincide entirely throughout.
어울리는 모습들이 아주 시종일관 조화롭다.

corporal/ corporeal
[kɔ́ːrpərəl]

육체의, 신체의

<syn> of the body, physical

Corporal punishment of children in public schools is bitterly resented by many parents.
공립학교에서 어린이들에 대한 체벌이 많은 학부모들로부터 심하게 분노를 샀다.

culpable
[kʌ́lpəbl]

비난받을 만한, 유죄의, 과실이 있는

<syn> faulty, deserving of blame, guilty
<ant> innocent, blameless

The *culpable* parties should not escape punishment.
과실이 있는 당사자들은 처벌을 피하지 말아야 한다.

deleterious
[dèlətíəriəs]

몸에 해로운, 유독한

<syn> injurious, harmful, hurtful, detrimental
<ant> beneficial, healthy, helpful

DDT, when taken internally, has a *deleterious* effect on the body.
DDT는 몸 안에 흡입되었을 경우, 신체에 유독한 영향을 끼친다.

devious
[díːviəs]

정도를 벗어난, 솔직하지 않은, 교활한

<syn> roundabout, indirect, underhanded, tricky

When no one would tell her anything, she resorted to *devious* means to uncover the truth.
아무도 그녀에게 무엇을 말해주지 않자, 그녀는 진실을 알기 위해 정도를 벗어난 수단에 의지하였다.

discernible
[disə́:rnəbəl]

식별할 수 있는, 분간할 수 있는

\<syn> perceivable, identifiable, noticeable

The other cars were barely *discernible* in the fog.
다른 자동차들은 안개 속에서 겨우 분간할 정도였다.

discrete
[diskrí:t]

별개의, 분리된, 독립된

\<syn> separate, unrelated, individually distinct, noncontinuous

The process is divided into six *discrete* steps.
그 과정은 6개의 분리된 단계로 나뉘어져 있다.

dissonant
[dísənənt]

불협화음의, 불화의

\<syn> inharmonious, discordant

Much contemporary music seems *dissonant* to unaccustomed ears.
많은 현대음악이 익숙하지 않은 귀에는 불협화음으로 들린다.

dormant
[dɔ́:rmənt]

잠자는, 정지된, 잠복한

\<syn> sleeping, inactive, quiescent, idle
\<ant> active, operative, moving, awake

Perennial flowers such as irises remain *dormant* every winter and burgeon in the spring.
붓꽃과 같은 다년생 꽃들은 겨울마다 동면하고 봄에 싹을 틔운다.

equivocal
[ikwívəkəl]

모호한, 다의적인

\<syn> ambiguous, obscure, vague, enigmatic, dark, uncertain

His *equivocal* statements left us in doubt as to his real intentions.
그의 모호한 진술이 우리를 그의 진짜 의도에 대해 의심하도록 하였다.

euphonic
[ju:fánik]

어조가 좋은, 발음이 좋은 (pleasant-sounding)

Her *euphonic* singing had a soothing effect on the guests.
그녀의 발음 좋은 노래는 손님들을 편안하게 하였다.

expansible
[ikspǽnsəbəl]

확장할 수 있는, 팽창성의

<syn> capable of being extended, dilated, diffused

Bodies are not *expansible* in proportion to their weight.
신체는 몸무게에 비례하여 팽창할 수 없다.

facile
[fǽsil]

손쉬운; 솜씨가 날랜, 유창한

<syn> expert, skillful, adroit, handy, quick, artful
<ant> clumsy, awkward, plodding, maladroit

He never turned down an opportunity to make a speech because he was such a *facile* orator.
그는 아주 유창한 연사이기 때문에 결코 연설할 기회를 거절하지 않았다.

fatuous
[fǽtʃuəs]

얼빠진, 어리석은

<syn> conceitedly foolish, silly, vacant in mine, stupid
<ant> sensible, prudent, judicious, wise

Insisting on a Cadillac you can't afford is *fatuous*.
네가 살 능력도 없는 캐딜락을 고집하는 것은 어리석다.

gratuitous
[grətjúːətəs]

불필요한, 이유 없는; 무료의, 무상의

<syn> uncalled for, unjustified, unprovoked; free, voluntary, for nothing
<ant> justified, warranted, provoked; paid, compensated, compulsory

His *gratuitous* insults were resented very highly.
그의 불필요한 무례가 대단한 분노를 샀다.

gregarious
[grigɛ́əriəs]

군집하는, 모여 사는; 사교적인, 집단적인

<syn> fond of company, sociable, extroverted, outgoing
<ant> unsociable, solitary, introverted

They were a *gregarious* couple who cultivate many friendships among diverse people.
그들은 다양한 사람들과 많은 우정을 나누는 사교적인 부부였다.

heterodox
[hétərədɑ̀ks]

이교의, 이단의

<syn> not orthodox; not conforming

Her *heterodox* opinions and outlandish behavior earned her a reputation as an eccentric.
그녀의 이교도적인 견해와 이국적인 행동은 기인이라는 평판을 얻었다.

hydrous
[háidrəs]

물을 함유하는 (containing water)

Watermelon is a *hydrous* gourd.
수박은 물을 함유하는 조롱박과 식물이다.

illicit
[ilísit]

불법의, 금지된

<syn> not licensed, unlawful, illegal, illegitimate, not permitted
<ant> licit, lawful, legal, legitimated

Illicit love is the root of many divorce actions.
금지된 사랑이 많은 이혼행위의 뿌리가 된다.

impassioned
[impǽʃənd]

감격한, 열렬한, 감동적인

<syn> ardent, fervent, excited, passionate, heated
<ant> dispassionate, objective, cool, impassive

The *impassioned* performance of the actor was thoroughly enjoyable.
그 배우의 열렬한 공연은 아주 재미있었다.

imperative
[impérətiv]

강제적인, 절대 필요한, 엄연한

<syn> important, essential, requisite, necessary, needful, mandatory, compulsory
<ant> unnecessary, unimportant, avoidable

This is an emergency; it is *imperative* that I reach them at once.
이것은 긴급상황이다. 즉각 그들에게 출동하는 것이 필요하다.

imprecise
[ìmprəsáis]

부정확한, 불명확한

<syn> not precise, vague, inaccurate

The description was *imprecise* because the witness had had only a fleeting glimpse of the man.
증인이 그 남자의 획 지나가는 희미한 모습만 기억하고 있어서 설명이 부정확했다.

inherent
[inhíərənt]

타고난, 선천적인

<syn> inborn, essential, innate, native, hereditary, intrinsic
<ant> foreign, alien, extrinsic

A love of hunting is *inherent* in cats.
고양이가 사냥을 좋아하는 것은 선천적이다.

inquisitive
[inkwízətiv]

호기심 많은, 탐구적인

<syn> curious, asking questions, inquiring, investigative
<ant> indifferent, unconcerned, incurious

Private eyes in detective fiction often get into trouble by being too *inquisitive*.
탐정소설에서 사설탐정은 흔히 너무 캐묻기 좋아해서 문제를 일으킨다.

insatiable
[inséiʃəbəl]

만족을 모르는, 탐욕스러운

<syn> never satisfied, always greedy, voracious
<ant> satiable, appeasable, satisfiable

His appetite for wealth was *insatiable*; no matter how rich he became, he always craved more.
부를 향한 그의 욕심은 끝이 없어서, 아무리 부자가 되어도 늘 더 갈망하였다.

insubordinate
[ìnsəbɔ́:rdənit]

고분고분하지 않는, 복종하지 않는

<syn> failing to obey, disobedient, insolent, defiant
<ant> obedient, docile, submissive, subdued

Ignoring a direct order is an *insubordinate* act with grave consequences.
직접적인 명령을 무시하는 것은 엄중한 결론에 복종하지 않는 행위이다.

intractable
[intræktəbəl]

고집 센, 다루기 어려운, (병이) 잘 낫지 않는

<syn> stubborn, perverse, headstrong, hard to cope with, obstinate
<ant> tractable, obedient, docile, submissive

An *intractable* person is slow to learn a new way of life.
고집 센 사람은 새로운 생활방식을 배우는 데 느리다.

irreconcilable
[irékənsàiləbəl]

화해할 수 없는, 조화되지 않는

<syn> beyond reconcilable, unable to be harmonized, unadjustable
<ant> reconcilable, appeasable

His statements about liking school were *irreconcilable* with the distaste he expressed for books in general.
공부를 좋아한다는 그의 말은 일반적으로 책에 대해 그가 표현한 혐오와 어울리지 않았다.

itinerant
[aitínərənt]

순회하는, 이동하는 (traveling on a circuit)

<syn> wandering, wayfaring, roving, migrant, traveling, nomadic
<ant> stationary, settled, resident, stay-at-home

The *itinerant* judge heard cases in Somerville on the first Tuesday of the month.
순회판사는 이 달 첫주 화요일의 서머빌 사건을 들었다.

jocose
[dʒoukóus]

우스꽝스러운, 익살맞은

<syn> humorous, joking, jocular, facetious

She had the sense not to take his *jocose* teasing seriously.
그녀는 그의 익살맞은 성가심을 심각하게 받아들이지 않는 감각이 있었다.

loquacious
[loukwéiʃəs]

말 많은, 수다스러운

<syn> talkative, garrulous, wordy, verbose
<ant> silent, reserved, taciturn, closemouthed, reticent

A *loquacious* employee is a double time-waster; he invariably engages others as listeners.
말 많은 직원은 시간을 곱절로 쓰는 사람이다. 항상 다른 사람들을 청중으로 끌어들이기 때문이다.

ludicrous
[lúːdəkrəs]

익살맞은, 우스운, 바보 같은

<syn> apt to raise laughter, ridiculous, crazy, comic
<ant> sensible, logical

The play was intended to be *ludicrous*.
연극은 익살스럽게 꾸며졌다.

malign
[məláin]

adj. 유해한, 악의적인

<syn> evil, malicious, very harmful, injurious
<ant> benign, benevolent, good

Malign comments are often motivated by jealousy.
악의적인 비평이 흔히 질투의 동기가 된다.

v. 비방하다, 헐뜯다, 해를 끼치다

<syn> speak ill of, slander, defame, abuse
<ant> praise, extol, eulogize, compliment

The students often *maligned* the strict professor.
학생들은 엄격한 교수를 자주 비방하였다.

malleable
[mǽliəbəl]

펴 늘일 수 있는, 순응하는, 유순한

<syn> easily shaped, adaptable, pliable, plastic, ductile, flexible
<ant> rigid, stiff, hard, firm, inflexible

Children are more *malleable* than adults and adapt to new environments more readily.
어린이들은 어른들보다 순응을 더 잘해서 새로운 환경에 더욱 잘 적응한다.

noxious
[nákʃəs]

유해한, 해를 끼치는, 불건전한

<syn> harmful, injurious, poisonous, unwholesome
<ant> wholesome, beneficial

The *noxious* fumes from the refinery poisoned the air.
정유공장에서 나오는 유해한 연기가 공기를 오염시켰다.

oblivious
[əblíviəs]

잊기 쉬운, 부주의한, 멍청한

<syn> unaware of, unconscious of, insensible, unobservant
<ant> aware, conscious, cognizant, heedful, concerned

The absentminded professor was *oblivious* of the fire caused by his experiment.
부주의한 그 교수는 자기의 실험으로 일어난 화재를 알지도 못했다.

obtuse
[əbtjúːs]

둔한, 무딘

<syn> dull, not sharp, blunt, not pointed
<ant> acute, sharp, pointed, intelligent, bright

The man did not understand because of his *obtuse* wit.
그 남자는 자신의 둔한 위트 때문에 이해할 수 없었다.

optimum
[áptiməm]

최적의, 적정한, 가장 알맞은 n. 최적조건 (pl. optima)

<syn> best for a purpose, most favorable, ideal, perfect, prime

Under *optimum* conditions of light and moisture, the plant will grow to over three feet.
그 식물은 빛과 습기의 최적조건에서 3피트 이상 자랄 것이다.

painstaking
[péinztèikiŋ]

근면한, 성실한, 수고를 아끼지 않는

<syn> careful, thorough, conscientious, diligent, earnest
<ant> careless, haphazard, slapdash

The search for the lost ring was long and *painstaking*.
잃어버린 반지를 찾는 일은 길고 수고스러웠다.

pending
[péndiŋ]

미결의, 심리중인, 현안의

<syn> awaiting decision, awaiting settlement, undecided

It required much patience to wait while the petition was *pending*.
청원서가 심리되는 동안 기다리는 것이 많은 인내를 요구하였다.

peremptory
[pərémptəri]

단호한, 엄연한, 확정된, 절대적인

<syn> imperative, absolute, final, decisive, domineering, imperious

The captain gave a *peremptory* command for a major advance.
대위는 주요 전위부대에 단호한 명령을 내렸다.

peripheral
[pərífərəl]

주위의, 주변의 (of an edge or boundary)

The man who notices people almost behind him has excellent *peripheral* vision.
자기 뒤에 있는 사람들을 거의 알아보는 사람은 훌륭한 주변 시력을 가지고 있다.

perpendicular
[pə̀:rpəndíkjələr]

직각을 이루는, 수직의

<syn> in an up-and-down direction, vertical, upright, at a right angle

The lamppost, having been grazed by the truck, was no longer *perpendicular*.
가로등 기둥이 트럭에 부딪쳐 더 이상 수직으로 서 있지 않았다.

pervious
[pə́:rviəs]

(물이나 빛을) 통과시키는, 투과성의, 받아들일 줄 아는

<syn> admitting of passage, open to influence

The man was *pervious* to criticism and often benefited from the constructive advice of his colleagues.
남자는 비평을 받아들일 줄 알아서 흔히 자기 동료들의 건설적인 충고로부터 이로운 것을 얻는다.

precipitous
[prisípətəs]

험한, 가파른, 벼랑의

<syn> steep like a precipice

The road had a *precipitous* drop on the south side.
도로는 남쪽으로 가파른 낭떠러지가 있었다.

precocious
[prikóuʃəs]

조숙한, 어른스러운

<syn> advanced in development, mature, smart, bright
<ant> slow, backward, retarded

Precocious children should be given enriched programs of study.
조숙한 아이들은 풍부한 학습프로그램이 주어져야 한다.

predominantly
[pərídámənəntri]

대부분, 크게, 주로

<syn> for the most part, mainly

Although there are a few older students, the class is *predominantly* made up of eighteen-year-olds.
소수의 나이 많은 학생들이 있지만, 그래도 그 학급은 주로 18세 아이들로 구성되어 있다.

preoccupied
[priːάkjəpàid]

몰두한, 열중한, 생각이 다른 데 있는

<syn> abstracted, absent, absentminded, inattentive

Preoccupied by her dilemma, she missed her stop on the train.
딜레마에 몰두하다가 그녀는 열차의 정거장을 놓쳤다.

prodigious
[prədídʒəs]

거대한, 막대한

<syn> large, vast, enormous, great
<ant> small, negligible

He had a *prodigious* nose and a tiny mouth.
그는 거대한 코와 작은 입을 가지고 있었다.

quiescent
[kwaiésənt]

정지한, 활동하지 않음

<syn> inactive, latent, dormant, potential, not aroused

The eternal problem of juvenile delinquency becomes *quiescent* during the excitement of war.
청소년 범죄라는 끊임없는 문제가 전쟁의 소용돌이 기간에 휴면상태에 들어갔다.

rampant
[ræmpənt]

무성한, 마구 퍼지는 (unchecked in growth or spread)

<syn> widespread, rife, prevalent, unchecked, raging, unrestrained
<ant> restrained, curbed, checked

The *rampant* growth of weeds made the lawn look extremely unsightly.
잡초가 무성하게 자라서 잔디를 대단히 모양사납게 만들어버렸다.

reactionary
[riːǽkʃənèri]

반동의, 반동주의의, 보수적인 (extremely conservative, marked by opposition to present tendencies and advocating a return to some previous or simpler condition)

<syn> reversionary, regressive, diehard, right-wing, ultraconservative

The pamphlet expressed a *reactionary* hatred of innovation and nostalgia for "the good old days."
팜플렛은 개혁에 대한 반동적 증오와 "과거 좋았던 시절"에 대한 항수를 표현하였다.

receptive
[riséptiv]

잘 받아들이는, 감수성이 예민한 (able and tending to receive and accept, open to influence)

<syn> favorably disposed, open-minded, accessible
<ant> unreceptive, illiberal, unresponsive, close-minded, narrow-minded

The manager, unsatisfied with the store's appearance, was *receptive* to the idea of a major remodeling.
지배인은 점포의 외양이 마음에 들지 않아서 개조할 생각을 하고 있었다.

reticent
[rétəsənt]

삼가는, 절제된, 과묵한 (restrained in speech, unwilling to talk)

<syn> taciturn, reserved, closemouthed, quiet, silent, sparing of words
<ant> voluble, talkative, communicative, unreserved

His *reticence* kept him from offering answers.
그의 과묵함이 대답을 못하게 하였다.

sentient
[sénʃənt]

감각력이 있는, 지각력이 있는 (capable of feeling, having perception)

Even a dog is *sentient*.
심지어 개도 감각이 있다.

strident
[stráidənt]

(소리가) 귀에 거슬리는, 삐걱거리는 (harsh sounding)

<syn> grating, harsh, piercing, jangling, shrill
<ant> soft, mellow, dulcet

She had a *strident* voice that sent shivers down my back.
그녀의 귀에 거슬리는 목소리는 내 등골을 오싹하게 하였다.

stringent
[stríndʒənt]

엄중한, 설득력 있는; 절박한

<syn> severe, strict, compelling; tight, sparing, frugal

The speaker presented *stringent* arguments for the unwelcome cutbacks.
연사는 환영받지 못하는 예산삭감을 위해 설득력 있는 주장을 폈다.

tacitly
[tǽsitli]

말없이, 암암리에, 잠자코

<syn> silently, by implication, without words

He *tacitly* assented to the arguments of his wife.
그는 아내의 주장에 말없이 동의하였다.

transitory
[trǽnsətɔ̀:ri]

오래가지 않는, 덧없는, 무상한, 일시적인

<syn> temporary, transient, fleeting, passing, not permanent
<ant> long, long-lived, lasting, persistent, durable

It is normal to feel a *transitory* depression over life's setbacks.
인생의 좌절에 일시적인 우울함을 느끼는 것은 일반적이다.

turbulent
[tə́:rbjələnt]

몹시 거친, 사나운, 난폭한

<syn> disturbed, agitated, violent, in wild motion, tempestuous

The *turbulent* stream claimed many lives.
사나운 조류가 많은 목숨을 빼앗았다.

unilateral
[jù:nəlǽtərəl]

한쪽만의, 일방적인, 치우친

<syn> one-sided, pertaining to one side

A *unilateral* bond is one that binds one party only.
일방적인 결합은 한쪽만을 묶는 것이다.

unmitigated
[ʌ̀nmítəgèitid]

누그러지지 않은, 경감되지 않은, 온전한 (not lessened, not softened in severity or harshness, not toned down)

<syn> unrelieved, unalleviated, unabated
<ant> mitigated, relieved, alleviated, abated

According to President Eliot of Harvard, inherited wealth is an *unmitigated* curse when divorced from culture.
하버드대학의 엘리엇 총장에 따르면, 물려받은 부가 문화로부터 분리될 때는 온전히 재앙이다.

unwieldy
[ʌ̀nwí:ldi]

다루기 힘드는, 무거운 (too bulky and clumsy to be moved easily)

<syn> ponderous, hard to handle, not handy, awkward
<ant> handy, convenient, comfortable

Four men were required to move the *unwieldy* rock.
네 남자는 무거운 바위를 옮겨야 했다.

vacuous
[vǽkjuəs]

빈, 공허한; 무위의

<syn> empty, vacant, blank; dull, stupid, inane

His *vacuous* speeches won him no converts.
그의 공허한 연설은 아무도 개종시키지 못하였다.

vapid
[vǽpid]

맛없는, 김빠진, 맥빠진, 재미없는

<syn> dull, flat, insipid, lifeless
<ant> lively, exciting, inspiring

The time was passed in *vapid* conversation about the weather.
날씨에 관한 재미없는 대화 속에 시간은 흘러갔다.

verbose
[və:rbóus]

말이 많은, 장황한 (using more words than are necessary, tedious from a multiplicity of words)

The audience was bored by the *verbose* politician.
청중은 말이 많은 정치인에 지겨워했다.

vigilant
[vídʒələnt]

자지 않고 지키는, 방심하지 않고 경계하는

<syn> alert, watchful, on guard, attentive, careful
<ant> negligent, neglectful, lax, careless, heedless

As a Supreme Court Justice he had always been *vigilant* against any attempt to encroach on the freedoms guaranteed by the Bill of Rights.
연방대법원 판사로서 그는 권리장전에 보장된 자유를 침해하는 어떤 도전에도 방심하지 않고 항상 경계해 왔다.

vociferous
[vosífərəs]

큰소리로 외치는, 소란스런 (making a noisy outcry)

<syn> crying loudly, clamorous, noisy, boisterous, uproarious
<ant> quiet

There are some who come to meetings merely to add to the *vociferous* din.
회의에 오는 사람들 중에는 시끄러운 소란을 더하기만 하게 될 사람들이 있다.

wayward
[wéiwərd]

제멋대로의, 고집 센; 변덕스러운

<syn> perverse, capricious, willful, erratic, fluctuating
<ant> obedient, manageable, docile, tractable, compliant

The *wayward* flight of the bat was difficult to trace.
박쥐는 제멋대로 날아서 따라가기가 어렵다.

wily
[wáili]

계략을 쓰는, 잔꾀를 부리는, 교활한

<syn> artful, cunning, devious, sly, tricky
<ant> open, candid, frank, sincere

He was *wily* enough to avoid detection.
그는 발각되지 않을 만큼 아주 교활하였다.

wont
[wɔːnt]

버릇처럼 된, 늘 …하는

<syn> accustomed, used, inclined

He was *wont* to stroll about the grounds before breakfast.
그는 아침식사 전에 운동장을 산책하는 것이 버릇이 되었다.

STEP 3 Practice Test 9

DIRECTIONS Select the word or phrase that means most nearly the same as the key word.

1 abortive
   (A) stuttering   (B) illegal
   (C) deadening   (D) ineffectual

2 abstruse
   (A) overweight   (B) stretched
   (C) obscure   (D) callow

3 ambivalent
   (A) divided   (B) two-handed
   (C) underwater   (D) agreed

4 antecedent
   (A) following   (B) necessary
   (C) preceding   (D) preclusive

5 biped
   (A) two-wheeled   (B) side-swiped
   (C) two-footed   (D) half-witted

6 concurrent
   (A) fluent   (B) coinciding
   (C) fleeing   (D) exodus

7 devious
   (A) prudent   (B) sideways
   (C) indirect   (D) naive

| ANSWER |

1. (A) 말 더듬는 (B) 불법의
   (C) 죽이는 (D) 효과 없는

2. (A) 중량 초과된 (B) 늘어난, 뻗은
   (C) 불명료한, 알기 어려운
   (D) 경험이 없는

3. (A) 둘로 나뉜 (B) 양손잡이인
   (C) 물 속의 (D) 동의한, 일치한

4. (A) 뒤이은 (B) 필요한
   (C) 앞서는 (D) 제외하는, 방지하는

5. (A) 두 바퀴의 (B) 옆을 스치듯 치는
   (C) 두 발 달린 (D) 둔한, 얼빠진

6. (A) 유창한 (B) 동시에 발생하는
   (C) 도망하는 (D) 집단이주

7. (A) 신중한 (B) 옆으로 향한
   (C) 간접적인 (D) 유약한

1. (D) 2. (C) 3. (A) 4. (C)
5. (C) 6. (B) 7. (C)

8 facile
   (A) quick   (B) inexpensive
   (C) deceptive   (D) expert

9 fatuous
   (A) obnoxiously foolish (B) excessively generous
   (C) obese   (D) gaseous

10 gratuitous
   (A) thankful   (B) inexpensive
   (C) dubious   (D) free

11 heterodox
   (A) paradoxical   (B) nonconforming
   (C) dilemma   (D) imperturbable

12 illicit
   (A) draw out   (B) barely perceivable
   (C) not necessary   (D) not licensed

13 imperative
   (A) subjective   (B) of great importance
   (C) belonging to emperors   (D) minuscule

14 hydrous
   (A) containing water   (B) digested
   (C) many-headed   (D) flooded

15 impassioned
   (A) animated   (B) apathetic
   (C) wary   (D) enamored

16 inherent
   (A) held tightly   (B) inborn
   (C) forgotten   (D) bequeathed

| ANSWER |

8. (A) 재빠른 (B) 값싼
   (C) 속이는 (D) 노련한

9. (A) 미울 정도로 어리석은
   (B) 아주 관대한 (C) 뚱뚱한
   (D) 가스의, 기체의

10. (A) 고마운 (B) 값싼
    (C) 의심스러운 (D) 무료의

11. (A) 역설적인, 모순된
    (B) 복종하지 않는
    (C) 궁지 (D) 침착한

12. (A) 끄집어내다
    (B) 가까스로 감지할 수 있는
    (C) 불필요한 (D) 허가되지 않은

13. (A) 주관적인 (B) 아주 중요한
    (C) 황제에게 속하는 (D) 소문자의

14. (A) 물을 함유하는 (B) 요약된, 소화된
    (C) 머리가 여러 개인 (D) 범람한

15. (A) 활기찬 (B) 냉담한
    (C) 주의 깊은 (D) 매혹된

16. (A) 꽉 붙잡다 (B) 타고난
    (C) 잊혀진 (D) 유산으로 남긴, 유증한

8. (D) 9. (A) 10. (D) 11. (B) 12. (D)
13. (B) 14. (A) 15. (A) 16. (B)

17 insatiable
　(A) kinetic　　(B) greedy
　(C) insomniac　(D) soundless

18 insubordinate
　(A) demote　　(B) reject
　(C) abusive　　(D) failing to obey

19 jocose
　(A) sarcastic　(B) bucolic
　(C) humorous　(D) complaining

20 inquisitive
　(A) curious　　(B) hopeless
　(C) circumstantial　(D) greedy

21 irreconcilable
　(A) lost
　(B) reckless
　(C) incomprehensible
　(D) unable to be harmonized

22 ludicrous
　(A) morbid　　(B) playful
　(C) rotund　　(D) ridiculous

23 malleable
　(A) posted　　(B) adaptable
　(C) vacillating　(D) unchanging

24 oblivious
　(A) powerful　(B) preoccupied
　(C) murky　　(D) mendacious

| ANSWER |

17. (A) 활동적인 (B) 탐욕의
　　(C) 불면증의 (D) 고요한

18. (A) 강등시키다 (B) 거절하다
　　(C) 악용하는 (D) 복종하지 않는

19. (A) 풍자의 (B) 목가적인
　　(C) 익살맞은 (D) 불평하는

20. (A) 호기심 많은 (B) 희망 없는
　　(C) 상황에 따른 (D) 탐욕의

21. (A) 잃어버린 (B) 무모한
　　(C) 이해할 수 없는
　　(D) 조화될 수 없는

22. (A) 음울한 (B) 즐거운
　　(C) 둥근 (D) 우스운

23. (A) 직위가 있는 (B) 적응하는
　　(C) 망설이는, 우유부단한
　　(D) 변함없는

24. (A) 영향력 있는
　　(B) 몰두한, 여념이 없는
　　(C) 어두운, (안개나 연기가) 자욱한
　　(D) 허위의, 거짓말 잘하는

17. (B) 18. (D) 19. (C) 20. (A)
21. (D) 22. (D) 23. (B) 24. (B)

25 peripheral
   (A) at the center   (B) halfway
   (C) distant   (D) on the boundary

26 noxious
   (A) repulsive   (B) unkind
   (C) injurious   (D) evil

27 obtuse
   (A) foreshortened   (B) frozen
   (C) dull   (D) whirling

28 peremptory
   (A) judicial   (B) decreed
   (C) imperative   (D) unnecessary

29 perpendicular
   (A) violent striking   (B) at a right angle
   (C) hanging   (D) transverse

30 precipitous
   (A) prevaricate   (B) presumptuous
   (C) steep   (D) climbing

31 rampant
   (A) impulsive   (B) angry
   (C) elegant   (D) growing unchecked

32 stringent
   (A) wound up   (B) severe
   (C) stingy   (D) puckered

33 strident
   (A) harsh-sounding   (B) brisk
   (C) long-legged   (D) gregarious

| ANSWER |

25. (A) 중심에 (B) 도중의
    (C) 떨어져 있는 (D) 경계의, 주변의

26. (A) 쌀쌀한 (B) 불친절한
    (C) 해가 되는 (D) 악의

27. (A) 줄어든, 원근을 넣어 그린
    (B) 얼어붙은 (C) 둔한, 무딘
    (D) 빙글빙글 도는

28. (A) 사법적인 (B) (법령이) 공포된
    (C) 엄연한 (D) 불필요한

29. (A) 폭력적인 충돌 (B) 직각의
    (C) 걸려있는 (D) 횡단하는

30. (A) 얼버무리다, 발뺌하다
    (B) 주제넘은, 뻔뻔한
    (C) 가파른, 벼랑의 (D) 기어오르는

31. (A) 충동적인 (B) 화난
    (C) 우아한 (D) 마구 자라는

32. (A) 결말을 낸 (B) 절박한, 호된
    (C) 자극 (D) 주름진

33. (A) 거친 소리가 나는 (B) 활발한
    (C) 다리가 긴 (D) 군집하는

25. (D) 26. (C) 27. (C) 28. (C) 29. (B)
30. (C) 31. (D) 32. (B) 33. (A)

34 tacitly
(A) politely (B) with few words
(C) stealthily (D) by implication

35 transitory
(A) affixed (B) fleeting
(C) dreamy (D) crosswise

36 unilateral
(A) one-level (B) wholesome
(C) undivided (D) one-sided

37 verbose
(A) wordy (B) handwritten
(C) terse (D) eloquent

38 unmitigated
(A) not lessened (B) not sent
(C) without stop (D) not understood

39 vacuous
(A) empty (B) hungry
(C) naive (D) opened

40 vapid
(A) vain (B) vacant
(C) dull (D) destitute

| ANSWER |

34. (A) 공손하게 (B) 말을 적게 하면서
    (C) 비밀히, 남모르게
    (D) 암묵적으로

35. (A) 첨부된 (B) 덧없는, 빨리 지나가는
    (C) 꿈같은 (D) 옆으로, 교차하여

36. (A) 한 등급의 (B) 전체의
    (C) 분리되지 않은
    (D) 한쪽만의, 일방적인

37. (A) 말이 많은 (B) (글씨를) 손으로 쓴
    (C) 간결한 (D) 설득력 있는, 웅변의

38. (A) 경감되지 않은 (B) 보내지 않은
    (C) 끊임없이 (D) 이해되지 않은

39. (A) 빈 (B) 배고픈
    (C) 순진한 (D) 열린

40. (A) 헛된 (B) 비어있는
    (C) 재미없는, 무딘 (D) 빈곤한

34. (D) 35. (B) 36. (D) 37. (A)
38. (A) 39. (A) 40. (C)

STEP 3 Mastery Test 3

[Synonym Test]

DIRECTIONS Choose the word or phrase that means most nearly the same as the key word or the underlined word.

1. abet
   - (A) gamble
   - (B) sanctify
   - (C) incite
   - (D) denounce

2. acumen
   - (A) intensity
   - (B) accuracy
   - (C) insight
   - (D) instinct

3. An ambiguous statement is one which is
   - (A) forceful and convincing
   - (B) capable of being understood in more than one sense
   - (C) based upon good judgment and sound reasoning processes
   - (D) uninteresting and too lengthy

4. The supervisor admonished the clerk for his tardiness.
   - (A) reproved
   - (B) excused
   - (C) transferred
   - (D) punished

5. The word divergent means most nearly
   - (A) simultaneous
   - (B) differing
   - (C) approaching
   - (D) parallel

6. The driver conceded that he was at fault. The word conceded means most nearly
   - (A) denied
   - (B) explained
   - (C) implied
   - (D) admitted

7. The word <u>cognizant</u> means most nearly
   (A) rare   (B) reluctant
   (C) aware   (D) haphazard

8. congruent
   (A) noisy   (B) agreeing
   (C) quarrelsome   (D) sticky

9. congenital
   (A) harmonious   (B) sympathetic
   (C) inherent   (D) fringed

10. culpable
   (A) dangerous   (B) soft
   (C) blameworthy   (D) easily perceived

11. edify
   (A) proclaim   (B) revise
   (C) whirl   (D) enlighten

12. equanimity
   (A) composure   (B) uniformity
   (C) equal justice   (D) indifference

13. enervated
   (A) neurotic   (B) weakened
   (C) cowardly   (D) strengthened

14. hypothetical
   (A) irrefutable   (B) conditional
   (C) triangular   (D) spellbound

15. engender
    (A) make inanimate   (B) imperil
    (C) manage skillfully (D) produce

16. He was not present at the <u>inception</u> of the program.
    (A) beginning   (B) finale
    (C) conclusion (D) rejection

17. He was unwilling to <u>impede</u> the work of his unit. The word impede as used in this sentence means most nearly
    (A) carry out (B) criticize
    (C) praise   (D) hinder

18. peccadillo
    (A) wild pig   (B) burrowing mammal
    (C) petty fault (D) bric-a-brac

19. levity
    (A) mediterranean (B) floatable
    (C) frivolity   (D) illumination

20. malign
    (A) defame   (B) break
    (C) separate (D) injure

21. loquacious
    (A) birdlike (B) winding
    (C) rich   (D) talkative

22. tenacity
    (A) firmness (B) temerity
    (C) sagacity (D) discouragement

23. renounce
    (A) mumble   (B) repeat
    (C) mimic   (D) disown

24. Employees are directed to exercise <u>vigilance</u>. The word vigilance means most nearly
    (A) strict discipline   (B) routine precaution
    (C) systematic practice   (D) alert watchfulness

] Antonym Test [

DIRECTIONS Choose the word or phrase that is most nearly opposite in meaning to the given word.

1. benign
    (A) captious   (B) relevant
    (C) robot   (D) malevolent

2. adjourn
    (A) convene   (B) declare invalid
    (C) investigate   (D) translate

3. capricious
    (A) active   (B) stable
    (C) opposed   (D) sheeplike

4. condone
    (A) condemn   (B) disregard
    (C) punish   (D) mistake

5. discern
    (A) misperceive (B) emit
    (C) expand (D) deploy

6. discrete
    (A) prudent (B) joined
    (C) crooked (D) stunted

7. dissonance
    (A) disapproval (B) disaster
    (C) harmony (D) disparity

8. disparage
    (A) applaud (B) degrade
    (C) erase (D) reform

9. itinerant
    (A) animosity (B) metaphor
    (C) perpetrator (D) resident

10. eulogize
    (A) attract (B) heed
    (C) defame (D) shun

11. imputation
    (A) assiduity (B) vindication
    (C) challis (D) raiment

12. equivocal
    (A) positive (B) medium
    (C) monotonous (D) musical

13. lassitude
    (A) tangle   (B) long-windedness
    (C) determination   (D) vitality

14. obviate
    (A) grasp   (B) reform
    (C) make necessary   (D) smooth

15. placate
    (A) amuse   (B) antagonize
    (C) embroil   (D) pity

16. mollify
    (A) fortify   (B) lullaby
    (C) shame   (D) intensify

17. reticent
    (A) fidgety   (B) repetitious
    (C) talkative   (D) restful

18. reactionary
    (A) chemically-induced (B) causal
    (C) innovative   (D) naive

19. sentient
    (A) emotional   (B) unfeeling
    (C) hostile   (D) sympathetic

20. wily
    (A) thin   (B) agile
    (C) stubborn   (D) inept

Sentence Completion Test

DIRECTIONS Select the word or phrase that will best complete the meaning of the sentence as a whole.

1. His remarks were so _____ that we could not decide which of the possible meanings was correct.
   (A) ambiguous (B) facetious
   (C) impalpable (D) congruent

2. Scattered around the dead dragon were mementos of the _____: heads, arms, and torsos of young maidens.
   (A) battle (B) relics
   (C) festivities (D) carnage

3. The Watergate scandal was the ostensible cause of Nixon's decision to _____ the presidency.
   (A) abandon (B) abdicate
   (C) aspire to (D) abort

4. Although the Delphic Oracle warned Agamemnon of storms in the Mediterranean, he did not heed its _____, and his fleet was destroyed.
   (A) admission (B) admonition
   (C) knowledge (D) suggestion

5. If we can arrange our schedules so that our vacations _____, we can make the trip together.
   (A) collaborate (B) coalesce
   (C) coerce (D) coincide

6. The effects of the drug were known to be _____ to pregnant women, so no doctor would prescribe them to her.
   (A) detoxifying (B) minor
   (C) deleterious (D) illegal

7. When one of the candidates avoided the issues during the debate, the other accused him of _____.
   (A) ambience (B) stridency
   (C) circumlocution (D) coherence

8. The _____ of the church choir was a result of the basso's cold and the tenor's lack of practice.
   (A) disunity (B) harmony
   (C) dissonance (D) discordance

9. His conclusions were so _____ that they helped no one.
   (A) imprecise (B) incalculable
   (C) unknown (D) impecunious

10. The patient's _____ pain could not be alleviated by medication.
    (A) bandaged (B) untraceable
    (C) intractable (D) imperturbable

11. The young socialite, forever seeking the company of other carefree young women, was extremely _____.
    (A) gregarious (B) visible
    (C) ungrateful (D) ostensive

12. His comments were unnecessary and _____; no one could understand why he added them.
    (A) gracious (B) gratuitous
    (C) grotesque (D) gregarious

13. When the judge invalidated the contract, depriving it of all legal force, he _____ it.
    (A) nullified
    (B) mitigated
    (C) rescinded
    (D) abolished

14. Because she prided herself on being of strong will, she quit smoking through her own _____, not because she was forced to.
    (A) malice
    (B) volition
    (C) paranoia
    (D) vocation

15. There was a _____ of gold-leafing on the mirror which made it look gaudy.
    (A) facade
    (B) quantity
    (C) depression
    (D) surfeit

16. The water was _____ from all the activity of the porpoises.
    (A) tranquil
    (B) sinking
    (C) turbulent
    (D) soothing

17. A conscientious employer does not _____ a troublesome employee in front of others.
    (A) upbraid
    (B) ignore
    (C) praise
    (D) upgrade

18. A security guard needs to be extra _____ on moonless nights.
    (A) chilly
    (B) vigilant
    (C) vibrant
    (D) unfriendly

ENGLISH FORUM

1000 essential words that often appear on the TOEFL
Step 4

STEP 4

verb 동사
vocabulary 1000

abnegate
[ǽbnigèit]

거절하다, 포기하다, 끊다

<syn> deny, renounce, relinquish
<ant> indulge, abandon

He must *abnegate* all his former friends.
그는 자신의 모든 전 친구들과 절교해야 한다.

abrogate
[ǽbrəgèit]

취소하다, 파기하다, 폐지하다

<syn> annul, abolish, cancel, do away with
<ant> institute, establish, confirm, ratify

Congress has the right to *abrogate* laws with the consent of the chief executive.
의회는 장관의 동의로 법률들을 폐지할 권한을 가지고 있다.

acclimate/ acclimatize
[ǽkləmèit]

(환경에) 적응하다

<syn> accustom to a new environment, get used to, adapt, adjust

Visitors to the dessert have a hard time *acclimating* themselves to the extreme variations in temperature.
사막을 여행하는 사람들은 극심한 기온변화에 적응하느라 어려움을 겪는다.

acquiesce
[ækwiés]

묵묵히 따르다, 묵인하다, 받아들이다

<syn> comply, accept, accede
<ant> resist, contest, refuse

One must often *acquiesce* to the demands of a superior.
우리는 종종 상관의 요구에 묵묵히 따라야 한다.

adjure
[ədʒúər]

엄명하다, 탄원하다

<syn> charge or command solemnly

The witness was *adjured* to weigh his words carefully.
증인은 신중하게 말해 줄 것을 엄명받았다.

agglomerate
[əglámərèit]

한 덩어리로 뭉치다, 모으다

<syn> gather into one mass

It was necessary to *agglomerate* all the minerals into one product to produce the necessary weight.
필요한 무게로 생산하기 위해서 모든 광물을 하나의 제품으로 모을 필요가 있었다.

aggravate
[ǽgrəvèit]

악화시키다

<syn> annoy, irritate, make worse, make more severe
<ant> improve, ease, soothe, relieve,

His sarcasm only *aggravated* an already touchy situation.
그의 풍자는 이미 손대기 힘든 상황을 악화시키기만 하였다.

annihilate
[ənáiəlèit]

전멸시키다, 소멸시키다, 폐지하다

<syn> destroy completely, wipe out, exterminate, liquidate
<ant> let live, build, construct, make

If the government does not act to preserve the few remaining herds, the whole species will have been *annihilated* by the end of the century.
정부가 얼마 남지 않은 무리들을 보존하는 조치를 하지 않으면, 금세기 말까지는 모든 종이 멸종될 것이다.

appease
[əpíːz]

달래다, 진정시키다

<syn> give in to satisfy, make peace, pacify, calm
<ant> aggravate, provoke, arouse, disturb, upset

Only a heartfelt apology will *appease* his rage at having been slighted.
진심 어린 사과만이 멸시받은 것에 대한 그의 분노를 진정시킬 것이다.

augment
[ɔːgmént]

증대시키다, 늘리다

<syn> increase, add to, raise
<ant> decrease, reduce, cut back

He *augments* his wealth with every deal.
그는 모든 거래마다 부를 늘린다.

belie
[bilái]

거짓으로 전하다, 속이다

<syn> lie about, show to be false, disprove, invalidate
<ant> prove, verify, validate, indicate

Her laughing face *belied* her pretense of annoyance.
그녀의 웃는 얼굴은 불쾌감을 감춘 모습이었다.

berate
[biréit]

호되게 꾸짖다

<syn> scold vehemently, upbraid, reprimand, rebuke
<ant> praise, compliment, laud, congratulate

The teacher who *berates* his class is rationalizing his own faults.
자기 학급을 심하게 야단치는 교사가 자기 자신의 잘못을 합리화한다.

burgeon
[bə́:rdʒən]

싹을 내다, 성장하다

<syn> sprout

Plants *burgeon* with the coming of spring.
봄이 오면 식물은 싹을 틔운다.

careen
[kərí:n]

한쪽으로 기울이다 (tip to one side)

The ship *careened* with each new wave.
배는 파도가 몰려올 때마다 기울어졌다.

castigate
[kǽstəgèit]

혹평하다, 징계하다

<syn> criticize severely, chastise, scold, punish
<ant> praise, laud, compliment, encourage

The judge *castigated* the plaintiff before he fined him for contempt of court.
판사는 법정 모독죄로 원고에게 벌금형을 내리기 전에 훈계를 주었다.

circumvent
[sə̀:rkəmvént]

회피하다, 방해하다

<syn> go around, frustrate, by pass, avoid
<ant> face, confront, meet, go through

By devious dealings, they were able to *circumvent* the regulations.
비정상적인 거래로 그들은 법규정을 피할 수 있었다.

coalesce
[kòuəlés]

연합하다, 합치다 (coalescence n. 연합)

<syn> unite, combine, join
<ant> separate, divide, part

The *coalescence* of the American states is one of the secrets of our nation's progress.
미국 주들의 연합은 나라 발전의 비밀 중의 하나이다.

coerce
[kouə́:rs]

강요하다 (coercion n. 강요)

<syn> compel, force, pressure
<ant> free, allow, permit, coax

The confession was obtained under *coercion*.
강요에 의해 자백을 받아냈다.

conciliate
[kənsílièit]

달래다, 무마하다, 화해시키다

<syn> gain good will, pacify, reconcile, appease
<ant> antagonize

The adjustor's task is to *conciliate* the client with a legitimate complaint.
조정자의 임무는 적법한 소송으로 고객을 화해시키는 것이다.

confiscate
[kánfiskèit]

압수하다, 징발하다

<syn> seize, appropriate, commandeer, preempt, take over
<ant> release, return, restore

The government has no right to *confiscate* private property without just compensation.
정부는 보상도 없이 사유재산을 몰수할 권리는 없다.

contort
[kəntɔ́:rt]

비틀다, 왜곡하다

<syn> twist out of shape, bend, distort, deform
<ant> straighten, unbend

Rage *contorted* her features into a frightening mask.
분노는 자기 모습을 무서운 얼굴로 바꿔놓았다.

debauch
[dibɔ́:tʃ]

타락시키다

<syn> corrupt, seduce, debase, demoralize, deprave, pervert

The temptations they offered could not *debauch* her.
그들이 유혹을 해도 그녀를 타락시킬 수 없었다.

deify
[díəfài]

신으로 모시다, 신성시하다

<syn> make as a god, worship, glorify

They would *deify* Caesar.
그들은 시저를 신성시할 것이다.

demote
[dimóut]

지위를 떨어뜨리다, 강등시키다

<syn> lower in rank, degrade

He was stripped of his rank and *demoted* to private.
그는 자신의 계급을 박탈당하여 이등병으로 강등되었다.

demur
[dimə́:r]

의의를 제기하다, 반박하다

<syn> hesitate, object, protest

Once he *demurred*, we knew we had the advantage of additional time to prepare.
일단 그가 의의를 제기하였고, 우리는 준비할 시간 여유가 있음을 알았다.

deprecate
[déprikèit]

비난하다, 반대하다, 나쁘게 말하다

<syn> detract from, condemn, disapprove of, belittle, depreciate

Do not *deprecate* what you cannot understand.
네가 이해할 수 없다고 하여 나쁘게 말하지 마라.

devolve
[diválv]

양도하다, 위임하다, 맡기다

<syn> be transferred, be handed down

The duties of the position *devolved* upon the new sales manager.
그 자리의 임무는 새로운 영업부장에게 맡겨졌다.

divest
[divést]

(옷을) 벗기다, 박탈하다

<syn> deprive, strip, remove, disrobe; deprive, dispossess, get rid of
<ant> clothe, dress, cover

After the court martial, he was *divested* of his rank and decorations.
군법회의가 끝난 뒤에 그는 자신의 계급과 훈장들을 박탈당했다.

educe
[idjú:s]

끄집어내다, 추출해내다

<syn> elicit, draw out, evoke, deduce, extract, evince, extort

Can you *educe* any information from her notes?
네가 그녀의 노트에서 어떤 정보를 끌어낼 수 있을까?

elate
[iléit]

기운을 돋구다, 의기양양하게 하다

<syn> make joyful, elevate in spirit

A grade of 100% will *elate* any student.
만점은 어떤 학생도 기운 나게 할 것이다.

elucidate
[ilú:sədèit]

밝히다, 명료하게 설명하다

<syn> make clear, explain, explicate, illuminate, illustrate, describe
<ant> confuse, obscure, becloud, muddle

The explanation served to confuse rather than to *elucidate*.
그 설명은 명확하게 하기보다는 혼돈되게 하였다.

elude
[ilú:d]

회피하다, 면하다

<syn> avoid, escape, escape the notice of, dodge, shun
<ant> confront, meet, encounter

The thief *eluded* the police by darting into a crowded theater.
도둑은 혼잡한 극장 안으로 돌진하여 경찰을 따돌렸다.

evince
[ivíns]

명시하다, 분명히 나타내다

<syn> make evident, display, reveal, show

His curt reply *evinced* his short temper.
그의 짤막한 대답은 자신의 급한 성질을 보여주었다.

exacerbate
[igzǽsərbèit]

악화시키다, 심화시키다

<syn> make worse, aggravate, make more violent

A generous portion of french fries is sure to *exacerbate* an upset stomach.
프렌치프라이의 기름진 부분은 분명히 배탈을 악화시킬 것이다.

exonerate
[igzánərèit]

결백을 증명하다, 혐의를 벗겨주다

<syn> free from blame, absolve, vindicate, acquit
<ant> prove guilty, condemn, blame

The confession of one prisoner *exonerated* the other suspects.
한 죄수의 자백이 다른 피의자들의 혐의를 벗겨 주었다.

explicate
[ékspləkèit]

해설하다, 가설을 전개하다

<syn> explain, develop a principle

He could not *explicate* a philosophy that depended on doing evil.
그는 악행에 기반을 두는 철학을 해설할 수 없었다.

extricate
[ékstrəkèit]

구출하다, 해방시키다

\<syn\> free from an entanglement, release, get out, loose, rescue, liberate
\<ant\> catch, trap, snare, tangle, tie up

Carefully removing each prickly branch, she *extricated* herself from the briars.
그녀는 가시 많은 가지들을 조심스럽게 제거하고서야 가시덤불에서 빠져 나왔다.

flout
[flaut]

비웃다, 놀리다

\<syn\> mock, show contempt for, scorn, laugh at
\<ant\> revere, regard, respect, esteem

He *flouted* public opinion by appearing with his lover in public.
그는 대중 앞에 애인과 함께 나타나 여론을 비웃었다.

gyrate
[dʒáiəreit]

선회하다, 회전하다

\<syn\> revolve around a point, whirl, spin around, rotate, twirl, circle

The tornado *gyrates* about a central point.
토네이도는 중심을 두고 회전한다.

infiltrate
[infíltreit]

침투시키다, 스며들게 하다 (pass through or into)

The radical organization had been *infiltrated* by federal agents who monitored its membership and activities.
그 급진 단체는 회원과 활동을 감시하던 연방 조직원들의 잠입을 받았다.

interpolate
[intə́:rpəlèit]

(원고의) 원문에 가필하다 (change a text by inserting new material)

The editor *interpolated* the latest news into the proofs.
편집자가 최신 소식을 교정쇄에 가필하였다.

menace
[ménəs]

위협하다, 으르다

\<syn\> endanger, threaten, imperil, jeopardize, risk, terrify, intimidate
\<ant\> benefit, help, aid, protect, guard, soothe

The periodic floods *menaced* the city with destruction.
주기적인 범람이 그 도시를 파괴적으로 위협하였다.

nauseate
[nɔ́:zièit]

메스껍게 하다, 염증을 느끼게 하다

\<syn\> cause nausea, sicken, disgust, upset

Food *nauseates* the patient.
음식이 환자를 메스껍게 한다.

obfuscate
[ɑbfʌ́skeit]

(마음을) 어둡게 하다, (판단을) 흐리게 하다

<syn> confuse, make obscure

Do not *obfuscate* the facts with irrelevant issues.
관계없는 문제를 가지고 사실을 흐리게 하지 마라.

palpitate
[pǽlpətèit]

심장이 뛰다, 가슴이 두근거리다

<syn> beat rapidly, flutter, throbs, pulse quickly

The *palpitation* of her heart was due to fright.
그녀의 심장이 뛰는 것은 공포 때문이었다.

proscribe
[prouskráib]

법률의 보호를 박탈하다, 금지하다

<syn> outlaw, forbid by law

Theft is *proscribed* mostly by state law.
도둑질은 주 법률로 금한다.

recapitulate
[rìːkəpítʃəlèit]

개괄적으로 말하다, 요약하다 (mention or relate in brief)

<syn> summarize, repeat in essence, sum up, reiterate

It is not my purpose to *recapitulate* all the topics that should find a place in democracy's message to the people.
사람들을 향한 민주주의의 메시지 속에서 어떤 위치를 찾아야 하는 모든 화제들을 요약하는 것이 나의 목적은 아니다.

recriminate
[rikrímənèit]

되받아 비난하다, 되받아 소송하다 (return accusation for accusation)

They *recriminated* constantly over the most trivial setbacks, each blaming the other whenever anything went wrong.
어떤 일이 잘못될 때마다 상대를 비난하면서 그들은 아주 사소한 차질에도 계속해서 되받아 비난하였다.

relegate
[réləgèit]

추방하다, 좌천시키다 (transfer to get rid of, assign to an inferior position)

He *relegated* the policeman to a suburban beat.
그는 그 경찰을 변두리 구역으로 좌천시켰다.

renege
[riníg]

약속을 어기다, 취소하다 (go back on a promise or agreement)

<syn> break a promise, break one's word, withdraw

Their assurances of good faith were hollow; they *reneged* on the agreement almost at once.
신의를 약속한 그들의 공언은 공허하였다. 그들은 아주 금방 합의를 어겼다.

traduce
[trədjúːs]

비방하다, 우롱하다

<syn> slander, publicly defame, malign, libel

Her reputation was *traduced* by malicious innuendo.
그녀의 명성은 악의적인 풍자로 비방을 받았다.

waive
[weiv]

포기하다, 보류하다 (give up voluntarily something to which one is entitled)

<syn> forego, surrender, relinquish a legal right; postpone, defer, put off
<ant> claim, demand, insist on, assert, maintain

In cases of unusual hardship, the normal fee may be *waived*.
비상의 어려운 경우에는 정규적인 급여가 보류될 수도 있다.

warp
[wɔːrp]

비틀다, 구부리다, 왜곡시키다 (bend slightly throughout)

<syn> bend, twist, deform, distort, pervert
<ant> straighten, unbend

The board *warped* in the sun.
판지가 햇볕에 뒤틀렸다.
The ideas were *warped* by a bad environment.
나쁜 환경으로 생각들이 왜곡되었다.

wield
[wiːld]

(도구를) 휘두르다, 사용하다; 지배하다, (힘을) 행사하다 (use with full command or power)

<syn> handle, play, manipulate, exert, exercise, employ

The soldier was skilled at *wielding* his sword.
병사는 자신의 칼을 사용하는 데 능숙하였다.

wince
[wins]

주춤하다, 움츠리다 (shrink from a blow or from pain)

<syn> shrink, flinch, grimace, shudder

He *winced* under her sarcasm.
그는 그녀의 비꼬는 말에 움츠러들었다.

winnow
[wínou]

키질하여 골라내다, 선별하다; 분석하다 (examine, sift for the purpose of separating the bad from the good)

His statement was so garbled that it was impossible to *winnow* the falsehoods from the truth.
그의 진술은 너무도 진실을 호도하고 있어서 진실과 거짓을 가려내기가 불가능하였다.

wrest
[rest]

비틀다, 잡아떼다, 억지로 빼앗다 (take by violence)

<syn> wrench, twist, wring, jerk, rep, force

It was impossible for the child to *wrest* his toy from the bigger boy.
어린이가 큰 아이에게서 장난감을 억지로 빼앗기란 불가능하였다.

STEP 4 Practice Test 10

DIRECTIONS Select the word or phrase that means most nearly the same as the key word.

1 abnegate
(A) forget (B) deny
(C) prevent (D) damage

2 abrogate
(A) insult (B) suffer
(C) abolish (D) breach

3 acquiesce
(A) pacify (B) comply
(C) disagree (D) solidify

4 agglomerate
(A) hardened (B) muddy
(C) stir up (D) gather

5 annihilate
(A) forget (B) damage
(C) destroy (D) disbelieve

6 annuity
(A) anniversary (B) friendliness
(C) blood relation (D) yearly payment

7 belie
(A) rest (B) excuse
(C) prove false (D) make appropriate

ANSWER

1. (A) 잊어버리다
   (B) 부정하다, 취소하다
   (C) 방지하다 (D) 손상을 입히다

2. (A) 모욕하다 (B) 고통을 겪다
   (C) 폐지하다 (D) 어기다

3. (A) 진정시키다 (B) 동의하다, 따르다
   (C) 동의하지 않다 (D) 단결시키다

4. (A) 단단해진, 굳어진
   (B) 진흙투성이의 (C) 젓다
   (D) 모으다

5. (A) 잊다 (B) 손상을 입히다
   (C) 파괴하다 (D) 믿지 않다

6. (A) 기념일 (B) 우호
   (C) 혈족 (D) 연금

7. (A) 쉬다 (B) 변명하다
   (C) 거짓으로 드러나다
   (D) 비용을 지출하다

1. (B) 2. (C) 3. (B) 4. (D)
5. (C) 6. (D) 7. (C)

8 berate
    (A) scold   (B) score
    (C) confuse   (D) confute

9 castigate
    (A) chatter   (B) encourage
    (C) criticize   (D) shut tight

10 coalesce
    (A) glow   (B) extinguish
    (C) grow together   (D) cleave

11 coerce
    (A) compel   (B) unite
    (C) invite   (D) propel

12 conciliate
    (A) confiscate   (B) appropriate
    (C) pacify   (D) exacerbate

13 confiscate
    (A) obfuscate   (B) seize
    (C) scatter   (D) collect

14 contort
    (A) mutate   (B) mutilate
    (C) twist   (D) spin

15 debauch
    (A) dehydrate   (B) steal away
    (C) remove   (D) corrupt

16 demote
    (A) harmonize   (B) mobilize
    (C) lower in rank   (D) raise in value

| ANSWER |

8. (A) 꾸짖다 (B) 성적
   (C) 혼동시키다 (D) 논박하다

9. (A) 잡담하다 (B) 격려하다
   (C) 비평하다 (D) 꽉 막다

10. (A) 빛나다 (B) 불을 끄다
    (C) 결합하다 (D) 쪼개다

11. (A) 강요하다 (B) 연합하다
    (C) 초대하다 (D) 추진하다

12. (A) 몰수하다
    (B) 사유화하다, 횡령하다
    (C) 안정시키다 (D) 악화시키다

13. (A) 어지럽게 하다
    (B) 붙잡다, 탈취하다
    (C) 흩뿌리다 (D) 수집하다

14. (A) 변화하다 (B) 절단하다
    (C) 비틀다 (D) 회전시키다

15. (A) 탈수하다 (B) 도망하다
    (C) 제거하다 (D) 타락시키다

16. (A) 조화하다 (B) 동원하다
    (C) 강등시키다 (D) 가치를 상승시키다

8. (A)　9. (C)　10. (C)　11. (A)　12. (C)
13. (B)　14. (C)　15. (D)　16. (C)

17 divest
 (A) disrobe   (B) deprive
 (C) plunge   (D) invest

18 educe
 (A) abscond   (B) elicit
 (C) usurp   (D) abdicate

19 evince
 (A) grimace   (B) display
 (C) convince   (D) understand

20 exonerate
 (A) blame   (B) free from blame
 (C) predict   (D) remove from office

21 flout
 (A) show off   (B) batter
 (C) mock   (D) smirk

22 gyrate
 (A) whirl   (B) twist
 (C) bend   (D) break

23 infiltrate
 (A) ventilate   (B) sift through
 (C) scatter   (D) pass through

24 interpolate
 (A) turn upside down   (B) annotate
 (C) add new material   (D) expurgate

25 recapitulate
 (A) invade   (B) procure
 (C) summarize   (D) truncate

| ANSWER |

17. (A) 옷을 벗기다 (B) 빼앗다
 (C) 뛰어들다 (D) 투자하다

18. (A) 도망하다
 (B) 유도해내다, 추출하다
 (C) 빼앗다 (D) 포기하다

19. (A) 얼굴을 찡그리다
 (B) 전시하다, 보여주다
 (C) 확신하다 (D) 이해하다

20. (A) 비난하다 (B) 비난을 면하다
 (C) 예언하다 (D) 직위해제하다

21. (A) 자랑하다 (B) 난타하다
 (C) 놀리다 (D) 능글맞게 웃다

22. (A) 회전하다 (B) 비틀다
 (C) 구부리다 (D) 깨트리다

23. (A) 환기하다 (B) 체질하다
 (C) 흩뿌리다 (D) 스며들다

24. (A) 거꾸로 향하게 하다
 (B) 주석을 달다
 (C) 새로운 것을 넣다 (D) 삭제하다

25. (A) 침입하다 (B) 획득하다
 (C) 요약하다 (D) (머리를) 잘라 줄이다

17. (B) 18. (B) 19. (B) 20. (B) 21. (C)
22. (A) 23. (D) 24. (C) 25. (C)

26 recriminate
(A) incarcerate (B) reprobate
(C) counter-accuse (D) countermand

27 relegate
(A) enact as law (B) reread
(C) assign to lower position (D) turn over

28 traduce
(A) put into a trance (B) cheat
(C) introduce (D) slander

29 waive
(A) forego (B) flutter
(C) warrant (D) detect

30 wrest
(A) wreck (B) wrench
(C) wretched (D) wrangle

| ANSWER |

26. (A) 투옥하다 (B) 비난하다, 배척하다
    (C) 되받아 소송하다
    (D) 취소하다, 철회하다

27. (A) 법제화하다 (B) 다시 읽다
    (C) 좌천시키다 (D) 뒤집다

28. (A) 황홀해지다 (B) 속이다
    (C) 소개하다 (D) 비방하다

29. (A) 보류하다, 포기하다
    (B) 펄럭거리다 (C) 보장하다
    (D) 방지하다

30. (A) 난파시키다 (B) 억지로 빼앗다
    (C) 비참한 (D) 논쟁하다

26. (C) 27. (C) 28. (D) 29. (A) 30. (B)

STEP 4

noun 명사
vocabulary 1000

aberration
[æbəréiʃən]

착오, 일탈, 정신이상

<syn> irregularity, deviation, abnormality
<ant> normality, regularity, sanity

Many hospital patients suffer from mental *aberrations*.
많은 병원의 환자들이 정신이상 증세를 겪고 있다.

abeyance
[əbéiəns]

중지, 정지

<syn> temporary suspension of action, postponement, deferral
<ant> continuance

The strike motion was held in *abeyance* pending contract negotiations.
계약협상이 진행 중인 가운데 파업이 보류되었다.

acclivity
[əklívəti]

오르막 비탈

<syn> upward slope

He viewed the great *acclivity* with dismay as their car chugged along.
자동차가 칙칙거리며 나아가자 그는 절망감으로 그 높은 오르막을 바라보았다.

adjunct
[ædʒʌŋkt]

부속물, 딸린 것

<syn> accessary, supplement, auxiliary part

A rider is an *adjunct* to a legislative bill.
추가조항이란 법률안의 부속항목이다.

affinity
[əfínəti]

유사성, 친근함, 친척

\<syn\> relationship, similarity, connection, kinship
\<ant\> dissimilarity

There is a close *affinity* among many European languages.
많은 유럽어들 사이에는 어떤 밀접한 유사성이 있다.

altercation
[ɔ̀ːltərkéiʃən]

언쟁, 격론

\<syn\> angry dispute, argument, quarrel
\<ant\> agreement, accord, concord

The *altercation* stopped just short of physical violence.
물리적인 폭력으로 가기 직전에 언쟁은 멈췄다.

annuity
[ənjúːəti]

연금, 연간 배당금 (an amount of money payable yearly)

Investment in an *annuity* provides an income for one's old age.
연금으로 투자된 것은 노년에 수입이 된다.

aperture
[ǽpərtʃùər]

벌어진 틈, 구멍

\<syn\> opening, hole, orifice, slit
\<ant\> closure

The woman walked through an *aperture* between two rocks and found herself in a cave.
그 여자는 두 개의 바위틈을 걸어서 동굴 속으로 들어섰다.

archives
[áːrkáivs]

기록보관소, 고문서, 기록

\<syn\> historic records, documents, library

A separate building houses the United States *archives* in Washington.
워싱턴에 있는 별도의 건물이 미국의 고문서들을 소장하고 있다.

aspersion
[əspə́ːrʒən]

비방, 중상

\<syn\> a disparaging remark, abuse, slander, detraction
\<ant\> praise, laudatory remark, compliment, commendation

Every pioneer in science has had *aspersions* cast on his work.
과학의 선구자들은 모두 자기 업적에 비방을 받아왔다.

cadence
[kéidəns]

운율, 박자, 억양

<syn> rhythmic flow, modulation of speech, measured movement

The low and musical *cadence* of her voice was a delight to hear.
그녀의 나지막하고 음악적인 억양은 듣기에 좋았다.

cataclysm
[kǽtəklìzəm]

지각변동; 대변동, 격변

<syn> a sudden and violent change in the earth, catastrophe, calamity, upheaval

Pompeii was visited by a *cataclysm* that destroyed the entire city.
폼페이는 도시전체를 파괴한 지각변동이 있었다.

celerity
[səlérəti]

신속함, 민첩함

<syn> swiftness

Act with all *celerity* to take advantage of the opportunity.
기회를 잡으려면 아주 민첩하게 행동하라.

commutation
[kàmjətéiʃən]

1. 교환, 대체 (substitution)

His prison sentence was *commuted* to hard labor.
그의 금고형은 징역으로 대체되었다.

2. 통근 (regular travel between home and work)

Commutation is a daily routine for most working people.
통근은 대부분의 직장인들에게 일상적인 일이다.

conduit
[kándjuit]

도관, 수로

<syn> pipe, main. tube, duct, canal, passage, watercourse, sewer, gutter, drain

The cables were inserted into a *conduit*.
케이블은 도관 속으로 연결되었다.

deterrent
[ditə́:rənt]

억제책, 방지책, 방해물

<syn> a thing that discourages, restraint, curb, check, hindrance

The absolute certainty of apprehension is a powerful *deterrent* to crime.
반드시 체포된다는 확신이 범죄에 대한 강력한 억제책이다.

dissension
[disénʃən]

불화, 의견차이

<syn> lack of harmony, disagreement, discord

There was *dissension* among the delegates about which candidate to support.
어느 후보를 지원할 것인가에 대해 대표자들 사이에 의견차이가 있었다.

emissary
[éməsèri]

사자, 밀사

<syn> delegate, ambassador, envoy, representative, agent, messenger

The rebels sent an *emissary* to negotiate a truce.
반란군들은 휴전을 협상하기 위해 밀사를 보냈다.

empathy
[émpəθi]

감정이입 (sense of identification with another person)

Her *empathy* with her brother was very strong; she generally knew what her sibling was feeling without his having to explain.
오빠에 대한 그녀의 감정이입은 너무나 강렬해서 그녀는 오빠가 설명해주지 않아도 그가 느끼는 것을 대체로 알고 있었다.

eugenics
[ju:dʒéniks]

우생학

Eugenics has provided us with improved animals in every class except the human race.
우생학은 인류를 제외한 모든 종의 개량된 동물을 우리에게 제공하였다.

hyperbole
[haipə́:rbəli:]

과장, 과장법

<syn> overstatement, exaggeration, extravagant statement, figurative statement
<ant> understatement

"He was as big as a house" is an example of *hyperbole*.
"그가 집채만하다"는 과장법의 예이다.

impediment
[impédəmənt]

장애, 방해물

<syn> delay, block, interference, obstruction, handicap, obstacle, defect
<ant> advantage, bolster, help, aid

The loss of two front teeth caused a speech *impediment*.
앞니 두 개가 없는 것이 언어장애의 원인이 되었다.

invocation
[ìnvəkéiʃən]

(도움을) 기원, 호소

<syn> calling on a deity for aid, prayer, appeal, plea, supplication

The minister delivered the *invocation* at the beginning of the ceremony.
총리는 의식행사의 서두에 기원을 올렸다.

itinerary
[aitínərèri]

여정, 여행계획 (plan or schedule of travel)

Our *itinerary* includes three days in Florence and a week in Rome.
우리의 여정에는 플로렌스에서 3일, 로마에서 1주일이 포함된다.

litigation
[lìtigéiʃən]

소송, 기소

<syn> lawsuit, process of carrying on a lawsuit

As long as the estate is tied up in *litigation* by the would-be heirs, no one has use of the property.
그 부동산이 자칭 상속인이라는 사람에 의해 소송에 묶여있는 한, 아무도 그 재산을 이용할 수 없다.

misnomer
[misnóumərs]

틀린 이름, 인명이나 지명의 오기

<syn> wrong or inaccurate name, inapplicable title, wrong designation

At this season Muddy River is a *misnomer*; the waters are sweet and crystalline.
이 계절에 머디강(진흙 투성이의 강)이란 이름은 틀린 이름이다. 강물이 아름답고 맑다.

nocturne
[náktəːrn]

야상곡 (a piece of music designed to be played at night)

The *nocturne* was particularly dreamy and expressive.
그 야상곡은 특별히 꿈결같고 표현이 풍부하였다.

obloquy
[ábləkwi]

욕지거리, 악담; 오명, 악평, 불명예

<syn> public disgrace, ill repute, dishonor, shame, infamy

He faced *obloquy* as a result of his ignoble actions.
그는 자신의 비열한 행위로 인한 악평을 받아야 했다.

orifice
[ɔ́ːrəfis]

구멍, 공간 (opening into a cavity)

The surgeon worked through an *orifice* below the ribs.
의사는 갈비 아래의 공간을 통해 작업을 하였다.

petulance
[pétʃələns]

성마름, 불쾌함, 토라짐

<syn> petty fretfulness, irritability, peevishness, fractiousness

Petulance is a vestige of childhood desire for more parental attention.
토라짐은 더 많은 부모의 관심을 갈망하는 어린이들의 특징적 표현이다.

predicament
[pridíkəmənt]

궁지, 곤경

<syn> dilemma, dangerous situation, troublesome, perplexing situation

Having promised to balance the budget, to cut taxes, and to increase defense spending, the newly-elected president found himself in a hopeless *predicament*.
예산을 맞추고, 감세를 하고, 국방비를 늘이겠다고 약속을 했기 때문에, 새로 선출된 대통령은 자신이 실망스런 곤경에 처해 있음을 알았다.

predilection
[prì:dəlékʃən]

편애, 역성, 선호

<syn> preference, predisposition, partiality, liking, love, fondness

He had a *predilection* for good food at any price.
그는 가격에 상관없이 좋은 음식을 선호했다.

premeditation
[pri:médətéiʃən]

미리 생각하기, 사전 계획 (the act of meditating beforehand, previous deliberation)

The *premeditation* of the crime was what made it so heinous.
범죄의 사전 계획은 더욱 악질적으로 만드는 것이었다.

prerogative
[prirágətiv]

특권, 특전, 특징적 권리

<syn> privilege, right, warrant, advantage

Going home after school is your *prerogative*.
방과후에 집으로 가는 것은 너의 권리이다.

proclivity
[prouklívəti]

경향, 성벽, 기질

<syn> tendency, inclination, leaning, liking
<ant> dislike, aversion, hatred

He had a *proclivity* for getting into trouble.
그는 문제를 일으키는 경향이 있었다.

prospectus
[prəspéktəs]

기업안내서, 사업설명서, 내용설명서

The *prospectus* for the real estate development was mailed to potential investors.
부동산개발을 위한 설명서가 예비투자자들에게 우송되었다.

quintessence
[kwintésəns]

정수, 진수, 에센스 (the purest essence of something, concentrated essence)

It is the *quintessence* of coffee flavor.
그것은 커피향의 진수이다.

rancor
[ræŋkər]

깊은 원한, 심한 증오 (bitter deep-seated ill will)

\<syn\> malice, ill will, antagonism, animosity, antipathy, hostility, resentment
\<ant\> amity, goodwill, friendship, friendliness, amicability

In spite of the insults of his opponent, the man remained calm and spoke without *rancor*.
상대편의 모욕에도 그 남자는 조용히 있다가 아무런 증오도 없이 말을 했다.

redress
[rí:dres]

배상, 보상 (compensation for a wrong done)

\<syn\> reparation, compensation, recompense, payment

The petitioners asked the state for a *redress* of grievances for which they had no legal recourse.
청원인은 주 정부에 자신들이 법률적으로 의지할 사람이 없는 피해에 대한 보상을 요구하였다.

restitution
[rèstət/ú:ʃən]

반환, 회복, 복원, 배상 (restoration to a rightful owner, reparation for an injury)

\<syn\> amends, redress, reparation, indemnity, atonement, compensation

He agreed to make *restitution* for the money he had stolen.
그는 자기가 훔친 돈을 반환하는 데 동의하였다.

rupture
[rʌ́ptʃər]

파열, 결렬, 불화

\<syn\> a breaking off, breach, split, fracture, crack, cleavage, separation
\<ant\> union, understanding, agreement, continuity

The bungling of the rescue operation, which resulted in the death of the ambassador, led to a *rupture* of diplomatic relations between the two nations.
구조작전의 미숙으로 대사가 사망하고, 두 나라 간의 외교관계가 결렬되었다.

stratagem
[strǽtədʒəm]

전략, 책략, 계략 (a scheme that outwits by trickery)

<syn> maneuver, scheme, plot, trick, intrigue, tactic, trickery

He presented another *stratagem* to overcome the lead of the opposition.
그는 반대파의 선두를 극복하기 위해 또 다른 책략을 펼쳤다.

torpidity
[tɔ́ːrpidəti]

둔감, 마비, 무감각

<syn> dullness, inactivity, sluggishness

His *torpidity* mounted to a total loss of sensation.
그의 마비는 감각을 완전히 잃어버리게 되었다.

umbrage
[ʌ́mbridʒ]

불쾌, 노여움 (suspicion of being slighted)

He takes *umbrage* if you look at him sideways.
그를 곁눈질로 보면 그는 화를 낸다.

usurpation
[jùːsərpéiʃən]

권리침해, 강탈, 횡령 (act of seizing and enjoying the power of property of another without right)

The *usurpation* of the kingdom by the conquerors caused much misery.
정복자들의 왕권찬탈이 많은 불행을 낳았다.

vernacular
[vərnǽkjələr]

자국어, 자기 지방의 말, 사투리, 일상언어

<syn> native language, the vulgar, common speech
<ant> formal speech, standard speech, educated speech

He spoke in the *vernacular* of southern Germany.
그는 남부 독일의 사투리를 썼다.

viability
[vaibiləti]

생존능력 (capacity to live)

The statistician compiled a chart that indicated the *viability* of male infants as compared with that of female infants.
통계학자는 여자 신생아의 생존능력과 비교해서 남자 신생아의 생존능력을 나타내주는 도표를 작성하였다.

welter
[wéltər]

뒹굴기, 굽이침; 소요, 동요

<syn> wallow, roll like a wave; jumble, commotion, tumult, turmoil

He took the *welter* of the crowds in stride, slipping down the street as quickly as he could.
그는 가능한 재빨리 거리로 달려나가 군중들의 동요를 무시히 진정시켰다.

STEP 4 Practice Test 11

DIRECTIONS Select the word or phrase that means most nearly the same as the key word.

1 abeyance
(A) distance (B) leave-taking
(C) postponement (D) hatred

2 aberration
(A) cloudiness (B) deviation
(C) stuttering (D) pacification

3 acclivity
(A) tendency (B) waywardness
(C) sleepiness (D) upward slope

4 affinity
(A) endlessness (B) slenderness
(C) distance (D) kinship

5 altercation
(A) dispute (B) change
(C) oscillation (D) permutation

6 annuity
(A) anniversary (B) friendliness
(C) blood relation (D) yearly payment

7 aperture
(A) exit (B) opening
(C) rip (D) hopefulness

ANSWER

1. (A) 거리 (B) 작별
   (C) 연기 (D) 증오

2. (A) 흐림 (B) 탈선, 일탈
   (C) 말더듬기 (D) 화해, 평정

3. (A) 경향, 추세
   (B) 제멋대로, 변덕(=willful)
   (C) 졸음 (D) 오르막 경사

4. (A) 무한 (B) 나약함
   (C) 거리 (D) 친족

5. (A) 논쟁 (B) 변화
   (C) 진동, 변동 (D) 교대

6. (A) 기념일 (B) 우호
   (C) 혈족 (D) 연금

7. (A) 비상구 (B) 틈
   (C) 찢어진 곳 (D) 희망

1. (C) 2. (B) 3. (D) 4. (D)
5. (A) 6. (D) 7. (B)

8 archives
(A) historic records (B) ancestors
(C) annotations (D) paraphrasings

9 burgeon
(A) sprout (B) bunion
(C) burnish (D) bury

10 cadence
(A) dialect (B) discordance
(C) rhythmic flow (D) harmonics

11 celerity
(A) swiftness (B) infamy
(C) wittiness (D) acidity

12 conduit
(A) pipe (B) leader
(C) surprise (D) window

13 empathy
(A) self-centered
(B) philanthropic
(C) magnanimity
(D) identification with another

14 hyperbole
(A) boomerang (B) overlooked
(C) overwhelmed (D) exaggeration

15 impediment
(A) cavity (B) aperture
(C) luggage (D) obstacle

| ANSWER |

8. (A) 고문서 (B) 조상
   (C) 주석 (D) 바꾸어 쓴 문장

9. (A) 싹 (B) 엄지발가락 안쪽의 염증
   (C) 닦다, 광내다 (D) 묻다

10. (A) 사투리, 방언 (B) 부조화, 불협화
    (C) 운율 (D) 화성악

11. (A) 민첩함 (B) 불명예
    (C) 재치 (D) 신맛, 산도

12. (A) 파이프 (B) 지도자
    (C) 놀람 (D) 창

13. (A) 자기중심적인 (B) 박애주의의
    (C) 너그러움
    (D) 다른 사람과의 동일시

14. (A) 부메랑 (B) 내려다 본
    (C) 압도된 (D) 과장법

15. (A) 구멍, 공동 (B) 구멍, 틈
    (C) 수화물 (D) 장애

8. (A) 9. (A) 10. (C) 11. (A)
12. (A) 13. (D) 14. (D) 15. (D)

16 invocation
- (A) prayer
- (B) career
- (C) hobby
- (D) invitation

17 itinerary
- (A) schedule
- (B) archives
- (C) bibliography
- (D) genealogy

18 litigation
- (A) fury
- (B) lawsuit
- (C) constraint
- (D) happenstance

19 misnomer
- (A) miscalculation
- (B) wrong address
- (C) unnamed
- (D) inaccurate name

20 predilection
- (A) expertise
- (B) spying out
- (C) susceptibility
- (D) preference

21 premeditation
- (A) forewarning
- (B) deliberation beforehand
- (C) execution
- (D) prevention

22 proclivity
- (A) tendency
- (B) aversion
- (C) precipice
- (D) speed

23 redress
- (A) change clothing
- (B) heal wounds
- (C) debt
- (D) compensation

| ANSWER |

16. (A) 기도 (B) 경력
    (C) 취미 (D) 초대

17. (A) 계획 (B) 공문서, 기록보관소
    (C) 참고문헌 (D) 혈통

18. (A) 분노 (B) 소송
    (C) 강제, 속박 (D) 우연한 일

19. (A) 계산 착오 (B) 잘못된 주소
    (C) 무명의 (D) 부정확한 이름

20. (A) 전문지식이나 기술 (B) 조사하다
    (C) 감수성, 다감 (D) 선호, 편애

21. (A) 예고하는 (B) 사전 논의
    (C) 실행, 집행 (D) 방지

22. (A) 경향 (B) 혐오
    (C) 절벽, 벼랑 (D) 속도

23. (A) 옷을 갈아입다
    (B) 상처를 치료하다
    (C) 빚 (D) 보상

16. (A) 17. (A) 18. (B) 19. (D) 20. (D)
21. (B) 22. (A) 23. (D)

24 restitution
(A) reward (B) reparation
(C) punishment (D) institutionalization

25 stratagem
(A) flim-flam (B) start
(C) afterthought (D) scheme

26 umbrage
(A) cloudiness (B) touchiness
(C) spreading out (D) rank growth

27 viability
(A) capacity to live (B) able to laugh
(C) true-to-life (D) capacity

28 quintessence
(A) dispersal (B) concentrated essence
(C) elevation (D) sacred objects

29 rancor
(A) malice (B) speed
(C) accusation (D) reprimand

| ANSWER |

24. (A) 보상 (B) 배상
    (C) 처벌 (D) 제도화

25. (A) 엉터리, 허튼 소리 (B) 출발
    (C) 뒤늦은 생각 (D) 계획, 책략

26. (A) 흐림 (B) 성마름, 까다로움
    (C) 벌리는 (D) 계급 발달

27. (A) 생존능력 (B) 웃을 수 있는
    (C) 현실적으로, 실생활에 맞게
    (D) 능력

28. (A) 분산, 해산 (B) 정수
    (C) 고도 (D) 제물

29. (A) 악의, 원한 (B) 속도
    (C) 비난, 고소 (D) 비난

24. (B) 25. (D) 26. (B) 27. (A)
28. (B) 29. (A)

STEP 4
adjective & adverb 형용사&부사

abstemious
[əbstíːmiəs]

(음식을) 절제하는, 자제하는

\<syn\> moderate in eating and drinking

The *abstemious* eater is seldom overweight.
식사를 절제하는 사람은 좀처럼 살이 찌지 않는다.

adamant
[ǽdəmənt]

굳은, 단단한

\<syn\> inflexible, hard insistent, firm
\<ant\> yielding, flexible, lax

A man must be *adamant* in his determination to succeed.
남자는 성공을 위한 자신의 결심에 철석같아야 한다.

ambidextrous
[æmbidékstrəs]

양손잡이인 (able to use both hands equally well)

Ambidextrous tennis players have a great advantage.
양손잡이 테니스 선수들은 큰 이점을 가지고 있다.

ambulatory
[ǽmbjulətɔ̀ːri]

이동하는, 활동 가능한, 걸을 수 있는

\<syn\> moving about, able to walk, mobile
\<ant\> bedridden, not walking, immobile

Ambulatory patients require organized activities to speed their recovery.
움직일 수 있는 환자들은 빠른 회복을 위해 단체 활동이 필요하다.

amenable
[əmíːnəbəl]

순종하는, 받아들이는

\<syn\> open to suggestion, agreeable, willing to listen
\<ant\> closed-minded, obstinate, stubborn

He was *amenable* to any proposition.
그는 어떤 제안도 받아들였다.

apposite
[ǽpəzit]

적절한, 적당한

<syn> fitting, relevant

Since he hadn't followed the discussion, his comments were not *apposite*.
그가 토론내용을 파악하지 못했기에 그의 발언은 적절치 못했다.

auspicious
[ɔːspíʃəs]

길조의, 경사스런, 상서로운

<syn> indicating success, being a good omen, benign, fortunate, lucky
<ant> ill-omened, ominous, sinister, unfortunate, unlucky

The first week's business was an *auspicious* start for the whole enterprise.
첫 주의 사업은 기업 전체로서는 기분 좋은 출발이었다.

averse
[əvə́ːrs]

싫어하는, 반대하는

<syn> opposed, reluctant disinclined, ill-disposed
<ant> agreeable, amenable, willing, inclined

The perennial bachelor is *averse* to matrimony.
오래 독신으로 지내는 남자는 결혼을 꺼린다.

blatant
[bléitənt]

소란스러운, 눈에 띄는

<syn> too noisy, obtrusive, loud
<ant> unobtrusive, acquiescent, agreeable

The herds of cattle filled the air with their *blatant* bellowing.
소 떼의 소란스런 울음소리가 공중에 가득 찼다.

callow
[kǽlou]

순진한, 경험이 없는, 풋내기의

<syn> immature, inexperienced, unseasoned, green
<ant> mature, grown-up, experienced, sophisticated

A *callow* youth often grows into a sophisticated man.
순진한 젊은이가 자라면서 닳은 인간이 된다.

circumspect
[sə́ːrkəmspèkt]

신중한, 주의 깊은

<syn> watchful in all directions, wary, careful, cautious
<ant> rash, reckless, heedless

A public official must be *circumspect* in all his actions.
공직자는 자신의 모든 행동에 신중해야 한다.

cogent
[kóudʒənt]

적절한, 설득력 있는

<syn> conclusive, convincing

A debater must present *cogent* arguments to win his point.
토론자가 자신의 요지를 관철시키기 위해서는 설득력 있는 논거를 제시해야 한다.

collateral
[kəlǽtərəl]

adj. 1. 부차적인 (secondary, subordinate, auxiliary) 2. 평행한 (side by side)

He cited *collateral* court decisions.
그는 부차적인 법원결정을 인용하였다.

n. 담보 (securities for a debt, pledge, warranty, insurance)

He offered bonds as *collateral* for his loan.
그는 자신의 대출을 위한 담보로 채권을 제공하였다.

concentric
[kənséntrik]

중심이 같은 (with the same center)

The orbits of the planets are *concentric*.
행성들의 궤도는 중심이 같다.

concerted
[kənsə́:rtid]

합의된

<syn> mutually agreed upon, cooperated, joint, united
<ant> disunited, separate, individual

The *concerted* plan of action was carried out by all the parties involved.
모든 관련 정당들은 합의된 결의안을 실행에 옮겼다.

conducive
[kəndjú:siv]

전도의, 도움이 되는

<syn> leading to, helping, contributive, favorable
<ant> harmful, hurtful, deleterious, beneficial

The waterbed was *conducive* to a restful sleep.
물침대가 편안한 수면에 도움이 되었다.

contiguous
[kəntígjuəs]

근접한, 인접한

<syn> next to, adjoining

Alaska is not *contiguous* to other states of the United States.
알래스카는 미국의 다른 주들과 인접해 있지 않다.

conversant
[kənvə́:rsənt]

정통하고 있는, 친한, 관련된

<syn> familiar, having knowledge of

The accountant is *conversant* with the tax laws.
그 회계사는 세법에 정통하고 있다.

copious
[kóupiəs]

풍부한, 많은

\<syn> plentiful, profuse, abundant, ample
\<ant> skimpy, sparse, meager, scanty

The table was *copiously* set.
식탁이 풍성하게 차려졌다.

corpulent
[kɔ́:rpjələnt]

뚱뚱한, 비만의

\<syn> very fat, obese, overweight
\<ant> thin, slender, slim, skinny

The *corpulent* individual must choose his clothes with great care.
뚱뚱한 사람은 자기 옷을 아주 주의해서 골라야 한다.

corrigible
[kɔ́:ridʒəbəl]

고칠 수 있는, 바로잡을 수 있는 (capable of being reformed)

Corrigible offenders should be separated from hardened criminals.
교화 가능한 경범자들은 중죄인들과 분리해야 한다.

defunct
[difʌ́ŋkt]

죽은, 소멸한

\<syn> dead, no longer functioning, extinct
\<ant> alive, live, living, in force

The business has been *defunct* since the big fire.
큰 화재가 있은 뒤로 회사는 소멸하였다.

derogatory
[dirágətɔ́:ri]

품위를 떨어뜨리는, 경멸적인

\<syn> disparaging, disdainful, belittling, uncomplimentary
\<ant> flattering, complimentary, favorable

His *derogatory* remarks hid feelings of envy.
그의 경멸적인 언사는 부러운 감정을 감추고 있었다.

didactic
[daidǽktik]

교훈적인, 가르치기 위한

\<syn> instructive, intended to teach, educational, tutorial

The *didactic* approach may be well suited for a textbook but should be avoided in books aimed at the general public.
교훈적인 접근이 교과서에는 잘 어울릴지 모르지만 일반대중을 겨냥한 책에는 피해야 된다.

dilatory
[dílətɔ́:ri]

더딘, 꾸물거리는

\<syn> delaying action, slow, tardy, sluggish
\<ant> diligent, assiduous, sedulous, prompt

The filibuster is an effective legislative tool in *dilatory* campaigns.
의사진행방해는 지연전술의 효과적이고 합법적인 수단이다.

discursive
[diskə́:rsiv]

산만한, 종잡을 수 없는

<syn> digressive, rambling, roundabout, wandering
<ant> direct, methodical, coherent

A debater must check the tendency to *discursive* remarks.
토론자는 산만한 소견으로 가는 경향을 주의해야 한다.

disquieting
[diskwáiətiŋ]

불안한, 걱정되는

<syn> disturbing, tending to make uneasy, unsettling, distressing

There have been *disquieting* reports of a buildup of forces along the border.
국경선의 군사력 증강에 관해 걱정하는 보고가 있었다.

divisive
[diváisiv]

불화를 일으키는, 분열을 일으키는

<syn> tending to divide, causing disagreement

The issue of abortion, on which people hold deep and morally-based convictions, was *divisive* to the movement.
깊고, 도덕적으로 기반이 확실한 낙태문제가 운동에서는 분열적이었다.

elusive
[ilú:siv]

붙잡기 어려운, 파악하기 어려운, 알 수 없는

<syn> hard to find or grasp, hard to comprehend

Because the problem is so complex, a definitive solution seems *elusive*.
문제가 너무 복잡하여 명확한 답을 알 수 없어 보인다.

ephemeral
[ifémərəl]

하루밖에 못사는, 단명한, 덧없는

<syn> lasting a day, short-lived, temporary, transitory

Ephemeral pleasures may leave lasting memories.
짧은 즐거움이 기억에 오래 남을 것이다.

erudite
[érjudàit]

박식한, 학식이 있는

<syn> scholarly, with bookish knowledge, learned, well-educated, literate
<ant> uninformed, uneducated, illiterate, unscholarly

The *erudite* person may find it difficult to communicate his thoughts to those less educated.
박식한 사람은 자기 생각을 학식이 적은 사람들에게 전달하는 것이 어렵다는 것을 알게 된다.

ethereal
[iθíriəl]

공기 같은, 천상의

<syn> spirit-like, celestial, sublime, exquisite, aerial, airy
<ant> earthly, mundane, worldly, monumental, solid
The heroine of his book was endowed with *ethereal* beauty.
그의 책의 여주인공은 천상의 아름다움을 지녔다.

expedient
[ikspí:diənt]

편리한, 편의적인

<syn> advantageous, appropriate, useful, practical
<ant> impractical, disadvantageous
Under pressure to reduce the deficit, the mayor found it *expedient* to cut funds for social services.
시장은 적자를 줄이기 위한 고민을 하다가 사회복지 부문의 자금을 삭감하는 것이 편하다는 것을 알았다.

extrinsic
[ekstrínsik]

외부로부터의, 본질적이 아닌

<syn> external, coming from the outside
Her complaints about one particular teacher are *extrinsic* to an evaluation of the program as a whole.
특정한 한 선생님에 대한 그녀의 불평은 전체적으로 프로그램의 평가에 부차적인 것이다.

feckless
[féklis]

무기력한, 무책임한

<syn> weak, spiritless, irresponsible, ineffective, worthless
A *feckless* soldier is a liability to his outfit.
아무리 무기력한 병사라도 자신의 장비에 책임을 져야한다.

generic
[dʒənérik]

속(屬)의, 종족의

<syn> pertaining to a race or kind
The *generic* characteristics of each animal enable us to distinguish them.
각 동물의 속(屬)의 특징으로 우리는 그것들을 구별할 수 있다.

herbivorous
[hə́rbívərəs]

초식성의 (feeding on plants)

A vegetarian is *herbivorous*.
채식주의자는 초식성이다.

heterogeneous
[hètərədʒíːniəs]

이종의, 이질적 성분으로 된 (composed of unlike elements)

<syn> mixed, varied, diversified, diverse, assorted, composite
<ant> homogeneous, uniform, same

The school favored *heterogeneous* groupings, so there was a very wide range of ability and achievement in every class.
학교는 이질적인 집단화를 좋아한다. 그래서 모든 학급이 매우 광범위한 능력과 성취를 보인다.

homogeneous
[hòumədʒíːniəs]

동질의, 동종의

<syn> of the same kind, all alike, of a piece, uniform, unmixed
<ant> heterogeneous, mixed, varied, different, diverse

The entering class was fairly *homogeneous*; nearly all the students were the same age and from similar middle-class homes.
입문반은 아주 동질적이었다. 거의 모든 학생들이 나이가 같고, 비슷한 중류 가정의 출신이었다.

imperturbable
[ìmpərtə́ːrbəbl]

침착한, 태연한

<syn> not easily excited, calm, cool, serene, undisturbed
<ant> perturbable, choleric, touchy

His poker face was aided by an *imperturbable* nature.
그의 무표정한 얼굴은 침착한 성격에 의한 것이었다.

inalienable
[inéiljənəbəl]

양도할 수 없는, 빼앗을 수 없는

<syn> not transferable, absolute, sacred, inherent

We are endowed with certain *inalienable* rights.
우리는 어떤 양도할 수 없는 권리들을 부여받았다.

incognito
[inkágnitòu]

암행의, 잠행의, 익명으로

The prince traveled *incognito*.
왕자는 신분을 숨기고 여행을 하였다.

ingenuous
[indʒénjuːəs]

솔직한, 꾸밈없는, 순진한

<syn> straightforward, frank, naive

An *ingenuous* approach is often better than guile.
솔직한 접근이 일반적으로 가식보다 더 좋다.

innocuous
[inákjuːəs]

무해한, 독이 없는, 악의 없는

<syn> harmless, not damaging, painless, not injurious
<ant> hurtful, harmful, deleterious, damaging

His words were *innocuous*, but his temper vile.
그의 말은 악의가 없었으나 성질은 고약했다.

insensate
[insénseit]

비정의, 무감각한, 잔인한

<syn> lacking sense or understanding, foolish, inanimate, brutal, inhuman

In his *insensate* rage he did not yet feel the pain of his injury.
비정한 분노로 그는 아직 상처의 고통도 느끼지 못했다.

laconic
[ləkánik]

간결한, 말 수 적은

<syn> terse, pithy, short, concise, brief, compact
<ant> voluble, wordy, loquacious, garrulous

His *laconic* replies conveyed much in few words.
그의 간결한 대답은 적은 단어로 많은 것을 전달하였다.

languid
[læŋgwid]

나른한, 활기 없는, 느린

<syn> listless, slow, weak, feeble
<ant> strong, active, energetic, vigorous

His *languid* walk irritated his companions, who were in a hurry.
그의 활기 없는 걸음은 바빠서 서두르는 동료들을 화나게 하였다.

lucrative
[lú:krətiv]

유리한, 수지맞는

<syn> profitable, moneymaking, remunerative, high-paying
<ant> unprofitable, low-paying, unremunerative

A *lucrative* enterprise is attractive to investors.
사업을 잘하는 기업은 투자자들에게 매력적이다.

magisterial
[mæ̀dʒəstíəriəl]

권위적인, 고압적인

<syn> authoritative, arrogant, dogmatical

One who is *magisterial* assumes the air of a master toward his pupils.
권위적인 사람은 학생들을 향해 거장의 모습을 나타낸다.

magnanimous
[mæɡnǽnimə s]

도량이 넓은, 관대한, 고결한

<syn> noble-minded, extremely generous, large-hearted
<ant> unforgiving, vindictive, resentful

The painter was *magnanimous* enough to praise the work of a man he detested.
화가는 자신이 싫어하는 사람의 작품을 칭찬할 만큼 아량이 있었다.

mediocre
[mìːdióukər]

보통의, 평범한

<syn> of middle quality, ordinary, medium, undistinguished
<ant> extraordinary, uncommon, distinguished, unique

A *mediocre* student in high school will rank low among candidates for college.
고등학교에서 평범한 학생이 대학입학 지원자들 가운데서는 하위에 놓인다.

mendacious
[mendéiʃəs]

허위의, 거짓말을 잘하는

<syn> lying, untruthful, dishonest, deceitful

Baron Munchausen was humorously *mendacious*.
바론 문초슨은 유머러스하게 거짓말을 잘하였다.

meritorious
[mèritɔ́ːriəs]

공적 있는, 칭찬할 만한, 갸륵한

<syn> deserving reward, commendable, laudable, noteworthy, praiseworthy
<ant> unpraiseworthy, discreditable, undeserving

Medals were awarded for *meritorious* service.
칭찬받을 만한 봉사활동으로 메달이 수여되었다.

miscreant
[mískriənt]

이단의, 사악한

<syn> villain, villainous

The *miscreant* kidnapper was caught and jailed.
사악한 유괴범이 잡혀서 투옥되었다.

mordant
[mɔ́ːrdənt]

신랄한, 독설적인

<syn> biting, sarcastic, burning, pungent

His *mordant* remarks hurt her vanity.
그의 신랄한 주장이 그녀의 허영심에 상처를 입혔다.

morose
[məróus]

까다로운, 기분이 언짢은, 침울한

<syn> gloomy, sulking, unreasonably unhappy
<ant> cheerful, blithe, happy, pleasant

The boy was *morose* for days over his failure to get tickets for the concert.
소년은 콘서트 티켓을 구하지 못해서 며칠동안 침울했다.

nonagenarian
[nùnədʒənɛ́əriən]

90대의 (a person in his 90s)

The *nonagenarian* looks forward to a century mark.
90대 노인들은 1세기 기록을 기대하고 있다.

obdurate
[ábdjurit]

고집 센, 완고한; 냉혹한

\<syn> stubborn, obstinate; callous, hardened
\<ant> obedient, agreeable, compliant

He was *obdurate* and resisted the pleadings of his friends.
그는 고집이 세어서 친구들의 탄원서를 반대하였다.

obstreperous
[əbstrépərəs]

시끄러운, 날뛰는

\<syn> noisy, boisterous, loud, disorderly, unruly, uncontrolled
\<ant> orderly, restrained, obedient, docile

The *obstreperous* customer was asked to leave.
그 시끄러운 고객은 떠나줄 것을 요청받았다.

onerous
[ánərəs]

부담이 되는, 귀찮은

\<syn> burdensome, oppressive, distressing, hard to endure
\<ant> easy, light, simple

His work was *onerous*.
그의 일은 부담스러웠다.

ostensible
[ɑsténsəbəl]

외면상의, 표면적인, 겉치레의

\<syn> avowed, apparent, outward, nominal, seeming
\<ant> real, true, actual, genuine

The *ostensible* purpose of the withdrawal was to pay a debt, but actually the money was used for entertainment.
출금의 표면적인 목적은 빚을 갚기 위한 것이었으나 실제로는 돈이 유흥에 사용되었다.

pedantic
[pidǽntik]

학자연하는, 현학적인 (making a needless display of learning)

\<syn> ostentatiously learned, pompous, academic, scholastic, didactic
\<ant> succinct, pithy, general

The *pedantic* pedagogue pedaled to the palace spouting Platonic principles.
현학적인 교육자는 플라톤의 원칙을 말하며 궁중으로 자전거를 달렸다.

penurious
[pinjúəriəs]

아주 인색한

\<syn> stingy, miserly, close, tightfisted, parsimonious

A poor man is *penurious* by necessity.
가난한 사람은 궁핍으로 인해 몹시 인색하다.

pernicious
[pəːrníʃəs]

유해한, 유독한, 치명적인

<syn> harmful, injurious, destructive, damaging, deadly, fatal
<ant> harmless, innocuous, beneficial, healthy

Excessive drinking is a *pernicious* habit.
과음은 해로운 습관이다.

portentous
[pɔːrténtəs]

전조의, 불길한, 무서운

<syn> foreshadowing future events, threatening, intimidating, ominous

The thunderstorm that broke as we were leaving seemed *portentous* but in fact the weather was lovely for the rest of the trip.
우리가 떠날 때 내리친 천둥소리가 불길하였으나 사실은 남은 여행기간 동안 날씨가 좋았다.

punctilious
[pʌŋktíliəs]

격식을 세심하게 차리는, 꼼꼼한 (exact in formalities and details)

<syn> meticulous, scrupulous, careful, punctual

Be *punctilious* in obeying your doctor.
의사의 말을 따를 때는 세심하게 주의해야 한다.

putative
[pjúːtətiv]

세평에 의한, 추정의, 소문의 (commonly accepted; assumed to exist or to have existed)

<syn> supposed, reputed

His *putative* wealth was exaggerated by his ostentation.
추정되는 그의 재산은 그의 겉치장 때문에 과장되었다.

retroactive
[rètrouǽktiv]

반동하는, 효력이 소급하는 (applying to what is past)

A law may not apply *retroactively*.
법률은 소급해서 적용할 수 없다.

salient
[séiliənt]

현저한, 두드러진

<syn> conspicuous, noticeable, prominent, obvious
<ant> low-lying, depressed, inconspicuous, minor

The *salient* points of the speech could not be forgotten by the audience.
연설의 두드러진 요점은 청중들에게 잊혀질 수 없었다.

sedulous
[sédʒuləs]

근면한, 정성을 다하는

<syn> diligent, painstaking, persevering

He was a *sedulous* worker.
그는 근면한 일꾼이었다.

sonorous
[sənɔ́ːrəs]

(목소리가) 낭랑한, (소리가) 울려 퍼지는

<syn> resonant, full-toned, deep, vibrant, resounding, eloquent, impressive

His *sonorous* voice helped make him a famous orator.
그의 낭랑한 목소리는 그를 유명한 연설가로 만드는 데 도움이 되었다.

specious
[spíːʃəs]

허울만 좋은, 그럴듯한, 가면을 쓴 (deceptively plausible)

He advanced his cause with *specious* arguments.
그는 그럴듯한 논지로 자신의 주장을 내세웠다.

supercilious
[sùːpərsíliəs]

거만한, 남을 깔보는, 거드름피우는

<syn> proud, haughty, contemptuous, disdainful, overbearing, arrogant

The *supercilious* attitude of wealthy families has been a cause of many social upheavals.
부잣집 사람들의 거드름피우는 태도는 많은 사회적 격변의 원인이 되어왔다.

surreptitious
[sə̀ːrəptíʃəs]

비밀의, 은밀한

<syn> underhand, unauthorized, clandestine, covert, secretive, furtive
<ant> open, aboveboard, candid, direct

They met *surreptitiously* in the night to exchange information.
그들은 정보를 교환하기 위해 밤에 은밀하게 만났다.

tangential
[tændʒénʃəl]

접선의, 지엽적인, 곁길로 새는

<syn> digressing, off the point, not central

Facts about the author's life, while they may be fascinating, are *tangential* to an evaluation of her works.
그들이 매혹될 수 있는 저자의 인생에 관한 사실들은 그녀의 작품에 대한 평가에서 지엽적인 부분이다.

tenable
[ténəbəl]

유지/방어할 수 있는, 지지할 수 있는 (capable of being held, maintained, or defended)

The club had no *tenable* reasons for the exclusion; it was purely a case of prejudice.
그 클럽은 배척에 어떤 지지할 수 있는 이유도 없었다. 순전히 편견의 사례이다.

tractable
[træktəbəl]

유순한, 다루기 쉬운 (easily led)

A *tractable* worker is a boon to the supervisor but is not always a good leader.
온순한 근로자가 늘 훌륭한 지도자가 못되는 관리자에게는 복이다.

trenchant
[tréntʃənt]

날카로운, 통렬한

<syn> sharp, penetrating, forceful; keen, caustic, sharply perceptive

His *trenchant* remarks were more dangerous than his sword.
그의 날카로운 소견은 그의 칼보다 더 위험하였다.

turgid
[tə́:rdʒid]

부어오른; 과장된

<syn> swollen, puffed up; pompous, bombastic, hyperbolic
<ant> shrunken; simple, modest

The man was in constant pain because his limbs were *turgid* as the result of an incurable disease.
남자는 치료가 어려운 질병으로 손발이 부어 올라 늘 고통에 시달렸다.

unscrupulous
[ʌnskrú:pjələs]

거리낌없는, 무절제한, 무도한 (not constrained by moral feelings)

<syn> unprincipled, dishonorable, devious, unethical
<ant> scrupulous, principled, moral, ethical

The *unscrupulous* landlord refused to return the security deposit, claiming falsely that the tenant had damaged the apartment.
무도한 집주인은 세입자가 아파트를 손상시켰다고 엉터리 주장을 하며 보증금을 돌려주기를 거절하였다.

verbatim
[vərbéitim]

말 그대로, 정확하게

<syn> word for word, in the same words, exactly, to the letter

The lawyer requested the defendant to repeat the speech *verbatim*.
변호사는 연설을 정확하게 다시 해줄 것을 피고에게 요청하였다.

vicarious
[vaikɛ́əriəs]

대신하는, 대리 체험한, 대리만족의 (experienced secondhand through imagining another's experience)

She enjoyed *vicariously* the achievements of her daughter.
그녀는 자기 딸이 이룬 성공을 대신하여 기뻐하였다.

vindictive
[vindíktiv]

복수의, 원한이 있는, 앙심을 가진 (showing a desire for revenge)

<syn> unforgiving, vengeful, revengeful, avenging, retaliative
<ant> forgiving, relenting, generous, magnanimous

Stung by the negative reviews of his film, the director made *vindictive* personal remarks about critics.
자기 영화에 대한 부정적인 평에 자극을 받은 감독은 앙심을 가지고 비평가들에 대한 개인적인 소견을 냈다.

STEP 4 Practice Test 12

DIRECTIONS Select the word or phrase that means most nearly the same as the key word.

1 abstemious
   (A) picky   (B) moderate
   (C) unpleasant   (D) demanding

2 amenable
   (A) irreparable   (B) open to suggestion
   (C) mitigated   (D) obstreperous

3 averse
   (A) eloquent   (B) lying across
   (C) reluctant   (D) gregarious

4 collateral
   (A) vertical   (B) collarbone
   (C) perpendicular (D) side by side

5 cogent
   (A) thoughtful   (B) convincing
   (C) conscious   (D) comatose

6 concentric
   (A) bizarre   (B) with the same center
   (C) with the same boundary (D) circular

7 concerted
   (A) symphony   (B) agreed upon
   (C) facile   (D) mollified

| ANSWER |

1. (A) 까다로운 (B) 삼가는, 절제하는
   (C) 기분 나쁜 (D) 모자라는

2. (A) 불치의, 돌이킬 수 없는
   (B) 제안을 받아들일 수 있는
   (C) 가라앉다 (D) 시끄러운, 난폭한

3. (A) 웅변적인 (B) 가로놓여 있는
   (C) 꺼리는, 싫어하는
   (D) 군집하는, 모여 사는

4. (A) 수직의 (B) 쇄골
   (C) 수직의 (D) 나란한

5. (A) 신중한
   (B) 확신시키는, 설득력 있는
   (C) 양심적인 (D) 혼수상태의

6. (A) 기괴한 (B) 같은 중심의
   (C) 같은 경계의 (D) 원형의

7. (A) 교향악 (B) 합의된
   (C) 손쉬운 (D) 진정된

1. (B) 2. (B) 3. (C) 4. (D)
5. (B) 6. (B) 7. (B)

8 conducive
   (A) compelling   (B) forceful
   (C) hypnotic   (D) helping

9 contiguous
   (A) adjoining   (B) noxious
   (C) sticky   (D) quarrelsome

10 copious
   (A) plentiful   (B) spacious
   (C) meretricious   (D) superfluous

11 corpulent
   (A) deceased   (B) obese
   (C) flesh-eating   (D) circular

12 corrigible
   (A) corroded   (B) eroded
   (C) malleable   (D) reformable

13 discursive
   (A) sinuous   (B) elliptical
   (C) rambling   (D) printed

14 ephemeral
   (A) celestial   (B) gaseous
   (C) temporary   (D) feverish

15 ethereal
   (A) celestial   (B) ephemeral
   (C) hard of hearing (D) fibrous

16 expedient
   (A) on foot   (B) protracted
   (C) extenuating   (D) advantageous

| ANSWER |

8. (A) 강제하는 (B) 강력한
   (C) 최면의 (D) 도움이 되는

9. (A) 인접하는 (B) 유해한
   (C) 집착하는 (D) 싸우기 좋아하는

10. (A) 많은 (B) 넓은
    (C) 저속한 (D) 여분의

11. (A) 죽은 (B) 살찐, 뚱뚱한
    (C) 육식의 (D) 원형의

12. (A) 침식된 (B) 부식된
    (C) 펴 늘일 수 있는 (D) 고칠 수 있는

13. (A) 굽이진 (B) 타원형의
    (C) 산만한, 종잡없는 (D) 인쇄된

14. (A) 천상의, 하늘의 (B) 가스의, 기체의
    (C) 임시의 (D) 열이 뜨거운

15. (A) 천상의 (B) 하루살이의
    (C) 청각장애의 (D) 섬유질의

16. (A) 도보로 (B) 오래 끈
    (C) 정상을 참작할 수 있는
    (D) 편의적인

8. (D) 9. (A) 10. (A) 11. (B) 12. (D)
13. (C) 14. (C) 15. (A) 16. (D)

17 generic
(A) communicable
(B) esoteric
(C) pertaining to race or kind
(D) variegated

18 homogeneous
(A) similarly shaped (B) variegated
(C) male gender (D) uniform throughout

19 herbivorous
(A) plant-eating (B) seeded
(C) plant-bearing (D) overweight

20 heterogeneous
(A) composed of unlike elements
(B) nonconforming
(C) severe
(D) composed of many parts

21 imperturbable
(A) ignorant (B) morbid
(C) unexcitable (D) terrified

22 incognito
(A) ignorant (B) disguised
(C) sly (D) wheedling

23 innocuous
(A) vaccinated (B) baleful
(C) harmless (D) daily

24 mediocre
(A) yellowish-brown (B) middle quality
(C) boiled (D) partially completed

| ANSWER |

17. (A) 전염성의, 전달하는
    (B) 비법전수의, 은밀한
    (C) 종족에 관련된 (D) 여러 가지 색의

18. (A) 비슷한 모양의 (B) 여러 가지 색의
    (C) 남성 (D) 완전히 동일한

19. (A) 초식성의 (B) 씨뿌린
    (C) 식물성 함유의 (D) 과체중의

20. (A) 서로 다른 요소들로 구성된
    (B) 복종하지 않는, 국교를 믿지 않는
    (C) 엄한 (D) 많은 부분으로 구성된

21. (A) 무식한 (B) 병적인
    (C) 흥분이 안 되는 (D) 겁에 질린

22. (A) 무식한 (B) 가장한
    (C) 교활한 (D) (감언이설로) 속이는

23. (A) 예방접종을 한 (B) 재앙의
    (C) 무해한 (D) 일상의

24. (A) 황갈색 (B) 중간급
    (C) 끓인 (D) 일부 완성한

17. (C) 18. (D) 19. (A) 20. (A)
21. (C) 22. (B) 23. (C) 24. (B)

25 mordant
(A) sarcastic (B) dying
(C) fallible (D) gloomy

26 nonagenarian
(A) night watchman (B) vegetarian
(C) ninety-year old (D) eighty-year old

27 obstreperous
(A) boisterous (B) infected
(C) stubborn (D) uninvited

28 pedantic
(A) hiker
(B) extravagantly wealthy
(C) intellectual showing-off
(D) jaywalker

29 penurious
(A) stingy (B) slow-moving
(C) ancient (D) happy-go-lucky

30 portentous
(A) obese (B) impressive
(C) foreshadowing (D) retroactive

31 retroactive
(A) wearing down (B) dangerous
(C) concealed activity (D) applying to past

32 supercilious
(A) absentminded (B) haughty
(C) punctual (D) jovial

| ANSWER |

25. (A) 풍자적인, 신랄한 (B) 죽어 가는
    (C) 틀리기 쉬운 (D) 우울한

26. (A) 야간경비원 (B) 채식주의자
    (C) 90세의 (D) 80세의

27. (A) 떠들썩한, 사나운 (B) 감염된
    (C) 완고한 (D) 초대받지 않은

28. (A) 도보여행자 (B) 지나치게 부유한
    (C) 지적으로 뽐내는
    (D) 교통규칙을 무시하고 걷는 사람

29. (A) 인색한 (B) 거동이 느린
    (C) 고대의 (D) 낙천적인

30. (A) 살찐, 뚱뚱한 (B) 인상적인
    (C) 전조가 되는
    (D) 반동하는, 효력이 소급하는

31. (A) 약화되는 (B) 위험한
    (C) 활동을 은폐하는
    (D) 과거로 소급적용

32. (A) 방심한 상태의, 멍한
    (B) 오만한, 건방진
    (C) 시간을 엄수하는 (D) 쾌활한

25. (A) 26. (C) 27. (A) 28. (C)
29. (A) 30. (C) 31. (D) 32. (B)

33 surreptitious
   (A) sleeping   (B) clandestine
   (C) flawed   (D) careful

34 turgid
   (A) slow   (B) stubborn
   (C) furious   (D) swollen

35 tenable
   (A) capable of being defended
   (B) swift
   (C) inhabitable
   (B) capable of withstanding pain

36 tractable
   (A) arable   (B) fertile
   (C) easily led   (D) easily broken

37 verbatim
   (A) forbidden   (B) paraphrased
   (C) translated   (D) word for word

38 vicarious
   (A) hilarious
   (B) experienced secondhand
   (C) remembered
   (D) spiteful

39 punctilious
   (A) on time   (B) whining
   (C) biting   (D) painstaking

40 rancor
   (A) malice   (B) speed
   (C) accusation   (D) reprimand

| ANSWER |

33. (A) 잠자는 (B) 비밀의, 은밀한
    (C) 결함 있는 (D) 주의 깊은

34. (A) 느린 (B) 고집 센
    (C) 분노한 (D) 부풀어 오른

35. (A) 방어할 수 있는 (B) 빠른
    (C) 살기 알맞은
    (D) 고통을 잘 견딜 수 있는

36. (A) 경작에 알맞은, 개간이 쉬운
    (B) 비옥한 (C) 다루기 쉬운
    (D) 쉽게 부러지는

37. (A) 금지된 (B) 문장 바꿔 쓴
    (C) 번역된 (D) 말 그대로

38. (A) 명랑한, 들뜬 (B) 간접 체험한
    (C) 기억하는
    (D) 악의가 있는, 원한 품은

39. (A) 제시간에 (B) 흐느껴 우는
    (C) 날카로운
    (D) 수고를 아끼지 않는, 근면한

40. (A) 악의, 원한 (B) 속도
    (C) 비난, 고소 (D) 비난

33. (B) 34. (D) 35. (A) 36. (C)
37. (D) 38. (B) 39. (D) 40. (A)

41 salient
(A) wise   (B) sympathetic
(C) secure   (D) conspicuous

42 sedulous
(A) painstaking   (B) discerning
(C) reticent   (D) receptive

43 trenchant
(A) timid   (B) troubled
(C) swollen   (D) penetrating

| ANSWER |

41. (A) 현명한 (B) 동정적인
    (C) 안전한 (D) 눈에 띄는, 특징적인

42. (A) 근면한, 수고하는
    (B) 식별하다, 인식하다
    (C) 과묵한, 삼가는
    (D) 잘 받아들이는, 감수성이 예민한

43. (A) 소심한 (B) 문제를 일으킨
    (C) 부어오른 (D) 꿰뚫는, 예민한

41. (D) 42. (A) 43. (D)

STEP 4 Mastery Test 4

[Synonym Test]

DIRECTIONS Choose the word or phrase that means most nearly the same as the key word or the underlined word.

1. acclimate
   - (A) predict weather
   - (B) become accustomed to
   - (C) enjoy good climate
   - (D) drill thoroughly

2. augment
   - (A) adopt
   - (B) increase
   - (C) modify
   - (D) predict

3. auspicious
   - (A) questionable
   - (B) well-known
   - (C) free
   - (D) favorable

4. dilatory
   - (A) slow
   - (B) enlarged
   - (C) aimless
   - (D) expansive

5. deprecate
   - (A) lower the worth
   - (B) express disapproval
   - (C) apologize for
   - (D) applaud

6. erudition
   - (A) coarseness
   - (B) scholarship
   - (C) pompousness
   - (D) elimination

7. expedient
   - (A) fair
   - (B) skillful
   - (C) advantageous
   - (D) objectionable

8. mendacious
   - (A) beggared
   - (B) dishonest
   - (C) intelligent
   - (D) laudable

9. miscreant
   - (A) aborted
   - (B) deformed
   - (C) villainous
   - (D) mistaken

10. His subordinates were aware of his <u>magnanimous</u> act. The word <u>magnanimous</u> as used in this sentence means most nearly
    - (A) insolent
    - (B) shrewd
    - (C) unselfish
    - (D) threatening

11. The visitor was <u>morose</u>. The word <u>morose</u> as used in this sentence means most nearly
    - (A) curious
    - (B) gloomy
    - (C) impatient
    - (D) timid

12. specious
    - (A) special
    - (B) deceptive
    - (C) genuine
    - (D) sporadic

13. salient
    - (A) mouth-watering
    - (B) salty
    - (C) marine
    - (D) conspicuous

14. sedulous
    - (A) diligent
    - (B) traitorous
    - (C) alluring
    - (D) ingenuous

] Antonym Test [

DIRECTIONS Choose the word or phrase that is most nearly opposite in meaning to the given word.

1. ambulatory
   - (A) confined to bed
   - (B) able to walk
   - (C) injured
   - (D) quarantined

2. cataclysm
   - (A) blunder
   - (B) status quo
   - (C) treachery
   - (D) triumph

3. auspicious
   - (A) condemnatory
   - (B) conspicuous
   - (C) unfavorable
   - (D) questionable

4. dilatory
   - (A) hairy
   - (B) happy-go-lucky
   - (C) ruined
   - (D) punctual

5. conversant
   - (A) terse
   - (B) pushy
   - (C) convinced
   - (D) unfamiliar

6. derogatory
   - (A) uneven
   - (B) equal
   - (C) opposite
   - (D) flattering

7. feckless
   - (A) intrepid
   - (B) spotless
   - (C) painstaking
   - (D) fickle

8. ingenuous
   (A) quick (B) guileless
   (C) talented (D) plotting

9. extrinsic
   (A) germ-proof (B) eccentric
   (C) uncultivated (D) internal

10. laconic
    (A) watery (B) musical
    (C) vivacious (D) verbose

11. languid
    (A) fluent (B) moist
    (C) sickly (D) vigorous

12. obfuscate
    (A) lame (B) placate
    (C) adulterate (D) clarify

13. petulant
    (A) irascible (B) cheerful
    (C) uncouth (D) abnormal

14. lucrative
    (A) debasing (B) unprofitable
    (C) influential (D) monetary

15. ostensible
    (A) showy (B) unintelligible
    (C) rust-free (D) blended

16. renege
- (A) runaway
- (B) honor
- (C) lighten
- (D) disown

17. sedulous
- (A) deceptive
- (B) religious
- (C) careless
- (D) hateful

18. usurp
- (A) abdicate
- (B) predict
- (C) pacify
- (D) declaim

Sentence Completion Test

DIRECTIONS Select the word or phrase that will best complete the meaning of the sentence as a whole.

1. To give in to the terrorists' demands would be a betrayal of our responsibilities; such _____ would only encourage others to adopt similar methods for gaining their ends.
   - (A) defeats
   - (B) appeasement
   - (C) appeals
   - (D) subterfuge

2. She was _____ in her determination to achieve her goals.
   - (A) sweet
   - (B) adamant
   - (C) amoral
   - (D) helpful

3. Although for years substantial resources had been devoted to alleviating the problem, a satisfactory solution remained _____.

   (A) costly
   (B) probable
   (C) elusive
   (D) esoteric

4. The ancient Romans so revered their emperors that they chose to _____ them.

   (A) question
   (B) deify
   (C) dethrone
   (D) terrify

5. He decided to _____ after he heard that several people would be fired if he took the job.

   (A) laugh
   (B) devolve
   (C) devote
   (D) demur

6. The plate began to _____ on top of the juggler's pole when he shook it gently.

   (A) wobble
   (B) hang
   (C) gallop
   (D) gyrate

7. Because everyone knew she tended to exaggerate when she got excited, no one took her _____ seriously.

   (A) hyperboles
   (B) hypertension
   (C) hypotension
   (D) hilarity

8. The brave police officer was honored for his _____ service.

   (A) mendacious
   (B) mediocre
   (C) meretricious
   (D) meritorious

9. He presented a _____ influence on the previously well-behaved child.

   (A) germane
   (B) far-reaching
   (C) pernicious
   (D) picky

10. The _____ child refused to change his opinion that the sky would fall during a rain storm, although his parents repeatedly told him otherwise.
    (A) odious
    (B) obdurate
    (C) objectionable
    (D) obligatory

11. Her comments were so _____ that we couldn't remember the real point of the discussion.
    (A) crude
    (B) unfriendly
    (C) wavering
    (D) tangential

12. The potion contained a powerful substance that caused _____ and allowed the enemy to walk past undisturbed.
    (A) rapidity
    (B) torpidity
    (C) arrogance
    (D) hesitance

13. The speaker's points were so _____ that the audience was convinced.
    (A) ambiguous
    (B) tenuous
    (C) trenchant
    (D) reactionary

14. Step-parents may exercise too little control over children for fear that they are _____ the rights of the child's natural parent.
    (A) vanquishing
    (B) vilifying
    (C) usurping
    (D) upbraiding

ENGLISH FORUM

1000 essential words that often appear on the TOEFL
Step 5

STEP 5

verb 동사
vocabulary 1000

abrade
[əbréid]

문지르다, 문질러 닳게 하다

<syn> rub off, wear away by friction

Sandpaper is used to *abrade* a rough surface.
사포는 거친 표면을 문지르는 데 사용된다.

adduce
[ədjú:s]

이유나 증거를 제시하다, 예증하다

<syn> bring forward as a reason or example

In their defense they *adduced* several justifications for their actions.
방어를 하기 위해 그들은 자신들의 행위에 대한 몇 가지 정당성을 제시하였다.

ameliorate
[əmí:ljərèit]

개선하다, 좋게 하다

<syn> make better, improve

It will take more than a few new textbooks to *ameliorate* the crisis in the schools.
학교의 위기를 개선하는 것은 몇 권의 새로운 교과서 이상의 것을 요구할 것이다.

arrogate
[ǽrəgèit]

남의 권리를 침해하다, 사취하다, 가로채다

<syn> claim without right

He *arrogates* to himself the judicial power.
그는 스스로 사법권력을 남용하고 있다.

belabor
[biléibər]

호되게 꾸짖다, 세게 때리다 (beat soundly)

In the book, the poor servant was constantly *belabored* without cause.
책에서는 불쌍한 하인이 늘 이유도 없이 매를 맞는다.

calumniate
[kəlʌ́mnièit]

비방하다, 중상하다

\<syn\> slander, defame, malign
\<ant\> praise, laud, applaud

He was known to *calumniate* anyone who disagreed with him.
그는 자신에게 동의하지 않는 사람은 누구든 비방하는 것으로 알려져 있다.

cogitate
[kάdʒətèit]

숙고하다, 궁리하다

\<syn\> think, ponder, contemplate, meditate

Take time to *cogitate* before you answer.
대답하기 전에 생각하는 시간을 가져라.

collate
[kəléit]

순서대로 정리하다, 책의 페이지를 확인하다; 대조하다

\<syn\> collect in order, assemble in proper order, check that pages of a text are in order; compare carefully

The photocopies have been *collated* and are ready to be stapled.
복사자료가 정리되었고, 묶을 준비가 되어있다.

congeal
[kəndʒíːl]

응결시키다, 굳히다

\<syn\> change from a fluid to a solid, curdle, harden, set, stiffen, solidify
\<ant\> dissolve, soften, melt, thaw

The horrible scene *congealed* his blood.
끔찍한 장면에 그는 피가 얼어붙는 것 같았다.

conjecture
[kəndʒéktʃər]

추측하다, 억측하다

\<syn\> guess, suppose, think, calculate, reckon
\<ant\> know

He *conjectured* that vocabulary questions would appear on the test.
그는 어휘문제들이 시험에 나올 거라고 생각하였다.

contravene
[kὰntrəvíːn]

반박하다, 위반하다, 무시하다

\<syn\> oppose by direct opposition

His actions *contravene* the policy set by the Board.
그의 행동들은 위원회에서 결정한 정책에 위반된다.

corroborate
[kərábərèit]

확증하다, 입증하다

<syn> provide added proof, prove, verify, confirm
<ant> disprove, contradict, refute

Laws of evidence require that evidence of a crime must be *corroborated* by other circumstances.
증거법은 범죄의 증거가 다른 상황에 의해 입증되어야 함을 요구하고 있다.

debilitate
[dibílətèit]

쇠약하게 하다

<syn> enfeeble, weaken, disable, undermine
<ant> strengthen, invigorate, energize, vitalize

Constant excesses will *debilitate* even the strongest constitution.
계속되는 무절제는 아무리 강한 조직이라도 쇠퇴하게 만든다.

decimate
[désəmèit]

(전염병이) 많은 사람을 죽이다 (destroy a large part of a population)

The Black Death had *decimated* the town.
흑사병이 도시 사람들을 죽였다.

delineate
[dilínièit]

윤곽을 그리다, 묘사하다

<syn> mark off the boundary of, sketch, portray, describe

They asked him to *delineate* the areas where play was permitted.
그들은 놀아도 되는 지역을 그려달라고 그에게 요구하였다.

descry
[diskrái]

발견하다, 찾아내다, 식별하다

<syn> spy out, discover by eye, catch sight of

In the distance we could *descry* a small cabin.
우리는 저 멀리 작은 오두막이 있는 것을 발견할 수 있었다.

desecrate
[désikrèit]

신성을 더럽히다, (신성한 것을) 속되게 쓰다

<syn> violate, profane, defile, dishonor
<ant> honor, esteem

Hoodlums attempted to *desecrate* the cemetery.
건달들이 공동묘지를 더럽히려 하였다.

diffuse
[difjúːz]

퍼뜨리다, 확산시키다

\<syn\> spread out, scatter widely, disperse
\<ant\> concentrate, compact, concise

When the bottle broke, the fragrance *diffused* throughout the room.
병이 깨져서 유리 파편들이 온 방안에 흩어졌다.

disconcert
[dìskənsə́ːrt]

당황케 하다, 쩔쩔매게 하다, 방해하다

\<syn\> throw into confusion, distract, ruffle, agitate, unsettle, upset, confuse

An apathetic audience may *disconcert* even the most experienced performer.
무관심한 청중이 경험 많은 연주자를 당황하게 만들기도 한다.

dissemble
[disémbəl]

숨기다, 감추다, 속이다

\<syn\> disguise, make pretense of, simulate, feign, conceal
\<ant\> show, manifest, reveal

A skillful publicity man will *dissemble* his propaganda to appear as impartial information.
노련한 홍보담당자는 자신의 선전을 치우치지 않은 정보로 보이도록 숨긴다.

disseminate
[disémənèit]

널리 퍼뜨리다, 유포하다

\<syn\> spread, broadcast, scatter, disperse, diffuse

With missionary zeal, they *disseminated* the literature about the new religion.
그들은 전도자적인 열정으로 새로운 종교에 관한 학문을 널리 퍼뜨렸다.

distend
[disténd]

넓히다, 부풀리다, 팽창시키다

\<syn\> stretch, swell, bloat, expand, bulge, inflate

If you *distend* a balloon beyond a certain point, it will break.
풍선을 어느 정도 이상 불면 터진다.

ensnare
[ensnɛ́ər]

함정에 빠뜨리다, 올가미에 걸다

\<syn\> catch, entrap, bag, capture

He was *ensnared* in the fabric of his lies.
그는 자신이 한 거짓말 그물에 걸렸다.

ensue
[ensúː]

(...의 결과로) 잇따라 일어나다

<syn> follow immediately, result, come afterward, succeed
<ant> herald, precede, introduce

One person raised an objection and a long argument *ensued*.
한 사람이 이의를 제기해서 긴 토론이 이어졌다.

eschew
[istʃúː]

피하다, 삼가다

<syn> avoid, shun, abstain from, forgo
<ant> seek, chase after, hunt out

She *eschewed* any social activities and lived in total seclusion.
그녀는 어떤 사회활동도 삼가고 완전한 은둔의 삶을 살았다.

excoriate
[ikskɔ́ːrièit]

피부를 벗기다; 심하게 비난하다

<syn> remove the skin from; denounce harshly

The principal *excoriated* the student as a juvenile delinquent.
교장선생님은 그 학생을 비행청소년으로 심하게 야단쳤다.

execrate
[éksikrèit]

심하게 욕하다, 저주하다

<syn> curse, abhor, denounce as evil

The captors who had lost all sense of humanity deserved to be *execrated*.
인간성을 모두 상실한 체포조들은 저주받을 만하였다.

expostulate
[ikspástʃulèit]

충고하다, 질책하다 (remonstrate)

He *expostulated* loudly and clearly with his students about their poor working habits.
그는 자기 학생들에게 크고 분명한 소리로 그들의 부족한 학업에 대해 질책하였다.

expurgate
[ékspərgèit]

삭제하다, 정화하다

<syn> remove, cut out, delete, censor, purge

The censors *expurgated* the portions of the book they considered obscene.
검열관들은 그 책의 음란하다고 생각되는 부분들을 삭제하였다.

extirpate
[ékstərpèit]

박멸하다, 근절시키다

<syn> destroy entirely, uproot, exterminate, eradicate, abolish, annihilate

The soldier threatened to *extirpate* the entire village if they refused to surrender.
그 병사는 그들이 항복하지 않으면 온 마을을 전멸시키겠다고 협박하였다.

flaunt
[flɔ:nt]

자랑하다, 과시하다

<syn> display, show off, brandish, vaunt, boast
<ant> conceal, hide, screen, cloak, disguise

Flaunting expensive jewelry in public may be an invitation to robbery.
대중 앞에 값비싼 보석을 과시하는 것은 강도를 초대할 수도 있다.

foreclose
[fɔ:rklóuz]

저당물을 찾는 권리를 상실시키다

<syn> rescind a mortgage for failure to keep up payments, shut out, preclude

The bank *foreclosed* the mortgage and repossessed the house, putting it up for sale.
은행은 담보물 찾을 권리를 상실시키고 그 집을 회수하여 경매에 올렸다.

importune
[ìmpərtjú:n]

성가시게 조르다, 괴롭히다

<syn> beg, urge, annoy

Do not *importune* me for what you can earn so easily.
네가 아주 쉽게 벌 수 있는 돈을 내게 달라고 조르지 마라.

inculcate
[inkʌ́lkeit]

주입시키다, 깨우치다, 가르치다

<syn> instill, to impress on the mind by repetition, teach

From earliest childhood they had been *inculcated* with the tenets of the community's belief.
그들은 어릴 때부터 공동체 신앙의 교리를 주입받아 왔다.

inculpate
[inkʌ́lpeit]

비난하다, 죄를 씌우다

<syn> blame, incriminate

To *inculpate* others in your troubles may bring some ego satisfaction, but it never brings a solution.
네 문제로 다른 사람을 비난하는 것은 어떤 이기적인 만족감은 가져올 것이나, 그것은 결코 문제해결을 가져오지 않는다.

ingratiate
[ingréiʃièit]

마음에 들도록 하다, 영합하다

<syn> establish in favor, gain favor

He tried to *ingratiate* himself with his teacher by bringing her apples.
그는 사과를 가져와서 선생님 마음에 들려고 애썼다.

lacerate
[læsərèit]

잡아 찢다 (tear tissue roughly)

<syn> slash, cut, lance, gash, tear, slice, scratch

The baby swallowed the safety pin, which caused an intestinal *laceration*.
아기가 안전핀을 삼킨 것이 장 파열의 원인이 되었다.

languish
[læŋgwiʃ]

기운이 없어지다

<syn> become weak, become languid, become dispirited, go into decline

He *languished* for weeks in miserable disappointment, refusing to leave the house or to see anybody.
그는 쓰라린 실망으로 기운이 없어져 몇 주일 간 외출을 하거나 누굴 만나기도 거절하였다.

metamorphose
[mètəmɔ́:rfouz]

변형시키다

<syn> transform, change, alter

Two months abroad *metamorphosed* him into a man of the world.
해외에서의 2개월이 그를 세계적인 인간으로 바꿔놓았다.

perambulate
[pəræmbjəlèit]

소요하다, 순회하다

<syn> walk about, stroll, promenade, ramble

We *perambulated* over the grounds for several hours.
우리는 몇 시간을 운동장을 걸어다녔다.

peruse
[pərú:z]

읽다, 음미하다

<syn> read carefully, study

She *perused* the text, absorbing as much information as she could.
그녀는 가능한 많은 정보를 흡수하면서 텍스트를 음미하였다.

pontificate
[pɑntífikit]

거드름 피면서 말하다 (speak pompously)

He would rise slowly, *pontificate* for half an hour, and sit down without having said a thing we didn't know before.
그는 천천히 일어나 30분을 거드름 피면서 말하고는, 우리가 전에 서로 모르는 사이라는 어떤 말도 없이 앉아버렸다.

prevaricate
[privǽrəkèit]

얼버무리다, 발뺌하다, 속이다

<syn> deviate from the truth, equivocate, be evasive

When questioned directly, the suspect was forced to *prevaricate*.
직접적인 질문을 받았을 때, 피의자는 얼버무리도록 강요받았다.

satiate
[séiʃièit]

충분히 만족시키다, 물릴 정도로 주다 (satisfy fully or to excess)

<syn> gratify completely, surfeit

Employees at candy factories soon get so *satiated* that they never eat the stuff.
과자공장의 근로자들은 과자에 금방 물려서 절대로 과자를 먹지 않는다.

sequester
[sikwéstər]

격리하다, 은퇴시키다 (seize by authority, set apart in seclusion)

<syn> set apart, seclude, segregate, isolate, withdraw

The jury was *sequestered* until the members could reach a verdict.
배심원단은 구성원들이 평결을 내릴 때까지 격리되었다.

truncate
[trʌ́ŋkeit]

잘라서 줄이다 (shorten by cutting, lop)

The shrubs were uniformly *truncated* to form a neat hedge.
관목이 가벼운 울타리를 형성하도록 일정하게 잘라졌다.

variegate
[vɛ́əriəgèit]

여러 가지 색으로 하다, 알록달록하게 하다 (diversify in external appearance, mark with different colors)

The builder created a *variegated* pattern with marble of different hues.
건축가는 여러 가지 색깔의 대리석으로 알록달록한 무늬를 만들었다.

wheedle
[hwíːdl]

유혹하여 …하게 하다, 속여서 …하게 하다

<syn> coax, cajole, flatter, beguile, lure
<ant> force, coerce, bully, intimidate

The woman knew exactly how to *wheedle* what she wanted from the man.
그 여자는 그 남자를 속여 자신이 원하는 것을 시켜먹는 방법을 정확히 알고 있었다.

STEP 5 Practice Test 13

DIRECTIONS Select the word or phrase that means most nearly the same as the key word.

1. **adduce**
   (A) provide reasons (B) compute
   (C) suspect (D) imply

2. **abrade**
   (A) wear away (B) plait
   (C) chide (D) wallow

3. **arrogate**
   (A) insult (B) claim unjustifiably
   (C) break into (D) abscond

4. **calumniate**
   (A) plaster (B) slander
   (C) complement (D) compliment

5. **cogitate**
   (A) gyrate (B) agitate
   (C) think (D) demand

6. **collate**
   (A) harness (B) late together
   (C) collect in order (D) annotate

7. **congeal**
   (A) friendly (B) family member
   (C) adhere (D) curdle

ANSWER
1. (A) 이유를 대다 (B) 계산하다 (C) 의심하다 (D) 함축하다
2. (A) 닳다 (B) 주름잡다 (C) 비난하다 (D) 뒹굴다
3. (A) 모욕하다 (B) 부당하게 요구하다 (C) 침입하다 (D) 도망하다
4. (A) (반죽을) 바르다 (B) 비난하다 (C) 보충, 보완 (D) 칭찬하다
5. (A) 나선으로 선회하다 (B) 동요시키다 (C) 생각하다 (D) 요구하다
6. (A) 말의 장비를 채우다 (B) 함께 늦다 (C) 순서대로 정리하다 (D) 주석을 달다
7. (A) 우호적으로 (B) 가족 (C) 고수하다 (D) 응결시키다
1. (A) 2. (A) 3. (B) 4. (B) 5. (C) 6. (C) 7. (D)

8 debilitate
(A) weaken (B) inhabit
(C) make poorer (D) reduce

9 decimate
(A) cut down many (B) divide
(C) reclaim (D) lower

10 delineate
(A) mark off (B) prohibit
(C) proscribe (D) descend

11 contravene
(A) intercept (B) interrupt
(C) approve (D) oppose

12 descry
(A) complain (B) censure
(C) scold (D) spy out

13 disconcert
(A) confuse (B) aggravate
(C) contemplate (D) impede

14 dissemble
(A) take apart (B) disparage
(C) disguise (D) disperse

15 distend
(A) drop (B) divide
(C) stretch (D) pull back

16 ensue
(A) litigate (B) follow
(C) flee (D) begin after a delay

| ANSWER |

8. (A) 약하게 하다
   (B) 서식하다, 거주하다
   (C) 가난하게 만들다 (D) 삭감하다

9. (A) 많은 사람을 죽이다 (B) 나누다
   (C) 교화시키다 (D) 낮추다

10. (A) 경계를 구분하다 (B) 금지하다
    (C) 추방하다 (D) 내리다

11. (A) 가로채다 (B) 방해하다
    (C) 인정하다 (D) 반대하다

12. (A) 불평하다 (B) 비난하다
    (C) 꾸짖다 (D) 찾아내다

13. (A) 혼동시키다 (B) 악화시키다
    (C) 숙고하다 (D) 방해하다

14. (A) 분석하다 (B) 다른
    (C) 감추다, 숨기다 (D) 흩뿌리다

15. (A) 떨어뜨리다 (B) 나누다
    (C) 늘이다 (D) 후퇴시키다

16. (A) 제소하다 (B) 뒤따르다
    (C) 도망하다
    (D) 연기된 뒤에 시작하다

8. (A) 9. (A) 10. (A) 11. (D) 12. (D)
13. (A) 14. (C) 15. (C) 16. (B)

17 eschew
 (A) masticate (B) denounce
 (C) shun (D) greet

18 excoriate
 (A) dishearten (B) encourage
 (C) remove (D) denounce harshly

19 expurgate
 (A) remove objectionable matter (B) expel
 (C) explicate (D) interpolate

20 importune
 (A) curse (B) beg
 (C) impose (D) suppose

21 inculcate
 (A) unfathomable (B) blameless
 (C) admonish (D) instill

22 ingratiate
 (A) establish in favor (B) mock
 (C) rebuff (D) pretend

23 lacerate
 (A) cover with oil (B) chew
 (C) tear roughly (D) fling

24 metamorphose
 (A) transfer (B) adulterate
 (C) gyrate (D) transform

25 pontificate
 (A) sanctify (B) speak pompously
 (C) greet warmly (D) hallow

| ANSWER |

17. (A) (음식물을) 씹다, 분쇄하다
    (B) 비난하다 (C) 피하다 (D) 인사하다

18. (A) 낙담시키다 (B) 격려하다
    (C) 제거하다 (D) 심하게 비난하다

19. (A) 불쾌한 것을 제거하다
    (B) 쫓아내다 (C) 해설하다
    (D) 원고에 가필하다

20. (A) 저주하다, 욕하다 (B) 애걸하다
    (C) 부과하다 (D) 가정하다

21. (A) 헤아릴 수 없는 (B) 결백한
    (C) 훈계하다 (D) 주입시키다

22. (A) 영합하다 (B) 조롱하다
    (C) 퇴짜놓다 (D) 가장하다

23. (A) 기름으로 뒤덮다 (B) 씹다
    (C) 거칠게 찢다 (D) 내던지다

24. (A) 운반하다 (B) 타락시키다
    (C) (나선형으로) 회전하다
    (D) 변형시키다

25. (A) 신성하게 하다
    (B) 거만하게 말하다
    (C) 따뜻하게 인사하다
    (D) 신성하게 하다

17. (C) 18. (D) 19. (A) 20. (B) 21. (D)
22. (A) 23. (C) 24. (D) 25. (B)

26 prevaricate
(A) wander (B) escape
(C) wonder (D) evade

27 truncate
(A) plant (B) cut in pieces
(C) cut short (D) put into containers

28 wheedle
(A) wield (B) yearn
(C) wince (D) coax

| ANSWER |

26. (A) 방랑하다 (B) 탈출하다
    (C) 궁금해하다
    (D) 회피하다, 얼버무려 넘기다

27. (A) (식물을) 심다
    (B) 여러 조각으로 자르다
    (C) 잘라서 줄이다 (D) 용기에 담다

28. (A) 휘두르다, 사용하다
    (B) 동경하다 (C) 주춤하다, 움츠리다
    (D) 달래서 ...하게 하다

26. (D) 27. (C) 28. (D)

STEP 5

noun 명사
vocabulary 1000

ablution
[əblúːʃən]

목욕재계

<syn> ceremonial washing, ritualistic cleansing, bathing

Ablutions are a part of many religious rites.
목욕재계는 여러 종교의식 가운데 일부이다.

absolution
[æbsəlúːʃən]

용서, 면제, 사면

<syn> pardon, forgiveness
<ant> restriction, limitation

The clergy has the right to grant *absolution*.
목사는 사면을 내릴 수 있는 권한을 가지고 있다.

acerbity
[əsə́ːrbəti]

신맛, 신랄함, 통렬함

<syn> bitterness, sourness, sarcastic irritability
<ant> good nature, cordiality, good humor

The *acerbity* of her wit won her many enemies.
그녀의 신랄한 위트는 자신의 많은 적들을 항복시켰다.

acrimony
[ǽkrəmòuni]

험악함, 모진 언행, 악의적 감정

<syn> harsh or biting language or temper, ill will, hard feelings
<ant> good will, good feelings, friendliness

His *acrimony* resulted from years of disappointment.
그의 험악함은 수년 간의 절망에서 비롯되었다.

adulation
[ædʒəléiʃən]

아첨

<syn> praise, flattery, fawning
<ant> condemnation, denunciation, defamation

The *adulation* tendered to the wealthy is often aimed at their purses.
부자들에게 행해지는 아첨은 흔히 그들의 지갑을 노린 것이다.

adumbration
[ædəmbréiʃən]

희미한 윤곽, 어렴풋한 예시

<syn> a faint outline, foreshadowing

The atomic bomb was an *adumbration* of a new era of destruction.
원자폭탄은 새로운 파괴의 시대를 나타내는 하나의 예시였다.

advent
[ǽdvent]

도래, 출현

<syn> coming, arrival

The *advent* of spring is always a gay time.
봄의 도래는 언제나 즐거운 시간이다.

agnostic
[ægnάstik]

불가지론자 (one who does not think it possible to know whether or not God exists)

Many *agnostics* are converted to religion in their later years.
많은 불가지론자들이 말년에 종교에 귀의한다.

alacrity
[əlǽkrəti]

활발함, 민활함

<syn> briskness, liveliness, agility, willingness
<ant> slowness, sluggishness, unwillingness

The *alacrity* shown by the new employee gratified the manager.
신입직원의 활발함은 부장을 만족시켰다.

altruism
[ǽltruìzəm]

이타주의 (regard for the interest of others)

<ant> egoism

The *altruism* of the nursing profession is taken for granted.
간호직의 이타주의는 당연한 것으로 여겨진다.

anachronism
[ənǽkrənìzəm]

시대착오, 시대에 뒤떨어진 (something out of its proper time)

An abstract picture in an early American home is an *anachronism*.
초기 미국 가정의 추상화 그림은 시대에 뒤떨어진 것이었다.

aplomb
[əplάm]

침착, 태연, 평정

<syn> self-assurance, poise, composure, calmness
<ant> awkwardness, confusion, embarrassment

His *aplomb* is characteristic of the successful urbanite.
그의 침착성은 성공적인 도시인의 특성이다.

approbation
[æproubéiʃən]

허가, 승인, 추천, 찬성

<syn> approval, praise, support, endorsement
<ant> censure, condemnation, disapproval, veto

The act was performed with the *approbation* of his superiors.
연극이 그의 선배들 추천으로 공연되었다.

ascetic
[əsétik]

금욕주의자, 고행자, 수도자

<syn> person who practices self-denial, abstainer, hermit, self-modifier
<ant> hedonist, sensualist, voluptuary

As an *ascetic*, he ate only the simplest foods and never touched alcohol.
금욕주의자로서 그는 소박한 음식만 먹고 술은 입에 대지를 않았다.

asperity
[æspérəti]

신랄함, 매서움

<syn> harshness

The *asperity* of his decisions made the judge no friends.
그의 매서운 의사결정들은 그 판사에게 친구가 없게 했다.

cadre
[kædri]

기초, 골격, 개요

<syn> a framework, a skeleton organization

A *cadre* of commissioned and non-commissioned officers was maintained.
장교와 하사관이라는 골격은 유지되었다.

calumny
[kæləmni]

중상, 비방

<syn> slander, false accusation
<ant> praise, applause

Many honest persons are the victims of *calumny*.
수많은 정직한 사람들이 중상모략에 희생된다.

casuistry
[kǽʒuistri]

궤변

[ex] If a man and wife are legally one, why must we buy two tickets?
한 남자와 아내가 법률적으로 하나라면, 왜 우리가 티켓을 두 장 사야하지?

chastisement
[tʃæstáizmənt]

체벌

<syn> physical punishment, discipline, penalty, whip
<ant> reward, honor, praise

Chastisement of delinquent children is considered necessary by some teachers.
일부 교사들은 비행 아동들에 대한 체벌이 필요하다고 생각한다.

clairvoyance
[klɛərvɔ́iəns]

투시력, 통찰력 (ability to foretell the future)

It was believed that the oracles had the power of *clairvoyance*.
오라클은 투시력이 있는 것으로 믿어진다.

clemency
[klémənsi]

관대함, 자비, 온순

<syn> leniency, indulgence, mercy
<ant> sternness, strictness, harshness

The governor granted *clemency* to the prisoners.
주지사는 죄수들을 관대하게 대했다.

collusion
[kəlú:ʒən]

공모, 담합

<syn> secret agreement, conspiracy, intrigue, guilty association

Higher prices were set by *collusion* among all the manufacturers.
모든 제조업자들끼리 담합하여 높은 가격이 책정되었다.

compunction
[kəmpʌ́ŋkʃən]

양심의 가책, 후회, 회한

<syn> remorse, uneasiness, pang of conscience, qualm, demur
<ant> pride, self-respect, righteousness, shamelessness

They showed no *compunction* over their carelessness.
그들은 자신들의 부주의에 대해 아무런 양심의 가책도 보이지 않았다.

conflagration
[kùnfləgréiʃən]

대화재, 큰불 (large fire, disastrous fire)

New York City was almost destroyed in the 1835 *conflagration*.
뉴욕시는 1835년 대화재 때 거의 파괴되었다.

dearth
[də:rθ]

부족, 결핍

<syn> scarcity, lack, shortage, deficiency
<ant> abundance, plenty, superabundance

A *dearth* of water can create a desert in a few years.
몇 년 지나면 물 부족으로 사막이 생길 수 있다.

deference
[défərəns]

존경, 경의

\<syn\> respect, reverence, honor, obedience, regard
\<ant\> disrespect, contempt, defiance, disobedience

Out of *deference* to her age, we rose when she entered.
나이에 대한 경의를 표하여 우리는 그녀가 들어올 때 일어섰다.

depredation
[dèprədéiʃən]

약탈, 침식

\<syn\> ravaging, plundering, laying waste

The *depredations* of the Huns left a bloody path across the continent.
훈족(흉노족)의 약탈은 대륙을 가로질러 피의 노정을 남겼다.

egress
[í:gres]

밖으로 나감, 탈출, 출구

\<syn\> exit, departure, escape, discharge, outflow
\<ant\> entrance

Barnum put the sign *"egress"* on the door so that the crowd would move on, expecting to see another exhibit.
바넘은 관중들이 또 다른 전시품 관람을 기대하며 이동하도록 문에 "출구" 라는 표지를 붙였다.

euphoria
[ju:fɔ́:riə]

행복감 (sense of well-being)

Their *euphoria* at being the first to ever climb the mountain was heightened by their narrow escape from death.
그 산에 최초로 올랐다는 행복감은 죽음에서 가까스로 탈출함으로써 더욱 고조되었다.

geriatrics
[dʒèriætriks]

노인병학 (science of care for the aged)

Our longer life span in modern times makes the study of *geriatrics* a necessity.
현대의 길어진 우리의 수명은 노인병학을 필수로 만든다.

imprecation
[ìmprikéiʃən]

저주 (a curse)

He uttered an *imprecation* that sent shudders through the superstitious mob.
그는 미신에 사로잡힌 군중을 통해 소름끼치는 저주를 내렸다.

inadvertence
[ìnədvə́:rtəns]

부주의, 태만, 소홀

\<syn\> heedlessness, inattentiveness, negligence
\<ant\> attentiveness, heedfulness, awareness

The bookkeeper's *inadvertence* caused several checks to be returned unpaid.
회계원의 부주의로 가계수표 몇 장이 지불되지 않고 돌아오게 되었다.

interregnum
[ìntərrégnəm]

통치 공백기간, 정치 공백기간 (interval between reigns of succeeding sovereigns)

He asked for a regency in the *interregnum*.
그는 통치 공백기간에 섭정을 요구하였다.

jettison
[dʒétəsən]

화물투기 (항공기나 선박이 긴급시 중량을 줄이기 위해 화물을 버리는 것)

<syn> cast overboard, pitch over, throw over, discard, dump

They had to *jettison* the cargo to lighten the plane.
그들은 비행기를 가볍게 하기 위해 화물을 투하하였다.

juxtaposition
[dʒʌ̀kstəpəzíʃən]

나란히 놓기, 병렬

<syn> placing close together, placing side by side

The *juxtaposition* of the Capitol and White House was avoided in planning the city of Washington to emphasize the separation of the legislature from the executive branch.
의사당과 백악관을 나란히 배치하여 행정부로부터 입법부의 분리를 강조하는 워싱턴 도시계획을 회피하였다.

malfeasance
[mælfíːzəns]

위법행위, (공무원의) 배임행위 (wrongdoing, especially in public office)

The governor was accused of acts of *malfeasance*, including taking graft.
주지사는 독직을 포함한 배임행위로 기소되었다.

misanthropy
[misǽnθrəpi]

사람을 싫어함, 인간혐오, 염세

<syn> dislike or distrust of mankind

The *misanthropy* of the hermit was known to all.
그 은둔자의 염세는 모두에게 알려져 있다.

mnemonics
[niːmɑ́niks]

기억을 돕는 공부, 기억술 (art of memory development)

Picture association is one of the keys to *mnemonics*.
그림 연상이 기억을 돕는 방법 가운데 하나이다.

neophyte
[níːəfàit]

새로운 개종자, 신임사제

<syn> new convert, new proselyte

He gave lessons each night to the *neophytes*.
그는 매일밤 새로운 개종자들에게 강의를 하였다.

noctambulist
[nɑktǽmbjəlist]

몽유병자 (one who walks in his sleep)

<syn> sleepwaker

The *noctambulist* had to be watched carefully.
몽유병자는 잘 돌봐야 한다.

nomenclature
[nóumənklèitʃər]

명명법, 학명, 전문어 (a system of terms used in a science or art)

The *nomenclature* of botany had to be studied carefully.
식물학의 학명은 주의해서 연구해야 했다.

non sequitur
[non-sékwitər]

[라틴어] 논리적으로 불합리한 추론, 관계없는 이야기
(Latin phrase meaning "it does not follow.")

His speech was a tissue of *non sequiturs* that appealed to his audience's emotions at the expense of their intelligence.
그의 연설은 청중들의 지성을 무시한 채 감정에 호소하는 불합리한 논리의 연속이었다.

onus
[óunəs]

[라틴어] 부담, 짐, 의무, 책임

<syn> burden, responsibility, obligation, load

The *onus* of proof is on the accuser; the defendant is presumed innocent until proved guilty.
증명의 책임은 고소인에게 있다. 피고는 유죄가 증명될 때까지 무죄로 추정된다.

opprobrium
[əpróubriəm]

불명예, 치욕, 악담, 비난

<syn> reproach for disgraceful conduct, infamy
<ant> compliment, praise, laud

He deserved all the *opprobrium* he received for turning his back on a friend.
그는 친구에게 등을 돌림으로써 모든 비난을 받아 마땅하였다.

panacea
[pæ̀nəsí:ə]

만병통치약

<syn> a remedy for all ills, cure all, universal cure, sovereign remedy

Even money is no *panacea*.
돈도 만병통치약은 아니다.

penchant
[péntʃənt]

경향, 기호, 좋아함

<syn> a strong inclination, liking, fondness, leaning, partiality, preference
<ant> hatred, dislike, loathing, aversion

He has a *penchant* for making friends.
그는 친구 사귀는 것을 좋아한다.

permutation
[pə̀ːrmjuːtéiʃən]

교환, 교대, 순열치환 (rearrangement of the order of a group of items)

The sequences CBA and BCA are *permutations* of ABC.
연속하는 CBA와 BCA는 ABC의 순열치환이다.

perspicuity
[pə̀ːrspikjúːəti]

(설명이) 명석함, 명료함, 명쾌함 (clearness in expression)

His *perspicuity* made him an excellent teacher.
명쾌한 설명이 그를 우수한 교사로 만들어주었다.

polemics
[poulémiks]

논쟁술, 논증법 (art of disputing)

He is an expert at *polemics* and is studying for a career in law.
그는 논증법에 전문가인데, 법률가가 되기 위해 공부하고 있다.

propinquity
[prəpínkwəti]

가까움, 근접

<syn> nearness, proximity

The *propinquity* of gas stations decreased the value of the property.
주유소가 근처에 있다는 것이 재산가치를 떨어뜨렸다.

protuberance
[proutjúːbərəns]

융기, 돌기

<syn> bulge, swelling; knob, knot, bump, hump

Jimmy Durante was proud of his facial *protuberance*.
지미 듀란트는 자기 얼굴의 돌기를 자랑으로 여겼다.

quorum
[kwɔ́ːrəm]

의결정족수 (the minimum number of members that must be present for an assembly to conduct business)

No votes may be taken until there are enough representatives present to constitute a *quorum*.
의결정족수를 구성할 수 있는 충분한 대표자들이 참석할 때까지 투표가 행해질 수 없다.

ramification
[ræ̀məfikéiʃən]

분지(分枝), 분파 (a division into subdivisions, a branching out)

The *ramifications* of the subject were complex.
주제가 지엽적으로 흘러 복잡했다.

rationale
[ræ̀ʃənǽl]

이론적 설명, 근본적 이유 (explanation or justification supposedly based on reason)

<syn> rational basis, underlying reason, logic, foundations, grounds

They defended their discrimination with the *rationale* that women were incompetent physically to handle the job.
그들은 여성들이 그 일을 처리하기에는 육체적으로 능력이 부족하다는 근본적인 이유를 들어 자신들의 차별을 옹호하였다.

rebuttal
[ribʌ́tl]

원고의 반박, 반증 (contradiction, reply to a charge or argument)

Each side was allowed five minutes for *rebuttal* of the other side's arguments.
양측은 상대편의 진술에 반박하도록 5분씩 허용되었다.

recourse
[ríːkɔːrs]

의지가 되는 것 또는 믿을 수 있는 사람 (seeking of aid or remedy in response to some action or situation)

<syn> a source of aid, resort

Unless you correct this error immediately, I will have no *recourse* but to complain to the manager.
당신이 이 잘못을 즉시 고치지 않으면 나는 부장에게 호소하는 것 밖에 다른 믿을 것이 없어요.

rectitude
[réktətjùːd]

정직, 청렴, 올바름 (moral integrity, strict observance of what is right)

<syn> honesty, virtue, goodness, morality, probity

Her unfailing *rectitude* in business dealings made her well trusted among her associates.
거래에서 굴하지 않는 그녀의 정직성이 동료들 사이에서 그녀를 신뢰하도록 만들었다.

risibility
[rìzəbíləti]

잘 웃는 성질, 웃는 버릇 (disposition to laugh)

His *risibility* increased with each act of the play.
연극의 막이 전개되면서 그의 웃는 버릇이 늘어났다.

sanctimony
[sǽŋktəmòuni]

성자연함, 거짓 신앙심 (assumed manner of holiness, pretense of piety)

His *sanctimony* served to hide the fact that he indulged in the very vices he publicly condemned.
그의 성자연하는 모습은 자신이 공공연히 비난하던 바로 그 악에 빠졌던 사실을 숨기는데 도움이 되었다.

subpoena
[səpíːnə]

소환장 (writ summoning a witness)

They issued *subpoenas* to all necessary witnesses.
그들은 필요한 모든 증인들에게 소환장을 발부하였다.

subterfuge
[sʌ́btərfjùːdʒ]

핑계, 속임수 (deceitful means of escaping something unpleasant)

<syn> fraud, deception, trickery, artifice
<ant> openness, honesty, straightforwardness

The lie about a previous engagement was a *subterfuge* by which they avoided a distasteful duty.
이전 약속에 관한 거짓말은 그들이 하기 싫은 임무를 회피하기 위한 속임수였다.

turpitude
[tə́ːrpitjùːd]

간악함, 비열 (depravity)

A person convicted of moral *turpitude* may not be permitted entry into the United States.
도덕적 간악함으로 유죄선고를 받은 사람은 미국 입국이 허용되지 않을 수 있다.

ubiquity
[juːbíkwəti]

언제 어디나 존재함, 예수의 편재 (existence everywhere at the same time)

<syn> omnipresence

The *ubiquity* of God has often been denied.
신이 언제 어디서나 존재한다는 것은 흔히 부인되어 왔다.

vacillation
[væ̀səléiʃən]

망설임, 우유부단함 (fluctuation of mind, unsteadiness of character, change from one purpose to another, inconstancy)

His *vacillation* in giving orders made him difficult to work for.
명령하달에 있어 우유부단함은 자신이 일을 하는 데 어렵게 만들었다.

verisimilitude
[vèrəsimílətjùːd]

정말 같음, 진실 같음 (appearance of truth)

There is a great *verisimilitude* here, but I still do not believe this is conclusive evidence.
여기에 아주 진실 같은 점이 있지만, 나는 여전히 이것을 결정적인 증거로 믿지 못한다.

vicissitude
[visísətjùːd]

변화, 교체, 흥망성쇠, 변화무쌍 (regular change or succession of one thing to another, a passing from one condition to another)

The *vicissitude* of fortune made him a poor man.
운명의 바뀌어 그는 가난하게 되었다.

wraith
[reiθ]

영혼, 망령, 귀신

<syn> ghost, spector, apparition, phantom, phantasm, spook

When the children entered the haunted house, they fully expected to encounter *wraiths*.
어린이들이 귀신 나오는 집에 들어갈 때는 꼭 귀신을 만나게 되리라 기대하였다.

xenophobia
[zènəfóubiə]

외국인 싫어하기 (fear and hatred of strangers or foreigners)

The *xenophobia* of the candidate expressed itself in his extreme and unrealistic isolationism.
그 후보의 외국인 혐오는 그 자체로 자신의 극단적이고 비현실적인 고립주의를 나타내주었다.

STEP 5 Practice Test 14

DIRECTIONS Select the word or phrase that means most nearly the same as the key word.

1. **adulation**
   (A) condemnation (B) derision
   (C) praise (D) fretfulness

2. **advent**
   (A) arrival (B) springtime
   (C) rental (D) perusal

3. **ablution**
   (A) cleansing (B) solution
   (C) forgetfulness (D) remuneration

4. **adumbration**
   (A) cloudiness (B) dawning
   (C) closure (D) foreshadowing

5. **approbation**
   (A) warning (B) thoughtfulness
   (C) delivery (D) approval

6. **asperity**
   (A) herbivorous (B) harshness
   (C) soporific (D) wishful thinking

7. **anachronism**
   (A) animosity (B) out of time
   (C) tardiness (D) timeless

| ANSWER |

1. (A) 비난 (B) 조롱
   (C) 칭찬 (D) 초조
2. (A) 도착 (B) 봄
   (C) 임대 (D) 정독
3. (A) 정화 (B) 해결책
   (C) 건망증 (D) 보수
4. (A) 흐림 (B) 새벽, 시작
   (C) 닫힘 (D) 전조, 예시
5. (A) 경고 (B) 사려 깊음
   (C) 배달 (D) 승인
6. (A) 초식성의 (B) 거칠음, 호됨
   (C) 최면의 (D) 희망적인 생각
7. (A) 원한 (B) 시대에 뒤떨어진
   (C) 느림 (D) 시간제한이 없는

1. (C) 2. (A) 3. (A) 4. (D)
5. (D) 6. (B) 7. (B)

8 clairvoyance
  (A) power to foretell (B) prudence
  (C) consonance (D) urbanity

9 collusion
  (A) impact (B) conspiracy
  (C) affirmation (D) infection

10 compunction
  (A) remorse (B) compensation
  (C) punctuality (D) incision

11 concomitant
  (A) accompaniment (B) culprit
  (C) agreed upon (D) lax

12 conflagration
  (A) gathering (B) public shaming
  (C) large fire (D) celebration

13 dearth
  (A) mortality (B) scarcity
  (C) morbidity (D) secrecy

14 deference
  (A) indifference (B) mockery
  (C) removal (D) respect

15 euphoria
  (A) well-being (B) trance
  (C) hysteria (D) coma

16 inadvertence
  (A) inaccuracy (B) happenstance
  (C) willful (D) oversight

| ANSWER |

8. (A) 점술력 (B) 신중함
   (C) 화음 (D) 도시풍

9. (A) 충격 (B) 공모
   (C) 확정 (D) 전염

10. (A) 후회, 양심의 가책
    (B) 보상 (C) 시간엄수
    (D) (칼로) 베기, 새김

11. (A) 부수적인 것 (B) 피의자
    (C) 의견을 같이하는 (D) 느슨한

12. (A) 집합 (B) 치욕
    (C) 큰불 (D) 축하

13. (A) 죽을 운명 (B) 결핍
    (C) 병의 사망률 (D) 비밀

14. (A) 무관심 (B) 조소
    (C) 제거 (D) 존경

15. (A) 행복 (B) 몽환, 혼수상태
    (C) 히스테리 (D) 혼수상태

16. (A) 부정확 (B) 우연한 일
    (C) 고의적인, 멋대로의
    (D) 빠뜨림, 못봄

8. (A) 9. (B) 10. (A) 11. (A) 12. (C)
13. (B) 14. (D) 15. (A) 16. (D)

17 geriatrics
    (A) study of motion   (B) economics
    (C) care of the aged   (D) care of infants

18 jettison
    (A) helicopter fuel   (B) cast overboard
    (C) hurl   (D) inflame

19 juxtaposition
    (A) confusion   (B) far apart
    (C) irreconciliation   (D) close together

20 malfeasance
    (A) wrongdoing   (B) maliciousness
    (C) disowning   (D) sorrowfulness

21 mnemonics
    (A) memory development
    (B) forgetfulness
    (C) ammunition
    (D) pain-killers

22 noctambulist
    (A) nine-legged   (B) sleepwalker
    (C) nurturer   (D) cripple

23 opprobrium
    (A) citation   (B) infamy
    (C) contemplation   (D) official rank

24 penchant
    (A) necklace   (B) secretive
    (C) clock   (D) inclination

| ANSWER |

17. (A) 운동학 (B) 경제학
    (C) 노인보호 (D) 유아보호

18. (A) 헬기 연료 (B) 밖으로 던지다
    (C) 집어던지다 (D) 불을 붙이다

19. (A) 혼란 (B) 멀리 떨어진
    (C) 대립 (D) 근접한

20. (A) 부정행위 (B) 악의, 심술
    (C) 소유권을 부인하다 (D) 슬픔

21. (A) 기억개발 (B) 망각
    (C) 탄약 (D) 진통제

22. (A) 다리 아홉의 (B) 몽유병자
    (C) 양육인 (D) 장애인

23. (A) 인용 (B) 불명예, 악평
    (C) 관조, 명상 (D) 관직

24. (A) 목걸이 (B) 숨기는
    (C) 시계 (D) 기울기, 경향, 좋아함

17. (C) 18. (B) 19. (D) 20. (A)
21. (A) 22. (B) 23. (B) 24. (D)

25 neophyte
(A) retiree (B) specialist
(C) new convert (D) heterodox

26 nomenclature
(A) inaccurate names (B) ruling
(C) technical names (D) marriage

27 non sequitur
(A) illogical conclusion (B) no exit
(C) nonconformist (D) illegal transaction

28 onus
(A) responsibility (B) aperture
(C) exclamation (D) monotone

29 panacea
(A) illogical statement (B) tranquility
(C) cure-all (D) belief in God

30 perspicuity
(A) wisdom (B) good humor
(C) far-sightedness (D) eloquence

31 recourse
(A) reroute (B) seeking remedy
(C) finding solutions (D) lacking acceptance

32 risibility
(A) feverishness (B) disposition to laugh
(C) lightness (D) ability to rise

33 subterfuge
(A) underground (B) explosives
(C) joyous arrival (D) deceitful escape

| ANSWER |

25. (A) 퇴직자 (B) 전문가
    (C) 새로운 개종자 (D) 이교의, 이단의

26. (A) 부정확한 이름 (B) 통치
    (C) 전문용어 (D) 결혼

27. (A) 비논리적인 결론 (B) 출구 없음
    (C) 규범에 따르지 않는 사람, 비국교도
    (D) 불법적인 거래

28. (A) 의무 (B) 구멍, 공간
    (C) 외침 (D) 단조음

29. (A) 논리적인 표현 (B) 고요함
    (C) 만병통치 (D) 신앙

30. (A) 지혜 (B) 좋은 유머
    (C) 원시의, 먼 눈이 밝은
    (D) 웅변, 설득력

31. (A) 다른 길로 수송하다
    (B) 구제안 찾기 (C) 해법 찾기
    (D) 수용 부족

32. (A) 열의 (B) 웃는 버릇
    (C) 가벼움 (D) 일어나는 능력

33. (A) 지하의 (B) 폭발적인
    (C) 즐거운 도착 (D) 거짓 발뺌

25. (C) 26. (C) 27. (A) 28. (A) 29. (C)
30. (D) 31. (B) 32. (B) 33. (D)

34 rebuttal
(A) knock again (B) refusal
(C) contradiction (D) controversy

35 sanctimony
(A) holiness (B) orthodoxy
(C) false piety (D) vocation

36 vacillation
(A) prevention
(B) whiskers
(C) fluttering in the wind
(D) fluctuation of mind

37 vicissitude
(A) likeness (B) misery
(C) ups and downs (D) foresightedness

38 ubiquity
(A) omnipresence (B) impudence
(C) sinfulness (D) curiosity

39 verisimilitude
(A) twinhood (B) appearance of truth
(C) approaching perfection (D) cheerfulness

40 ramification
(A) concentration (B) battering
(C) branching out (D) clearing out

41 rectitude
(A) solicitude (B) integrity
(C) compensation (D) reconciliation

| ANSWER |

34. (A) 다시 두드리다 (B) 거절
    (C) 반박 (D) 논쟁

35. (A) 성스러움 (B) 정설, 정교
    (C) 성자연함, 거짓 신앙심 (D) 직업

36. (A) 방지 (B) 구렛나루
    (C) 바람에 펄럭이는 (D) 우유부단

37. (A) 동일 (B) 불운
    (C) 흥망성쇠, 기복 (D) 선견지명

38. (A) 언제 어디나 있음 (B) 뻔뻔함
    (C) 죄스러움 (D) 호기심

39. (A) 쌍둥이 (B) 진실 같음
    (C) 완벽에 가까움 (D) 기분좋음

40. (A) 집중 (B) 연타하는
    (C) 분지(分枝), 지엽적으로 흐름
    (D) 정리하기

41. (A) 염려 (B) 성실, 정직
    (C) 보상 (D) 화해

34. (C) 35. (C) 36. (D) 37. (C)
38. (A) 39. (B) 40. (C) 41. (B)

STEP 5
adjective & adverb 형용사&부사

abrasive
[əbréisiv]

문지르는, 마모시키는, 신경을 건드리는

<syn> scraping, rubbing

The high-pitched whine of the machinery was *abrasive* to my nerves.
기계의 시끄러운 쇳소리는 내 신경을 건드렸다.

adventitious
[æ̀dvəntíʃəs]

외래의, 우연의, 우발적인

<syn> coming from outside

The *adventitious* economic aid given by the United States was instrumental in saving many nations from Communism.
미국에서 제공되는 외래 경제원조는 많은 국가들을 공산주의로부터 구하는 데 도움이 되었다.

amoral
[eimɔ́:rəl]

초도덕적인, 도덕과는 관계없는

<syn> nonmoral, with no sense of sin

To the new settlers, the islanders seemed to lead a carefree, *amoral* existence, doing whatever they pleased.
새 정착민들에게는 섬사람들이 무엇이든 자기들 좋을 대로 하는 태평스런 초도덕적인 생활을 하는 것으로 보였다.

anomalous
[ənámələs]

변칙적인, 파격적인, 이례적인, 이상한

<syn> out of place, inappropriate, incongruous, bizarre, irregular, abnormal
<ant> common, usual, typical, normal, familiar

An *anomalous* jukebox stood rusting in the square of the primitive village.
이상하게 생긴 주크박스가 원시 마을의 한복판에 놓여 녹슬어가고 있었다.

antipathetic
[æntípəθitik]

괜히 싫은, 상반되는 (opposite in disposition)

Siblings are often *antipathetic*.
형제자매도 종종 정반대의 성질을 갖기도 한다.

arbitrary
[á:rbitrèri]

임의의, 멋대로의, 독재적인

<syn> despotic, absolute, unrestrained, autocratic
<ant> objective, constitutional, lawful

An *arbitrary* ruling of a civil commission may be reviewed by the courts.
민간위원회의 전횡적인 운영은 법원의 심사를 받게 될 수도 있다.

baleful
[béilfəl]

재앙의, 해로운, 파괴적인

<syn> destructive, sinister, ominous, malignant
<ant> benevolent, beneficient, benign

The *baleful* glance of a witch was feared.
마녀가 불길하게 흘겨보는 모습은 두려웠다.

banal
[bənǽl]

평범한, 진부한

<syn> commonplace, trite, ordinary
<ant> original, unusual, extraordinary

The use of *banal* remarks will dull any conversation.
진부한 표현을 사용하면 어떤 대화라도 따분하게 만들 것이다.

bellicose
[bélikòus]

호전적인, 싸움 잘하는

<syn> warlike, belligerent, aggressive, hostile
<ant> peaceful, friendly, pacific

The *bellicose* attitude of the man involved him in many fights.
그 남자의 호전적인 태도는 자신을 수많은 싸움판으로 끌어들였다.

bombastic
[bɑmbǽstik]

과장된, 호언장담하는, 허풍떠는

<syn> pompous, grandiloquent, using inflated language
<ant> temperate, modest, quiet

The *bombastic* politician sounds like a fool on television.
허풍떠는 정치인은 텔레비전에 나오는 광대 같다.

bucolic
[bju:kálik]

목가적인, 전원 생활의, 시골의

<syn> pertaining to a farm, rural

The *bucolic* personality is usually thought of as hearty, simple, and lusty.
목가적인 성품은 흔히 마음씨 좋고, 소박하고, 활발한 것으로 여겨진다.

captious
[kǽpʃəs]

헐뜯는, 흠잡기 좋아하는

<syn> fault-finding

His *captious* criticisms were motivated by an unreasoning jealousy.
그의 흠잡기 좋아하는 비평은 비이성적인 질투가 원인이었다.

cerebral
[sérəbrəl]

뇌의, 두뇌와 관련된 (pertaining to the brain)

The stroke was the result of a *cerebral* hemorrhage.
뇌졸중은 뇌출혈의 결과였다.

commensurate
[kəménʃərit]

같은 정도의, 비례하는, 상응하는

<syn> equal, equivalent, even, balanced
<ant> unequal, inappropriate, uncomparable

He asked for compensation *commensurate* with his work.
그는 자신의 작업에 상응하는 보상을 요구하였다.

compliant
[kəmpláiənt]

남이 시키는 대로 하는, 복종하는, 따르는

<syn> yielding to others, obedient, give in, submit
<ant> disobedient, resistant

A *compliant* person may gain popularity at the cost of character.
남의 말을 잘 듣는 사람은 인품의 대가로 인기를 얻을 수 있다.

concomitant
[kɑnkámətənt]

동반하는, 부수적으로 생기는, 공존하는

<syn> attendant, accompanying, contributing, additional, related
<ant> noncontributory, unconnected

Due consideration must be given to *concomitant* conditions.
부수적인 상황들이 마땅히 고려되어야 한다.

contingent
[kəntíndʒənt]

사정 나름의

<syn> dependent, subject to, controlled by, conditioned

His plans were *contingent* upon the check's arriving on time.
그의 계획은 수표가 제시간에 도착하느냐에 달려있었다.

convivial
[kənvívi əl]

연회를 좋아하는, 연회의, 흥겨운

<syn> gay, festive, jovial, gregarious, merry, sociable

Class reunions are *convivial* affairs.
반창회는 흥겨운 행사이다.

cursory
[kə́:rsəri]

서두른, 엉성한

<syn> superficial, hurried, hasty, random
<ant> careful, slow, painstaking, scrupulous

Cursory examination of the scene revealed little information.
그 장면을 서둘러 살펴보았기에 정보가 거의 드러나지 않았다.

demure
[dimjúər]

점잔빼는, 진지한, 얌전한

<syn> serious, sober, modest, reserved, shy
<ant> brazen, brash, impudent, shameless, immodest

The *demure* maiden was an object of their admiration, but not their affection.
얌전한 처녀는 그들의 존경의 대상이었지 애정의 대상은 아니었다.

desultory
[désəltɔ̀:ri]

일관성 없는, 산만한, 종작없는

<syn> jumping around, aimless, disconnected

Desultory reading will seldom create a well-read individual; reading must be planned.
목적 없는 독서는 결코 훌륭한 독서인을 만들지 못한다. 독서는 계획적이어야 한다.

dissolute
[dísəlù:t]

방종한, 방탕한

<syn> immoral, dissipated, corrupt, loose, debauched
<ant> moral, upright, temperate, sober, prudent

The *dissolute* young man was soon without friends or reputation.
방종한 젊은이는 곧 친구와 명성을 잃게 된다.

distraught
[distrɔ́:t]

괴로운, 마음이 산란한

<syn> crazed, distracted, distressed, agitated

The young woman, *distraught* at the tragedy of her husband's death, threatened suicide.
남편의 죽음이라는 비극에 괴로워하는 젊은 여성은 자살의 위험성이 있다.

ductile
[dʌ́ktil]

연성의, 늘이기 쉬운, 유연한 (capable of being drawn out or hammered)

The *ductile* quality of gold makes it possible to manufacture fine gold leaf for artists' frames.
황금의 유연한 성질은 예술가들의 액자를 멋진 금박으로 제작하는 것을 가능하게 해준다.

eclectic
[ekléktik]

절충하는, 얽매이지 않는, 폭넓은, 취사선택하는

<syn> drawing from diverse sources or systems, selecting

His *eclectic* record collection included everything from Bach cantatas to punk rock.
그의 폭넓은 음반수집은 바하의 칸타타에서 펑크록에 이르기까지 모든 것을 포함하였다.

efficacious
[èfəkéiɣəs]

효능이 있는, 의도된 효과가 있는

<syn> producing a desired effect, effective, effectual, efficient

The drug is *efficacious* in the treatment of malaria.
그 약은 말라리아 치료에 효능이 있다.

effusive
[efjúːsiv]

감정이 넘쳐나는, 과장된, 심정을 토로하는

<syn> gushing, demonstrative, lavish, profuse
<ant> restrained, reserved, sparing

Her *effusive* greeting seemed overdone.
그녀의 감정이 넘치는 인사는 과장되어 보였다.

endogenous
[endádʒənəs]

내부로부터 성장하는, 내부에서 비롯된 (originating from within)

An ulcer is usually *endogenous*.
종기는 흔히 내부에서부터 자란다.

esoteric
[èsoutérik]

비법을 전수하는, 은밀한

<syn> limited to a few, secret, undisclosed, hidden, concealed, covert
<ant> public, open, exoteric

The *esoteric* rites of the fraternity were held sacred by the members.
남학생클럽의 은밀한 의식이 회원들에 의해 신성하게 거행되었다.

execrable
[éksikrəbəl]

저주할, 지겨운, 밉살스러운

<syn> extremely bad, detestable

Although her acting was *execrable*, she looked so good on stage that the audience applauded.
그녀는 행동은 밉살스러워도 무대 위에서는 훌륭했기에 관객들이 갈채를 보냈다.

exogenous
[eksádʒənəs]

밖으로부터 생긴, 외부적 원인에 의한 (derived externally)

His delusions seemed to have no internal cause and were thus termed *exogenous*.
그의 망상은 내부적인 원인은 없어 보이므로 외부적인 원인에 의한 것이었다.

exorbitant
[igzɔ́ːrbətənt]

터무니없는, 과대한

<syn> excessive, enormous, unreasonable, outrageous
<ant> fair, equitable, cheap, reasonable

The *exorbitant* rates of the moneylenders kept the peasants in a state of poverty.
사채업자들의 터무니없는 이자율이 농민들의 가난을 지속시켰다.

extemporaneous
[ikstèmpəréiniəs]

즉흥적인, 준비 없는, 즉석의

<syn> impromptu, improvised, extempory, ad-lib, without notice, unprepared
<ant> well-rehearsed, prepared, planned

The speaker who was expected to make the presentation didn't show up, so he gave an *extemporaneous* speech.
발표를 하기로 된 연사가 나타나지 않아서 그가 즉석에서 연설을 하였다.

gauche
[gouʃ]

솜씨가 서투른, 세련되지 못한

<syn> without social grace, tactless, awkward, ill-mannered, unpolished
<ant> polite, well-mannered, well-bred, elegant, polished

It is considered *gauche* to ask acquaintances how much they earn or how much they paid for something.
알고 지내는 사람들일지라도 얼마나 벌고, 얼마나 쓰는지 물어보는 것은 세련되지 못하게 여겨진다.

germane
[dʒəːrméin]

적절한, 밀접한 관계의

<syn> pertinent, relevant, appropriate, connected, relative
<ant> irrelevant

The facts were not *germane* to the argument.
그 사실들은 논쟁에 관계가 없다.

heinous
[héinəs]

가증스런, 악질의

<syn> hateful, atrocious, abhorrent
<ant> good, beneficial, lovable

The deed was so *heinous* that everyone despised him for it.
그 행동은 너무나 악질적이라서 모두가 그를 경멸하였다.

hortatory
[hɔ́ːrtətɔ̀ːri]

권고하는, 장려하는

<syn> giving advice, encouraging, inciting

With his *hortatory* speech, the orator incited his listeners to riot.
격려사를 통해 그 연사는 청중들이 폭동을 일으키도록 선동하였다.

igneous
[ígniəs]

화성암의, 화성의, 불같은

<syn> formed by great heat, fiery

The Palisades of the Hudson Valley are of *igneous* origin.
허드슨강 계곡 서안의 암벽은 화성암으로 되어있다.

ignominious
[ìgnəmíniəs]

수치스러운, 불명예의

<syn> discrediting, disgraceful, shameful
<ant> creditable, honorable, reputable

His *ignominious* activities could lead only to his removal from office.
그의 비열한 행동들은 자신을 사무실에서 쫓겨나게 할 것이다.

impeccable
[impékəbəl]

잘못이 없는, 나무랄 데 없는

<syn> faultless, flawless, immaculate, unblemished, perfect
<ant> deficient, defective, faulty, tarnished

Successful comedy depends on *impeccable* timing.
성공적인 코미디는 적절한 타이밍에 달려있다.

impecunious
[ìmpikjúːniəs]

돈이 없는, 무일푼의

<syn> penniless, having no money

His *impecunious* aunt was a drain on his purse.
그의 가난한 작은어머니는 그의 지갑의 배수관이었다.

impervious
[impə́ːrviəs]

(공기, 물, 광선이) 스며들지 않는, 손상되지 않는

<syn> not to be passed through, impenetrable, impermeable
<ant> susceptible, vulnerable, open, exposed

Heavy cardboard is *impervious* to light.
두꺼운 카드보드는 빛이 통과하지 않는다.

impetuous
[impétʃuəs]

격렬한, 맹렬한, 성급한

<syn> impulsive, rash, hasty, headlong, violent
<ant> cautious, wary, moderate, slow, mild

The *impetuous* action often leads to trouble.
격렬한 행동은 가끔 문제를 일으킨다.

incorrigible
[inkɔ́:ridʒəbəl]

교정할 수 없는, 어쩔 수 없는

<syn> beyond reform, uncontrollable, intractable, delinquent
<ant> correctable, manageable, tractable

Some delinquents are *incorrigible*.
일부 비행청소년들은 상습적이다.

indigenous
[indídʒənəs]

토착의, 자생의, 타고난

<syn> native to a country, growing naturally, endemic, homebred
<ant> exotic, foreign, alien, imported

The *indigenous* trees of the Rockies are largely evergreens.
로키산맥의 자생 수목들은 대체로 상록수들이다.

indurate
[índjurèit]

무감각하게 굳어진 (hardened)

He was an *indurate* criminal.
그는 무감각해진 범죄자였다.

inexorable
[inéksərəbəl]

무정한, 냉혹한 (relentless)

The *inexorable* logic of history points to a period of decadence for every satisfied nation.
역사의 무정한 이치는 모든 만족하는 국가들에게 쇠락의 시기를 지적해 준다.

inscrutable
[inskrú:təbəl]

헤아릴 수 없는, 수수께끼 같은

<syn> unknowable, incomprehensible, unfathomable, mysterious
<ant> obvious, palpable, plain, clear

His face was *inscrutable* when he doubled his bet.
내기를 두 배로 걸었을 때 그는 알 수 없는 얼굴이었다.

intransigent
[intrǽnsədʒənt]

비타협적인

<syn> uncompromising, stubborn, intractable, unyielding, inflexible
<ant> compromising, yielding, flexible

The *intransigent* attitude of the abolitionists did much to antagonize the South.
노예폐지론자들의 비타협적인 태도가 남부의 반감을 많이 샀다.

intravenous
[ìntrəvíːnəs]

정맥 내의 (through a vein)

The patient was given an *intravenous* feeding of glucose because he could not swallow.
그 환자는 삼킬 수 없었기 때문에 포도당을 정맥으로 투여받았다.

lethargic
[liθáːrdʒik]

혼미한, 나른한, 활발하지 못한

<syn> drowsy, slothful, languid, torpid, listless, sleepy
<ant> energetic, vigorous, alert, active

The convalescent moved in a *lethargic* manner.
회복기의 환자가 활발하지는 못한 거동에 들어갔다.

lugubrious
[luːgjúːbriəs]

많이 슬퍼하는, 애처로운, 가엾은

<syn> excessively mournful, sad

The bloodhound had an endearingly *lugubrious* look.
영국경찰견 블러드하운드는 사랑스럽게도 애처로운 표정을 가지고 있다.

macabre
[məkáːbrə]

섬뜩한, 기분 나쁜

<syn> gruesome, ghastly, grim, frightening, dreadful
<ant> pleasant, lovely, appealing, delightful

The cannibals joined in a *macabre* dance around the boiling pot.
식인종들이 끓는 솥 주위로 섬뜩한 춤을 추는 대열에 합류하였다.

mellifluent
[məlífluənt]

감미로운, 부드럽게 흐르는

<syn> sweetly flowing, sweet-sounding, euphonious, mellifluous
<ant> harsh, discordant, grating, hoarse

The soprano had an extremely *mellifluent* voice.
그 소프라노는 대단히 감미로운 음색을 가졌다.

meretricious
[mèrətríʃəs]

야한, 저속한

<syn> superficially attractive, enticing by false charms, tawdrily, specious

Her heavy makeup and the dim light combined to give her a *meretricious* allure.
그녀의 짙은 화장과 희미한 불빛이 결합하여 그녀에게 야한 매력을 주었다.

minuscule
[mínʌskjùːl]

아주 작은, 하찮은; 필기체 소문자

<syn> very small, tiny, minute (after a small cursive script)

Such *minuscule* particles cannot be viewed with the usual classroom microscope.
아주 작은 분자들은 교실에서 일반적으로 쓰는 현미경으로 보이지 않는다.

moribund
[mɔ́(:)rəbʌ̀nd]

죽어 가는, 정체된, 소멸해 가는

<syn> dying, doomed, waning, stagnating, fading out

The *moribund* king called for the prime minister.
죽어 가는 임금이 총리를 불렀다.

mundane
[mʌ́ndein]

현세의, 세속적인, 세계의, 보통의

<syn> worldly, unexciting, ordinary, prosaic, commonplace, terrestrial, earthly
<ant> heavenly, celestial, ethereal, spiritual

The film was undistinguished, a *mundane* exercise in horror movie clichés.
그 영화는 공포영화의 진부한 표현들로 특별하지가 않았다.

nebulous
[nébjələs]

성운 모양의; 흐린, 불투명한, 모호한

<syn> vague, hazy, indistinct, obscure, unclear, dim

He had a *nebulous* theory about memorizing key words as an aid to study.
그는 학습에 도움을 준다는 기억핵심어에 관한 모호한 이론을 가지고 있다.

nonchalant
[nὰnʃəlάːnt]

무관심한, 태연한, 냉정한

<syn> indifferent, cool, unconcerned, unmoved
<ant> concerned, moved, affected

The woman acted in a *nonchalant* manner, pretending not to notice the stars.
그 여자는 스타들을 알지 못하는 것처럼 무관심한 태도로 행동하였다.

obsequious
[əbsíːkwiəs]

아첨하는, 비굴한, 순종하는

<syn> servile, fawning, menial, slavish, subservient
<ant> domineering, overbearing, lordly, proud

His *obsequious* obedience to the conquerors turned our stomachs.
정복자에 대한 그의 비굴한 복종은 우리를 역겹게 하였다.

omnipotent
[ɑmnípətənt]

전능한, 무엇이든 할 수 있는, 절대권력을 가진

<syn> all-powerful, almighty, supreme
<ant> powerless, helpless, impotent

By the end of the third match, he felt *omnipotent*.
세 번째 경기가 끝날 때까지 그는 힘이 넘치는 것 같았다.

ostentatious
[àstentéiʃəs]

과시하는, 화려한

<syn> pretentious, showy, gaudy, flashy
<ant> modest, reserved, somber

Some people abhor large diamonds as being too *ostentatious*.
어떤 사람들은 큰 다이아몬드를 너무 과시하는 듯해서 싫어한다.

pantoscopic
[pǽntəskòupik]

각도가 넓은, 광각도의, 시야가 넓은 (affording a wide scope of vision, seeing everything)

Pantoscopic spectacles are spectacles that are divided into two segments, of which the upper is for distant vision and the lower is for reading or viewing near objects.
광각 스펙터클은 두 부분으로 나뉘는데, 위의 것은 먼 거리의 모습을, 아래 것은 독서나 가까운 물체를 보기 위함이다.

parsimonious
[pɑ̀ːrsəmóuniəs]

인색한

<syn> frugal, stingy, thrifty, miserly
<ant> extravagant, wasteful, lavish

Although she lived in prosperous comfort, she seemed *parsimonious* to her more extravagant relatives.
그녀는 부유하고 안락하게 살았는데도 더 낭비적인 그녀의 친척들에게는 지나치게 인색해 보였다.

pecuniary
[pikjúːnièri]

금전상의, 재정상의

<syn> financial, relating to money, monetary

He had no *pecuniary* interest in the project.
그는 그 프로젝트에서 아무런 금전적인 이익이 없었다.

primordial
[praimɔ́ːrdiəl]

원시의, 최초의, 근본적인

<syn> first created or developed, original, primitive, primeval

The *primordial* world had no human beings.
최초 원시 세계에는 인간이 없었다.

profligate
[práfligit]

방탕한, 품행이 나쁜

<syn> utterly immoral, dissipated, licentious
<ant> moral, decent, upright

The *profligate* son was a regular source of income for his father's attorney.
그 방탕아는 자기 아버지 변호사의 정규 수입원이었다.

pusillanimous
[pjùːsəlǽnəməs]

무기력한, 겁 많은, 소심한

<syn> faint-hearted, cowardly, lily-livered, fearful, timorous
<ant> courageous, brave, valorous, bold, daring

A young *pusillanimous* infantryman is a danger to an entire company.
젊은 소심한 보병 한 사람이 전 중대에 위험인물이다.

quixotic
[kwiksɑ́tik]

돈키호테식의, 공상가의, 비현실적인

<syn> extravagantly chivalrous, impractical, absurdly romantic, fanciful
<ant> realistic, down-to-earth, practical, serious

His actions were *quixotic* and thoroughly useless.
그의 행동은 비현실적이고 완전히 쓸데없었다.

quotidian
[kwoutídiən]

매일의, 매일같이 일어나는

<syn> daily, recurring daily, commonplace, ordinary

He had a *quotidian* fever.
그는 매일같이 열이 났다.

recalcitrant
[rikǽlsətrənt]

반항하는, 말을 잘 안 듣는, 고집 센

<syn> stubborn, refusing to obey, obstinate, unsubmissive, willful
<ant> obedient, compliant, amenable, submissive

A *recalcitrant* child is a difficult pupil.
말을 잘 안 듣는 아이는 힘든 학생이다.

sagacious
[səgéiʃəs]

총명한, 현명한, 영민한 (of kin mind) (n. sagacity 현명함, 총명)

<syn> wise, discerning, shrewd, intelligent
<ant> stupid, ignorant, dumb, silly, foolish

Teachers have more *sagacity* than students give them credit for.
선생님들은 학생들이 선생님들을 생각하는 것보다 더 현명해야 한다.

somatic
[soumǽtik]

신체의, 육체의 (bodily)

Psychological disturbances often result in *somatic* symptoms.
심리적 불안이 흔히 육체적 증상으로 나타나기도 한다.

soporific
[sɑ̀pərífik]

졸린, 최면성의 (causing sleep or drowsiness)

<syn> hypnotic, somniferous, sleepy, drowsy, lethargic

Because of the drug's *soporific* effect, you should not try to drive after taking it.
그 약은 수면 효과가 있으니 복용 후에 운전하지 않도록 하세요.

spurious
[spjúəriəs]

가짜의, 위조의, 겉치레의

<syn> not genuine, fake, false, forged, counterfeit, phony

The junta's promise of free elections was *spurious*, a mere sop to world opinion.
정권의 자유선거 약속은 단순히 세계의 여론을 호도하는 거짓이었다.

stentorian
[stentɔ́:riən]

큰 목소리의 (extremely loud and powerful)

His *stentorian* voice carried across the auditorium without aid.
그의 큰 목소리는 확성기 없이도 강당 끝까지 전달되었다.

subcutaneous
[sʌ̀bkju:téiniəs]

피하의 (beneath the skin)

Injections of most vaccines are made *subcutaneously*.
대부분의 백신 주사는 피하에 놓는다.

tenuous
[ténjuəs]

엷은, 빈약한, 가느다란 (held by a thread, flimsy)

<syn> weak, flimsy, slight, slim, thin, slender, frail, fragile, unsubstantial
<ant> strong, solid, valid, substantial

Some legislators made a rather *tenuous* argument against the bill.
일부 입법 의원들이 그 법안에 반대하는 빈약한 논지를 폈다.

transcendent
[trænséndənt]

뛰어난, 탁월한, 초월적인, 초절적인

<syn> excelling, surpassing, superlative, supreme, peerless, incomparable

The high cost of the house was due to its obviously *transcendent* worth.
그 주택의 고비용은 명백히 탁월한 가치 때문이다.

truculent
[trʌ́kjələnt]

야만스런, 모질게 사나운, 가혹한

<syn> ferocious, savage, harsh, pugnacious
<ant> peaceful, gentle, kind

The champion affected a *truculent* manner to intimidate the young challenger.
챔피언은 젊은 도전자를 겁주기 위해 사나운 태도를 취했다.

uncanny
[ʌnkǽni]

엄청난, 기괴한, 초인적인 (so acute as to appear mysterious)

<syn> extraordinary, remarkable; mysterious, weird, unearthly, spooky
<ant> normal, common, usual; natural, obvious

After a lifetime of fishing those waters, the old man was able to predict weather changes with *uncanny* precision.
그 바다에서 평생 낚시를 한 터라 노인은 초인적으로 정확하게 날씨변화를 예감할 수 있었다.

uncouth
[ʌnkúːθ]

조잡한, 거친

<syn> unrefined, awkward, crude, rude, discourteous, ill-mannered, impolite
<ant> refined, polite, genteel, cultivated, well-mannered

His *uncouth* behavior was marked by a simple inability to handle a knife and fork.
그의 거친 행동은 단순히 나이프와 포크를 사용할 줄 모르는 데서도 나타났다.

undulating
[ʌ́ndʒəlèitiŋ]

물결이 이는, 굽이치는 (having a form or outline resembling that of a series of waves)

<syn> waving, vibrating

A stretch of country is said to be *undulating* when it presents a succession of elevations and depressions resembling waves of the sea.
펼쳐진 전원의 높낮이가 물결치는 파도처럼 오르막 내리막으로 이어지는 모습을 보일 때, 굽이친다고 말한다.

uxorious
[ʌksɔ́ːriəs]

애처가인, 아내에게 무른 (excessively or foolishly fond of one's wife)

He was described as an *uxorious* husband.
그는 애처가로 묘사되었다.

volatile
[vɑ́lətil]

휘발성의, 폭발하기 쉬운, 흥분하기 쉬운

<syn> changing to vapor, evaporating quickly; quickly changeable, fickle
<ant> stable, clam, peaceful, constant

She had a *volatile* temper — easily angered and easily appeased.
그녀는 흥분하기 쉬운 성격이라서 쉽게 화내고 쉽게 누그러진다.

wry
[rai]

뒤틀린, 비뚤어진, 왜곡된 (produced by distortion of features)

<syn> twisted, crooked, contorted
<ant> straight, direct, symmetrical

He made a *wry* face when I suggested castor oil.
내가 아주까리 기름을 권했을 때 그는 얼굴을 찌푸렸다.

Practice Test 15

DIRECTIONS Select the word or phrase that means most nearly the same as the key word.

1 adumbration
   (A) cloudiness   (B) dawning
   (C) closure   (D) foreshadowing

2 anomalous
   (A) inappropriate   (B) in disrepair
   (C) magnificent   (D) secretive

3 antipathetic
   (A) opposite feeling   (B) dispassionate
   (C) sympathetic   (D) apathetic

4 arbitrary
   (A) despotic   (B) definite
   (C) capacious   (D) mendacious

5 compunction
   (A) remorse   (B) compensation
   (C) punctuality   (D) incision

6 commensurate
   (A) monthly   (B) collaborate
   (C) equal   (D) dissonant

7 compliant
   (A) adamant   (B) innovative
   (C) whining   (D) yielding

| ANSWER |

1. (A) 흐림 (B) 새벽, 시작
   (C) 닫힘 (D) 전조, 예시

2. (A) 부적절한
   (B) 황폐한, 수리해야 하는
   (C) 장대한 (D) 비밀의

3. (A) 반감 (B) 침착한
   (C) 동정적인 (D) 냉담한

4. (A) 독재의, 전횡하는 (B) 명확한
   (C) 널찍한 (D) 허위의

5. (A) 후회, 양심의 가책 (B) 보상
   (C) 시간엄수 (D) (칼로) 베기, 새김

6. (A) 월별 (B) 협동하다
   (C) 동등한 (D) 불협화음의

7. (A) 철석같이 굳은 (B) 혁신적인
   (C) 흐느끼는 (D) 순종하는

1. (D) 2. (A) 3. (A) 4. (A)
5. (A) 6. (C) 7. (D)

8 demure
   (A) gregarious   (B) taciturn
   (C) vivacious   (D) sober

9 contingent
   (A) contiguous   (B) cerebral
   (C) celebration   (D) depending upon

10 didactic
   (A) instructive   (B) medicinal
   (C) repetitious   (D) wholesome

11 dissolute
   (A) immoral   (B) show disrespect
   (C) dissolve   (D) revolution

12 efficacious
   (A) meretricious   (B) able to sustain life
   (C) ignoble   (D) able to produce results

13 endogenous
   (A) originating from within
   (B) originating from outside
   (C) diseased
   (D) suspected

14 heinous
   (A) ridiculous   (B) atrocious
   (C) of the blood   (D) somber

15 ignominious
   (A) flammable   (B) disgraceful
   (C) unschooled   (D) highly explosive

16 impeccable
   (A) persnickety   (B) faultless
   (C) painstaking   (D) unadulterated

| ANSWER |

8. (A) 군집하는, 모여 사는
   (B) 말없는 (C) 쾌활한 (D) 침착한

9. (A) 끊이지 않는 (B) 대뇌의, 지적인
   (C) 축하 (D) 사정 나름의

10. (A) 교육적인 (B) 의약의
    (C) 반복적인 (D) 건전한, 건강한

11. (A) 부도덕한, 행실 나쁜
    (B) 무례를 표하다
    (C) 녹이다, 용해시키다 (D) 혁명

12. (A) 저속한 (B) 삶을 지탱할 수 있는
    (C) 천박한 (D) 결과를 낳을 수 있는

13. (A) 내부에서 비롯되는
    (B) 외부에서 비롯되는
    (C) 병에 걸린 (D) 의심스러운

14. (A) 우스꽝스러운 (B) 흉악한
    (C) 피의 (D) 어두침침한

15. (A) 인화성의 (B) 불명예스러운
    (C) 학교교육을 받지 않은
    (D) 폭발성이 높은

16. (A) 까다로운 (B) 흠 없는
    (C) 수고를 아끼지 않는, 성실한
    (D) 다른 것이 안 섞인, 순수한

8. (D) 9. (D) 10. (A) 11. (A) 12. (D)
13. (A) 14. (B) 15. (B) 16. (B)

17 impervious
(A) accepting (B) hopeful
(C) unwilling (D) impenetrable

18 impecunious
(A) without fault (B) insensitive
(C) penniless (D) not possible

19 impetuous
(A) impulsive (B) sulky
(C) haphazard (D) recalcitrant

20 incorrigible
(A) not rusted (B) uninterrupted
(C) beyond reform (D) beyond repair

21 indurate
(A) hardened (B) lazy
(C) native (D) comforting

22 inexorable
(A) inexcusable (B) loathesome
(C) relentless (D) refreshing

23 inscrutable
(A) near-sighted (B) invisible
(C) unfathomable (D) vigilant

24 lugubrious
(A) mournful (B) laughable
(C) deeply cut (D) accented

25 macabre
(A) festive (B) gruesome
(C) difficult (D) bird-like

| ANSWER |

17. (A) 받아들이는 (B) 바라는
    (C) 내키지 않는 (D) 통과하지 못하는

18. (A) 잘못이 없는 (B) 무감각한
    (C) 무일푼의 (D) 불가능한

19. (A) 충동적인 (B) 뚱한, 골난
    (C) 우연의 (D) 반대하는, 고집 센

20. (A) 부식되지 않은 (B) 끊임없는
    (C) 교정할 수 없는 (D) 수리할 수 없는

21. (A) 굳어진 (B) 게으른
    (C) 토착의 (D) 위안이 되는

22. (A) 용서할 수 없는 (B) 싫은
    (C) 잔인한 (D) 상쾌한

23. (A) 근시안적인 (B) 보이지 않는
    (C) 헤아릴 수 없는
    (D) 자지 않고 지키는, 부단히 경계하는

24. (A) 슬픈 (B) 우스운
    (C) 깊이 패인
    (D) 강조된, 액센트를 붙인

25. (A) 축제의 (B) 섬뜩한, 무시무시한
    (C) 어려운
    (D) 새와 같은, 날씬한, 민첩한

17. (D) 18. (C) 19. (A) 20. (C) 21. (A)
22. (C) 23. (C) 24. (A) 25. (B)

26 minuscule
(A) subtracted (B) tiny
(C) mediocre (D) organism

27 moribund
(A) biting (B) wrapped
(C) dying (D) archaic

28 onerous
(A) solitary (B) indebtedness
(C) relieving (D) burdensome

29 ostentatious
(A) pretentious (B) deep voiced
(C) animated (D) retiring

30 pantoscopic
(A) panoramic (B) chaotic
(C) omniscient (D) underwater

31 profligate
(A) spendthrift (B) stingy
(C) impeccable (D) immoral

32 recalcitrant
(A) mendacious (B) helpful
(C) immoral (D) stubborn

33 somatic
(A) pertaining to sleep (B) rock-like
(C) powerful (D) bodily

34 soporific
(A) ridiculous (B) causing sleep
(C) tendentious (D) wise

| ANSWER |

26. (A) 감소된 (B) 작은
    (C) 평범한 (D) 기관, 유기체

27. (A) 날카로운 (B) 포장한
    (C) 죽어 가는 (D) 고풍의

28. (A) 외로운 (B) 신세, 은혜
    (C) 구제하는 (D) 부담이 되는

29. (A) 우쭐하는 (B) 저음의
    (C) 활기찬 (D) 은퇴하는

30. (A) 파노라마 같은 (B) 혼돈의
    (C) 전지의, 무엇이든 알고 있는
    (D) 수중의

31. (A) 씀씀이가 헤픈, 낭비하는
    (B) 인색한 (C) 나무랄 데 없는
    (D) 비도덕적인

32. (A) 허위의 (B) 도움이 되는
    (C) 비도덕적인 (D) 고집 센

33. (A) 수면에 관하여 (B) 바위 같은
    (C) 힘있는 (D) 육체의

34. (A) 웃기는 (B) 졸리게 하는
    (C) 편향된, 의도가 있는 (D) 현명한

26. (B) 27. (C) 28. (D) 29. (A) 30. (A)
31. (D) 32. (D) 33. (D) 34. (B)

35 sonorous
(A) resonant (B) snoring
(C) whispered (D) silent

36 subcutaneous
(A) beneath the rose (B) underground
(C) beneath the skin (D) submerged

37 undulating
(A) softening (B) splitting
(C) waving (D) burying

38 quixotic
(A) inactive (B) proportional
(C) swift (D) impractical

39 spurious
(A) proud (B) false
(C) specific (D) stringent

40 tenuous
(A) persistent (B) brief
(C) flimsy (D) flagrant

41 uncanny
(A) awkward (B) ponderous
(C) weird (D) unnecessary

42 meretricious
(A) praiseworthy
(B) dishonest
(C) superficially attractive
(D) impecunious

| ANSWER |

35. (A) 공명하는 (B) 코를 고는
    (C) 속삭인 (D) 고요한

36. (A) 장미 아래의 (B) 지하의
    (C) 피하의
    (D) (물 속에) 가라앉다, 잠기다

37. (A) 부드럽게 하는 (B) 분열시키는
    (C) 물결이 이는 (D) 매장하는

38. (A) 활기 없는, 활동 없는
    (B) 비례의, 균형잡힌 (C) 재빠른
    (D) 비실제적인

39. (A) 자랑으로 여기는 (B) 가짜의
    (C) 특정한 (D) 절박한, 엄중한

40. (A) 지속적인 (B) 간단한
    (C) 취약한, 박약한
    (D) 극악무도한, 악명 높은

41. (A) 거북한, 어색한 (B) 무거운
    (C) 불가사이한 (D) 불필요한

42. (A) 칭찬할 만한 (B) 정직하지 못한
    (C) 겉으로 매력인 (D) 무일푼의

35. (A) 36. (C) 37. (C) 38. (D) 39. (B)
40. (C) 41. (C) 42. (C)

STEP 5 Mastery Test 5

[Synonym Test]

DIRECTIONS Choose the word or phrase that means most nearly the same as the key word.

1. adventitious
   - (A) exciting
   - (B) hazardous
   - (C) accidental
   - (D) presumptuous

2. acerbic
   - (A) harsh
   - (B) abstemious
   - (C) mocking
   - (D) aggressive

3. ameliorate
   - (A) improve
   - (B) aggrandize
   - (C) amend
   - (D) cure

4. captious
   - (A) headstrong
   - (B) grasping
   - (C) enchanting
   - (D) critical

5. bellicose
   - (A) amusing
   - (B) pugnacious
   - (C) resounding
   - (D) obese

6. corroboration
   - (A) expenditure
   - (B) compilation
   - (C) confirmation
   - (D) reduction

7. desultory
   - (A) errant
   - (B) dejected
   - (C) aimless
   - (D) destitute

8. imprecation
   - (A) extemporaneous musical composition
   - (B) prodigality
   - (C) hint
   - (D) curse

9. indigenous
   - (A) angry
   - (B) impoverished
   - (C) native
   - (D) insulting

10. lethargic
    - (A) romantic
    - (B) sluggish
    - (C) oily
    - (D) melodic

11. nebulous
    - (A) cloudy
    - (B) subdued
    - (C) awkward
    - (D) careless

12. nonchalant
    - (A) unattainable
    - (B) excitable
    - (C) nonessential
    - (D) indifferent

13. spurious
    - (A) halting
    - (B) false
    - (C) galloping
    - (D) pending

] Antonym Test [

DIRECTIONS Choose the word or phrase that is most nearly opposite in meaning to the given word.

1. calumnious
   - (A) disastrous
   - (B) conspiratorial
   - (C) querulous
   - (D) complimentary

2. alacrity
   - (A) fearfulness
   - (B) languor
   - (C) celebrity
   - (D) sobriety

3. acrimonious
   - (A) sprightly
   - (B) intelligent
   - (C) soothing
   - (D) bitter

4. cursory
   - (A) thorough
   - (B) impolite
   - (C) honest
   - (D) quickly

5. debilitate
   - (A) encourage
   - (B) insinuate
   - (C) prepare
   - (D) strengthen

6. eclectic
   - (A) brilliant
   - (B) exclusive
   - (C) pastoral
   - (D) conclusive

7. corroborate
   - (A) correct
   - (B) strengthen
   - (C) broaden
   - (D) undermine

8. depredation
   - (A) plethora
   - (B) gross
   - (C) restoration
   - (D) glamour

9. flaunt
   - (A) mock
   - (B) hide
   - (C) irritate
   - (D) defend

10. gauche
    - (A) western
    - (B) frivolous
    - (C) tactful
    - (D) terse

11. germane
    - (A) teutonic
    - (B) sown
    - (C) cowardly
    - (D) irrelevant

12. extemporaneous
    - (A) energetic
    - (B) foreign
    - (C) grave
    - (D) rehearsed

13. intransigent
    - (A) impassable
    - (B) reconcilable
    - (C) harsh
    - (D) fly-by-night

14. extirpate
    - (A) besmirch
    - (B) clean
    - (C) implant
    - (D) favor

15. polemic
    - (A) arctic
    - (B) electrochemical
    - (C) agreeable
    - (D) statistical

16. obsequious
    - (A) respectful
    - (B) bold
    - (C) hereditary
    - (D) murky

17. parsimony
    - (A) contradiction
    - (B) prodigality
    - (C) clinch
    - (D) penury

18. sagacious
    - (A) ignorant
    - (B) hazardous
    - (C) articulate
    - (D) verbose

19. rectitude
    - (A) immorality
    - (B) fortitude
    - (C) cowardice
    - (D) attitude

20. satiated
    - (A) satirical
    - (B) hungry
    - (C) gorgeous
    - (D) delectable

21. truculent
    - (A) brilliant
    - (B) fawning
    - (C) automotive
    - (D) unruly

22. risibility
    - (A) melancholy
    - (B) timidity
    - (C) arrogance
    - (D) excitability

Sentence Completion Test

DIRECTIONS Select the word or phrase that will best complete the meaning of the sentence as a whole.

1. The woman, a lover of sweets, disliked the taste of the drill pickles because of their _____.
   (A) celerity   (B) celibacy
   (C) acerbity   (D) juiciness

2. Some historians contend that Hitler was a tyrant, unlike Franklin Roosevelt, who might have been considered an _____ ruler.
   (A) egotistic   (B) absorbed
   (C) absurd   (D) altruistic

3. The people felt the infidels' throwing of mud upon the statue to be a _____.
   (A) detestation   (B) desecration
   (C) delinquency   (D) delegation

4. A(n) _____ to the street was found through a broken bay window after the front door had been blocked by falling debris.
   (A) egress   (B) regress
   (C) exodus   (D) elopement

5. The director did not have the time today to give the report more than a _____ reading.
   (A) peripheral   (B) concentrated
   (C) dubious   (D) cursory

6. Because coal is formed when molten material from beneath the earth's surface dries, it is an _____ rock.
   (A) indigenous   (B) indispensable
   (C) igneous   (D) inscrutable

7. The vicious attack on the old couple was denounced as _____, horrible, and unforgivable.
   (A) haphazard   (B) hesitant
   (C) happenstance   (D) heinous

8. A parent tries to _____ children with sound morals and respect for others.
   (A) inculcate   (B) calculate
   (C) incubate   (D) inoculate

9. Having some free time, she decided to _____ the hats in the department store.
   (A) steal   (B) invest in
   (C) peruse   (D) propel

10. Anyone who walks about or takes a stroll is _____.
    (A) percussive   (B) peregrine
    (C) perambulating   (D) progressive

11. The school teacher's fawning behavior toward parents made the headmaster wonder why he was so _____ to parents and so strict with his pupils.
    (A) obovoid   (B) oblivious
    (C) obsessed   (D) obsequious

12. The God of the Christian religions has unlimited, universal power and is thus _____.
    (A) omnipresent   (B) omniscient
    (D) omnivorous   (D) omnipotent

13. The _____ hated and distrusted mankind for what he perceived to be its spiteful actions towards him.
    (A) misanthrope   (B) magnate
    (C) miser   (D) miscreant

14. After emerging from its cocoon, the caterpillar completed its _____ to a butterfly.

    (A) metaphrase (B) metaphase
    (C) metamorphosis (D) metaphor

15. Our understanding of the finances involved was so _____ that we needed outside advice.

    (A) tenuous (B) astute
    (C) sure (D) worried

16. His _____ manners offended the hostess.

    (A) unnoticed (B) uncovered
    (C) undone (D) uncouth

ENGLISH FORUM

1000 essential words that often appear on the TOEFL

Commonly
Misused Words

COMMONLY MISUSED WORDS

accept	v. 받아들이다 = receive, undertake They *accept* my invitation. 그들은 나의 초대를 받아들였다.
except	prep. 제외하는 = excluding, but Everyone *except* me attended the meeting. 나를 제외한 모두가 회의에 참석하였다.
access	n. 접근 = admittance, entrance The teachers had no *access* to the students' files. 교사들은 학생들의 파일에 접근을 하지 않았다.
excess	adj. 과잉의, 초과되는 = surplus, extra, excessive We paid a surcharge on our *excess* baggage. 우리는 초과 화물에 대한 추가비용을 지불하였다.
advice	n. 충고 = counsel, opinion, suggestion His *advice* was very useful. 그의 충고는 아주 유용하였다.
advise	v. 충고하다 = counsel, recommend, suggest I *advised* him to buy a car. 나는 그에게 자동차를 사라고 충고하였다.
affect	v. (1) 영향을 주다 = influence (n. affection 애정, 호의) Air pollution *affects* everyone. 대기오염은 모든 사람들에게 영향을 미친다. (2) 가장하다 = assume, feign, pretend (n. affectation 가장) She's from Chicago but she *affect* a British accent. 그녀는 시카고 출신인데도 영국억양으로 가장하였다.
effect	n. 결과, 효과 = result, consequence, impact The *effect* of the drug is well known. 그 약의 효능은 유명하다. v. …을 초래하다, 일으키다 = cause, bring about, produce To *effect* a change in city government we must all vote on Friday. 시청을 변화시키기 위해서 우리는 모두 금요일에 투표해야 한다.

almost	adv. 거의 = nearly *Almost* all the students work very hard. 거의 모든 학생들이 아주 열심히 공부한다.
most	adj, pron. 대부분 = the majority *Most* students work very hard. 대부분의 학생들이 아주 열심히 공부한다.

already	adv. 이미, 벌써 The movie had *already* begun by the time we arrived. 우리가 도착하였을 때 영화는 벌써 시작되었다.
all ready	adj. 완전히 준비된 = completely prepared The president was *all ready* to go on vacation. 회장은 휴가를 떠날 준비가 완전히 되어있었다.

among	prep. 셋 이상 중에 It was difficult to select a winner from *among* so many contestants. 아주 많은 출연자들 가운데서 우승자 한 사람을 뽑기가 어렵다.
between	prep. 둘 중에, between ... and로 연결 There is little difference *between* the two ideas. 두 생각은 다르지 않다. *Between* writing and teaching, Mary had little time for anything else. 글쓰기와 가르치기 가운데 메리는 어느 것도 시간이 없었다.

amount	n. 양 = quantity (불가산명사) The *amount* of money you have is not enough. 자네가 가진 금액으로는 부족하다
number	n. 수 (가산명사) The *number* of students in the program is increasing. 그 프로그램의 학생수가 증가하고 있다.

comparable	adj. 비교할 만한, ...에 필적하는 = similar, match for This dinner is *comparable* to the best French cooking. 이 만찬은 최고의 프랑스 요리에 필적한다.
comparative	adj. 비교의, 비교적인 = by comparison, relative I'm a *comparative* newcomer. 나는 비교적 신인이다. ∗comparative linguistics 비교언어학

beside	prep. 옆 = next to He sat *beside* the pretty girl. 그는 예쁜 여자 옆에 앉았다.
besides	prep,adv. 게다가 = in addition to, also, moreover He has a bicycle *besides* a car. 그는 자동차 외에 자전거도 가지고 있다.
aside	adv. 따로, 한쪽에 = to one side Harry sets money *aside* every payday for his son's education. 해리는 아들의 교육을 위해 봉급날마다 돈을 따로 모은다.

benediction	n. 감사기도, 축복 = blessing, closing prayer At the end of service the bishop gave the *benediction*. 예배가 끝날 때 주교는 감사기도를 드렸다.
benefactor	n. 자선사업가, 은혜를 베푸는 사람 = support, patron The new wing of the hospital is the gift of a *benefactor*. 병원의 새로운 병동은 어느 자선사업가의 선물이다.
beneficiary	n. 수혜자, 혜택을 받는 사람 = receiver, inheritor Fill in the name of your *beneficiary* on the insurance policy. 보험약관에 당신 수혜자의 이름을 적으시오.
benedictional	adj. 축복 받은
benedictory	adj. 축복의
beneficient	adj. 선행을 하는, 인심 좋은
beneficial	adj. 유익한, 도움이 되는 = helpful, favorable Exercise is *beneficial* to good health. 운동은 건강에 도움이 된다.
benevolent	adj. 자비심 많은, 인정 많은 = charitable, compassionate

consecutive	adj. 연속적인, 중단 없는 연속 The streets of New York City are numbered in *consecutive* order. 뉴욕시의 거리는 연속적인 순서로 번호가 매겨져 있다.
successive	adj. 연속적인, 일련의 각기 다른 사건의 연속 He underwent four *successive* operations in two weeks. 그는 2주일에 4번의 수술을 연속해서 받았다.

capital	1. n. 부, 재산 = wealth, funds He invested a lot of his *capital* in the project. 그는 프로젝트에 자기 재산을 많이 투자하였다. 2. 수도, 서울 = seat of government, chief city London is the *capital* of England. 런던은 영국의 수도이다. 3. 대문자 = capital letter The child wrote his name in *capitals*. 아이는 자기 이름을 대문자로 썼다.
capitol	n. 미 국회의사당(Capitol Hill), Capitol : 로마의 Jupiter 신전 The *capitol* building is near the downtown shopping area. 의사당은 시내 쇼핑지역 근처에 있다.

close	v. 닫다, 닫히다, 끝나다 = shut, stop The store *closes* at midnight. 상점은 한밤중에 문을 닫는다.
close	adj. (1) 가까운 = near, nearby She lives *close* to the university. 그녀는 대학 근처에 산다. (2) 단단한, 정밀한, 친한 = tight, firm, attentive, intimate Keep a *close* grip on your purse. 지갑을 단단히 쥐고 있어라. Keep a *close* watch on the children. 아이들을 잘 보고 있어라. The two brothers are very *close*. 두 형제가 아주 친하다.

compare	v. 비교하다 = show similarities *Compare* food costs today with those of a year ago. 오늘날의 음식물 비용을 일년 전과 비교해 봐. The canned soup can't *compare* to homemade. 캔에 든 수프는 집에서 만든 것과 비교할 수 없다. He *compared* the crowd to a swarm of angry bees. (비유하다) 그는 군중들을 성난 벌떼들에 비유하였다.
contrast	v. 대조하다 = show differences *Contrast* Keats's poetry with Dylan Thomas's. 키츠의 시를 딜란 토머스의 시와 대조해 봐. This cold weather *contrasts* with last week's heat. 이렇게 추운 날씨는 지난주의 더위와 대조된다.

costume	n. 복장 = clothing, apparel, garments, dress	
	She wore a beautiful *costume* to the party.	
	그녀는 예쁜 옷을 입고 파티에 갔다.	
custom	n. 관습, 풍습 = convention, habitual practice	
	Customs differ from country to country.	
	관습은 나라마다 다르다.	
customs	n. 관세, 세관 = tariff	
	You must pass through *customs* when you enter a country.	
	다른 나라에 입국할 때는 세관을 통과해야 한다.	

cloth [klɔ(:)θ]	n. 천, 옷감 = fabric	
	Two yards of *cloth* will be enough for the dress.	
	옷감 2야드면 드레스를 만드는 데 충분할 것이다.	
clothe [klouð]	v. 옷을 입히다, 덮다 = dress, cover, wrap	
	After showering, I *clothed* myself for the party.	
	샤워를 한 다음, 나는 파티복장을 입었다.	
	The charity feeds and *clothes* the needy.	
	자선단체에서 가난한 사람들을 먹여주고 입혀준다.	
clothes [klouðz]	n. (복수명사) 옷, 의복(복수취급) = clothing, apparel, garments	
	The man was wearing old, dirty *clothes*.	
	그 남자는 낡고 더러운 옷을 입고 있었다.	
	Fine *clothes* make the man.	
	좋은 옷이 사람을 만든다.	
clothing [klóuðiŋ]	n. (집합명사) 옷, 의복(단수취급) = clothes, attire, costume	
	I need a new *clothing*.	
	나는 새 옷이 필요하다.	

detract	v. 가치를 떨어뜨리다 = reduce, lower, lessen	
	The peeling walls *detract* the beauty of the room.	
	벽의 껍질이 벗겨져 나가는 것은 방의 아름다움을 떨어뜨린다.	
distract	v. 미혹하게 하다, 빗나가게 하다 = divert, trouble, agitate	
	The clowns *distracted* the children.	
	광대들은 어린이들을 미혹시킨다.	
	Fear *distracted* her so that she could hardly think straight.	
	두려움이 그녀를 너무 미혹시켜서 똑바로 생각을 할 수 없었다.	

council	n. 회, 의회 = convention, conference, assembly
	The city *council* meets every week.
	시의회는 매주 모인다.

counsel	n. 조언, 충고 = advice, consultation
	His *counsel* was very useful to us.
	그의 조언은 우리에게 매우 유익하였다.
	v. 조언하다 = advise, recommend
	His doctor *counseled* him to stop smoking.
	의사는 그에게 담배를 끊으라고 충고하였다.

desert [dézə:rt]	n. 사막 = wasteland, barren wilderness
	It is very hot and dry in the *desert*.
	사막에서는 매우 덥고 건조하다.
	adj. 불모의, 황량한 = barren, desolate waste
	The speculators bought a large *desert* tract and sold lots.
	투자가는 넓은 불모지를 사서 많이 팔았다.

desert [dizə́:rt]	v. 버리다, 도망하다 = abandon, forsake, run away from
	The police are looking for a woman who *deserted* her children.
	경찰은 자기 아이들을 버린 여인을 찾고 있다.

dessert [dizə́:rt]	n. 후식
	My favorite *dessert* is chocolate ice cream.
	내가 제일 좋아하는 디저트는 초콜릿 아이스크림이다.

later	adj, adv. late의 비교급, 나중에, 후에
	The movie began *later* than we expected.
	영화는 우리가 예상했던 것보다 나중에 시작하였다.

latter	adj, pron. late의 비교급, 둘 중에 뒤의 것
	Both Frank and Philip are likeable, but the *latter* is the more intelligent.
	프랭크와 필립은 닮았으나 필립이 더 똑똑하다.

last	adj. 맨 마지막
	December is the *last* month of the year.
	12월은 일년의 마지막 달이다.

| considerable | adj. 중요한, 상당한 = important, significant, great
Jane had *considerable* experience in the field.
제인은 그 분야에서 상당한 경험을 가지고 있다. |
|---|---|
| considerate | adj. 사려 깊은, 인정 있는 = thoughtful, kind, mindful
It was very *considerate* of you to send me a get-well card.
자네가 내게 안부카드를 보내다니 참 고마웠네. |

| contemptible | adj. 천시, 경멸할 만한, 비열한 = mean, vile, unworthy
Spreading ugly gossip is *contemptible*.
추문을 퍼뜨리는 것은 비열하다. |
|---|---|
| contemptuous | adj. 경멸하는 = scornful, insolent, snobbish
Snobs are usually *contemptuous* of people they feel to be beneath them.
속물들은 보통 자기보다 아래로 생각되는 사람들을 경멸한다. |

| complement | n, v. 보충(하다) = completion, supplement, make complete
A subject *complement* follows the verb 'to be'.
주격보어는 동사 'to be' 뒤에 온다.
Travel can be an excellent *complement* to one's education.
여행은 사람의 교육을 훌륭히 보충할 수 있다.
The dessert *complemented* the dinner.
디저트가 만찬을 보충하였다. |
|---|---|
| compliment | n. 칭찬, 축하 = praise, commendation, congratulations, regards, respects
She got many *compliments* on her new ring.
그녀는 자신의 새 반지에 많은 찬사를 받았다.
Please give my *compliments* to your parents.
부모님께 나의 칭찬을 전해라.
v. 칭찬, 축하하다 = praise, applaud, commend
He *complimented* her on her cooking.
그는 그녀의 요리를 칭찬하였다. |

| decease | n, v. 사망(하다) = death
He mourned the *decease* of his best friend.
그는 가장 친한 친구의 사망을 슬퍼하였다. |
|---|---|
| disease | n. 질병, v. 병들게 하다 = illness
Doctors hope that someday they can eradicate *disease*.
의사들은 그들이 언젠가 질병을 뿌리뽑을 수 있게 되기를 바란다. |

contend	v. 경쟁하다, 다투다, 주장하다 = struggle, compete, contest, assert (n. contention) Three students *contended* for the prize. 세 명의 학생이 우승을 다투었다. The suspect *contended* that the witness was lying. 피의자는 증인이 거짓말한다고 주장하였다.
content	adj. 만족하여 = satisfied, pleased, happy Many men are *content* with a routine life. 많은 사람들이 일상생활에 만족한다. n. (1) 만족 = satisfaction, gratification, contentment The children ate to their heart's *content*. 아이들은 자기들의 성에 찰 때까지 먹었다. (2) 내용, 목차, 요지 = insides, capacity, essence, thoughts The *content* of this can is seven ounces of tuna fish. 이 통조림의 내용물은 참치 7온스이다. The *content* of his argument was weak. 이 토론의 요지는 약하였다.

credible	adj. 신용할 수 있는 = believable, reliable, trustworthy Is the witness's story *credible*? 증인의 이야기는 믿을 수 있나?
creditable	adj. 칭찬할 만한 = admirable, commendable, respectable The coach did a *creditable* job in bringing the team in the championship. 감독은 팀을 우승팀으로 끌어올리는 훌륭한 일을 하였다.
credulous	adj. 남을 쉽게 믿는 = ready to believe, easily convinced Ann is so *credulous* she'll believe anything you tell her. 앤은 너무 쉽게 믿는 탓에 네가 그녀에게 무슨 말을 하든지 믿을 것이다.

literal	adj. 문자의, 글자그대로의 = word-for-word, faithful, exact The students were asked to make a *literal* translation of the French story. 학생들은 프랑스 소설을 글자그대로 번역하도록 지시받았다.
literary	adj. 문학적인 = of literature The *literary* club meets once a month. 문학동아리는 한 달에 한 번 모인다.
literate	adj. 학식 있는 = able to read and write, educated, learned Only a few of the nation's peasants are *literate*. 그 나라의 농부들은 소수만이 글을 알았다.

device	n. 고안, 장치 = invention, apparatus, mechanism, scheme	
	She invented a *device* that automatically closes windows when it rains.	
	그녀는 비가 올 때 자동으로 창문을 닫아주는 장치를 발명하였다.	
devise	v. 고안하다 = invent, design, plot	
	He tried to *devise* a foolproof plan for getting rid of termites.	
	그는 흰개미들을 제거하는 아주 간단한 계획을 고안하려고 애썼다.	

differ	v. 다르다
	My current teacher *differs* in method from my last one.
	현재 우리 선생님은 지난번 선생님과 가르치는 방법이 다르다.
different	adj. 다른
	The ending of the book was *different* from what I expected.
	책의 끝 부분이 내가 기대했던 것과 달랐다.

elicit	v. 유도해내다, 불러일으키다 = evoke, bring forth, cause
	The mayor's remark *elicited* a flood of letters.
	시장의 발언은 편지를 쇄도하게 만들었다.
illicit	adj. 불법의, 부정한 = illegal, prohibited, criminal
	The police began to crack down on *illicit* drug traffic.
	경찰은 불법약품거래를 엄중히 단속하기 시작하였다.

emigrate	v. 다른 나라로 이주하다 = move, migrate, depart, leave
	The British doctor *emigrated* to Canada.
	영국 의사가 캐나다로 이민갔다.
emigrants	n. 떠나는 이주민
	After World War II many *emigrants* left Europe to go to the U.S.
	제2차 세계대전 후에 많은 이민자들이 유럽을 떠나 미국으로 갔다.
immigrate	v. 다른 나라로부터 이주하다 = move, migrate, settle
	Many Italians *immigrated* to the United States and Canada.
	많은 이탈리아인들이 미국과 캐나다로 이민을 왔다.
immigrants	n. 들어와 정착하는 이주민
	The United States is a country composed of *immigrants*.
	미국은 이민자들로 구성된 나라이다.

example	n. 예, 보기 Picasso's Guernica is an excellent *example* of expressionism in art. 피카소의 Guernica는 표현주의 예술의 뛰어난 예이다.
sample	n. 표본 The dairy lady always gives me a *sample* of cheese. 목장 여자는 늘 내게 치즈 표본을 준다.

farther	adj. adv. (거리) 더 멀리 = further, to a greater distance Chicago is *farther/further* north than Austin. 시카고는 오스틴보다 북쪽으로 더 멀리 있다.
further	adj. adv. (시간, 정도, 양) 더 많은 = to a greater degree, extent, deepe I will give you *further* information later. 내가 나중에 더 많은 정보를 줄게. * farther와 further는 구분 없이 쓰기도 한다.

fewer	adj, pron. 가산명사에 사용 (few-fewer-fewest) He spent *fewer* hours studying for the exam. 그는 시험공부에 몇 시간 쓰지 못했다.
less	adj, pron. 불가산명사에 사용 (little-less-least) He spent *less* time studying for the exam. 그는 시험공부에 시간을 많이 쓰지 못했다.

former	adj, n. 둘 중에 앞의 것 = earlier, preceeding, anterior Both Mary and Jane were invited, but only the *former* came. 메리와 제인 둘 다 초대받았는데 메리만 왔다.
first	adj, n. 셋이나 그 이상 열거된 것 중에 첫째 = earliest, foremost Ann, Jane, and Amy are sisters, but the *first* was adopted. 앤과 제인, 에미가 자매간인데 첫째가 입양되었다.

formerly	adv. 이전에는 = previously, originally Elizabeth was *formerly* called Betty. 엘리자베스는 전에 베티라 불렀다.
formally	adv. 공식적으로 = officially You are too *formally* dressed for an outdoor picnic. 너는 야외소풍인데 너무 공식적으로 차려입었다.

forth	adv. 앞으로 = forward She rocked the baby back and *forth* until he fell asleep. 그녀는 아이가 잠들 때까지 앞뒤로 흔들어주었다.
fourth	adj. 네 번째 You are the *fourth* person to ask that question. 너는 그 질문을 하는 네 번째 사람이다.

had better	v. (권유) …하는 게 좋겠다 I *had better* study tonight. 난 오늘밤에 공부나 하겠다.
would rather	v. (선택) 차라리 …하겠다 I *would rather* watch television than study. 난 공부보다는 텔레비전이나 보겠다.

helpless	adj. 어쩔 수 없는, 무력한, 의지할 데 없는 Because I could not understand English, I felt *helpless* trying to understand his lecture. 영어를 이해하지 못하기 때문에 나는 그의 강의를 이해하려해도 잘 되지 않았다.
useless	adj. 쓸모 없는, 소용없는 = of no use, worthless An umbrella is *useless* in a hurricane. 우산이 허리케인에는 소용없다.

house	n. 집(실제 건물) He is building a new *house* in the fourth street. 그는 4번가에 새집을 짓고 있다.
home	n. 가정(관념상의 조직) *Home* is where the heart is. 가정이란 마음이 머무는 곳이다. * 실제로는 흔히 구분 없이 쓴다.

imaginary	adj. 실제가 아닌, 상상의 = unreal, fictitious, invented All characters in the book are *imaginary*. 책 속에 있는 모든 인물은 실제가 아니다.
imaginative	adj. 상상이 풍부한 = creative, inventive, original Star Wars was created by a highly *imaginative* writer. 스타워즈는 매우 상상력이 풍부한 작가가 창작하였다.

immortal	adj. 죽지 않는, 불멸의 = undying, eternal, divine The *immortal* works of Shakespeare are still being read. 셰익스피어의 불멸의 작품들은 아직도 읽혀지고 있다.
immoral	adj. 비도덕적인, 악한 = corrupt, evil, wrong, bad, wicked The committee banned two *immoral* movies. 위원회는 비도덕적인 두 편의 영화를 금지하였다.
implicit	adj. 함축적인, 암시적인 = hinted, inherent, innate The crew had *implicit* faith in the captain's judgement. 선원들은 선장의 판단에 암묵적인 믿음을 가지고 있었다.
explicit	adj. 명백한, 노골적인 = specific, distinct, clear She gave *explicit* directions about the way the rug should be cleaned. 그녀는 카펫을 세탁하는 방법에 대한 확실한 안내를 해주었다.
industrial	adj. 산업의 Paul had an *industrial* accident and was in the hospital for three months. 폴은 산업재해를 입어서 석 달 간 병원에 있었다.
industrious	adj. 부지런한 = diligent, hard working Mark was such an *industrious* student that he received a four-year scholarship. 마크는 아주 부지런한 학생이어서 4년 장학금을 받았다.
inflict	v. (폐를) 끼치다, (해를) 입히다 = lay on, impose, put upon The hurricane *inflicted* severe damage in the island. 허리케인은 섬에 심한 피해를 입혔다.
afflict	v. 육체적, 정신적으로 괴롭히다 = distress, oppress, torment Famine and war still *afflict* mankind. 기근과 전쟁이 여전히 인류를 괴롭힌다.
ingenious	adj. 재능 있는, 영리한 = clever, artful Digital watches are *ingenious* devices. 디지털시계는 똑똑한 물건이다.
ingenuous	adj. 솔직한, 순진한 = frank, naive Children are more *ingenuous* than adults. 어린이가 어른보다 더 순수하다.

inspiration	n. 영감, 착상 = incentive, impulse, incitement, idea The painter's *inspiration* came from nature. 그 화가의 영감은 자연에서 왔다.
aspiration	n. 지적인 열망, 포부 = ambition, object, intention His *aspiration* was to establish democracy in Korea. 그의 포부는 한국에 민주주의를 수립하는 것이었다.

intelligent	adj. 지적인, 똑똑한 = bright, smart He was so *intelligent* that he received good grades. 그는 아주 똑똑해서 좋은 성적을 받았다.
intelligible	adj. 알기 쉬운, 명료한 = clear, easily understood The teacher's explanations were so *intelligible* that students had no problems doing their assignments. 선생님의 설명이 아주 명쾌해서 학생들이 숙제를 하는 데 아무 문제가 없었다.
intellectual	n. 지식(인) = intellect, scholar, intelligentsia He was considered an *intellectual* by most voters. 그는 대부분의 유권자들에게 지식인으로 생각되었다. adj. 지성적인 = wise, intelligent, academic I admire her *intellectual* achievements. 나는 그녀의 업적을 존경한다.

intense	adj. 강렬한, 진지한 = extreme, strong, earnest The patient has an *intense* will to recover. 환자는 회복하려는 강한 의지를 가지고 있다.
intensive	adj. 강력한, 집중적인 = concentrated Before going to Mexico, I took an *intensive* course in Spanish. 멕시코로 가기 전에 나는 스페인어 고급반 강좌를 받았다.

learn	v. 배우다, 지식을 얻다 = master, acquire knowledge of We haveto *learn* how to operate the computer. 우리는 컴퓨터 작동법을 알아야 한다.
study	v. 학습하다, 연구하다 = educate oneself, school oneself The committee will *study* the tax plan. 위원회는 조세계획을 연구할 것이다.

lend	v. 빌려주다 = lease, loan Could you *lend* me five dollars until payday? 봉급날까지 5달러 빌려줄 수 있니?
borrow	v. 빌다, 임대하다 = lease, take May I *borrow* your car? 자네 차를 좀 빌릴 수 있겠나?
lie	vi. 눕다, 놓여있다 (lie-lay-lain-lying) He *lay* down on the bed. 그는 침대에 누워있었다.
lay	vt. 놓다, 두다 (lay-laid-laid-laying) He *laid* the book on the table. 그는 탁자 위에 책을 놓았다.
lie	vi. 거짓말하다 (lie-lied-lied-lying) He *lies*, cheats, and steals. 그는 거짓말하고, 속이고, 훔치기까지 한다.
like	adj, prep. …처럼 He looks *like* his father. 그는 자기 아버지를 닮았다.
the same as	adj. …과 같은 = like That car is almost *the same as* mine. 그 자동차는 내 것과 거의 똑같다.
alike	adj, adv. 〈서술적〉서로 같은, 똑같이 He and his brother are very much *alike*.(형용사) 그와 그의 동생은 아주 똑같다. A good teacher treats all his students *alike*.(부사) 좋은 선생은 자기 학생들을 모두 똑같이 대한다.
such as	adj. …와 같이 Fruits *such as* oranges and grapefruit grow in Texas. 오렌지와 자몽 같은 과일이 텍사스에서 자란다.
as if	conj. 마치 …처럼 He looks *as if* he is tired. 그는 지친 것 같다.

liquefy	v. 녹이다, 액화하다 The ice cream began to *liquefy* in the intense heat. 아이스크림이 강한 열에 녹기 시작하였다.
liquidate	v. 청산하다, 정리하다 = settle, pay, clear, eliminate The inheritance allowed him to *liquidate* his debts. 유산이 자신의 빚을 청산하게 해주었다. The dictator brutally *liquidated* all his political opponents. 독재자는 자신의 모든 정적들을 잔인하게 숙청하였다.

lonely	adj. (감정) 외로운 = lonesome, solitary Robinson Crusoe spent many *lonely* days on the desert island. 로빈슨 크루소는 황량한 섬에서 많은 외로운 날들을 보냈다.
alone	adj, adv. (상태) 혼자인 = by oneself, single, isolated She is too young to go to the party *alone*. 그녀는 너무 어려서 파티에 혼자 갈 수 없다.

loose [luːs]	adj. 느슨한, 풀어진 = freed, unbound (opp. fast) I need a screwdriver to tighten the *loose* screws. 나는 풀린 나사를 조이기 위해 드라이버가 필요하다.
loosen	v. 풀다, 느슨하게 하다 (opp. tighten) I am *loosening* the screws. 나는 스크루를 풀고 있다.
lose [luːz]	v. 잃다, 놓치다 = miss, forget, fail He is *losing* weight very quickly. 그는 금방 몸무게를 줄인다.
loss	n. 손실 = wreck, ruin (opp. gain) She was saddened by the *loss* of her wedding ring. 그녀는 결혼반지를 잃어버려서 슬펐다.

maybe	adv. 아마 = possibly, perhaps *Maybe* you will find the wallet you lost. 아마 자네는 잃어버린 지갑을 찾게 될 거야.
may be	She *may be* late. 그녀는 늦을 거야.

momentary	adj. 순간의, 덧없는 = temporary, transient, brief It was only a *momentary* infatuation. 그것은 순간적으로 심취될 것일 뿐이었다.
momentous	adj. 중요한 = important, significant The conference was a *momentous* occasion for both countries. 회의는 두 나라를 위해 중요한 일이었다.

near	prep, adv. 가까운 = close to My biology class meets *near* the Student Union. 생물학 수업이 학생회관 근처에서 있다.
nearly	adv. 거의 = almost We were *nearly* hit by the speeding car on the turnpike. 우리는 고속도로에서 과속차량에 거의 부딪칠 뻔했다.

object	n. 대상; 물체 = thing, goal, point The bright moving *object* appeared in the sky at sunset. 움직이는 밝은 물체가 석양의 하늘에 나타났다. What is the *object* of the research? 연구대상이 뭔가? v. 반대하다 = oppose, protest, disapprove of Mother *objects* to cigar smoking. 어머니는 시가를 피는 것을 반대하신다.
objection	n. 반대 = opposition, disapproval The boy kept the dog despite his sister's *objection*. 소년은 여동생의 반대에도 불구하고 개를 가두고 있다.

observance	n. (1) 준수 = obeying, following, compliance *Observance* of the rules is important in this game. 규정을 지키는 것이 이 경기에서 중요하다. (2) 관례 = ceremonial, commemoration, celebration Christmas is one of our religious *observances*. 크리스마스는 종교적인 관례 중의 하나이다.
observation	n. 관찰, 주시 = watching, viewing, examination This telescope is used for the *observation* of distant stars. 이 망원경은 멀리 떨어진 별들을 관찰하는 데 사용된다.

passed	v. 지나가다 (pass의 과거형)
	The car *passed* the house very slowly.
	자동차가 집을 아주 느리게 지나갔다.
past	adj, prep. 지나간, (시간, 공간적으로) …을 지나서
	The boy ran *past* the house.
	소년은 집을 지나쳐 달렸다.

persecute	v. 박해, 학대하다, 괴롭히다 = harass, torture, oppress
	Throughout history many people have been *persecuted* for their beliefs.
	역사적으로 많은 사람들이 자신들이 신념 때문에 박해를 받아왔다.
prosecute	v. 일을 수행하다, 기소하다 = carry on, bring suit
	Shoplifters will be *prosecuted* to the fullest extent of the law.
	들치기들은 법정 최대한도로 기소될 것이다.

personal	adj. 개인적인 = private, individual, exclusive
	It is difficult to discuss *personal* problems.
	개인적인 문제를 논의하는 것은 어렵다.
personnel	n. 조직에 속한 사람, 직원 = members, staff, employees
	All *personnel* must attend the meeting.
	모든 직원이 회의에 참석해야 한다.

physician	n. 내과의사
	The *physician* is a doctor of medicine.
	physician은 내과의사이다.
physicist	n. 물리학자
	The *physicist* is an expert in physics.
	physicist는 물리학의 전문가이다.

pleasant	adj. 즐거운, 유쾌한 = happy, pleasing, enjoyable
	Have a *pleasant* weekend.
	즐거운 주말을 보내세요.
pleased	adj. 기쁜, 만족한, 마음에 든
	The children were *pleased* when they got presents.
	아이들은 선물을 받을 때 기뻐했다.

precede	v. …에 앞서다 = go before, antecede The subject usually *precedes* the verb. 주어는 흔히 동사 앞에 온다.
proceed	v. 나아가다 = go forward, go ahead, progress, advance After a brief interruption, we *proceeded* with class. 우리는 잠시 중단하였다가 수업을 계속했다.
principal	n, adj. (조직의) 장, 중요한 = master, chief, important The *principal* side effect of the drug is drowsiness. 약의 중요한 부작용은 졸음이다. He has been *principal* of that high school for many years. 그는 수년 간 저 고등학교의 교장이었다.
principle	n. 원칙 = rule, fundamental The experiment demonstrated a basic scientific *principle*. 그 실험은 기본적인 과학적 원칙을 보여주었다.
quality	n. 질, 품질, 특성 = value, grade, characteristic The furniture was of poor *quality*. 그 가구는 질이 떨어지는 것이었다.
quantity	n. 양 = amount, sum, bulk Put a small *quantity* of sugar into the batter. 반죽에다 설탕을 조금 넣어라.
quiet	adj. 조용한 = silent, calm, serene After children left, the house was *quiet*. 아이들이 떠나자 집이 조용하였다.
quite	adv. 완전히, 아주 = completely, really 꽤, 매우 = very, fairly She was quite beautiful. The film was *quite* good. 그녀는 매우 예뻤다. 영화는 아주 좋았다.
raise	vt. 올리다, 일으키다, 기르다 = elevate, lift, breed (raise-raised-raised-raising) They *raised* the flag. 그들은 깃발을 올렸다.
rise	vi. 일어서다, 오르다 = stand, ascend, climb (rise-rose-risen-rising) Prices have *risen* sharply. 가격이 가파르게 올랐다.

regretful	adj. 후회하는 = full of regret Father was *regretful* he couldn't send us to college. 아버지는 우리를 대학에 보내지 못해 후회하였다.
regrettable	adj. 유감스런, 슬퍼할 만한, 안된 = lamentable, deplorable, unhappy Overpopulation has caused a *regrettable* situation. 인구과밀은 유감스러운 상황을 초래하였다.
remember	v. 생각해내다 = recall, recollect, keep in mind I do not *remember* what time he asked me to call. 나는 그가 몇 시에 나에게 전화를 했는지 기억하지 못한다.
remind	v. ...을 생각나게 하다 = awaken memories of Henry *reminds* me of my uncle. 헨리는 나에게 아저씨를 생각나게 한다.
respectable	adj. 존경할 만한, 훌륭한 = honorable, noble, decent My parents are *respectable* people. 우리 부모님은 존경할 만한 분들이다.
respectful	adj. 경의를 표하는, 공손한 = polite, reverent You can be *respectful* without being obsequious. 자네는 아첨하지 않고 공손해질 수 있다.
respective	adj. 각각의 They have their *respective* merits. 그들은 각각의 장점을 가지고 있다.
(e)special	adj. 특별한 This is a *special* day in my life. 오늘은 내인생의 특별한 날이다.
especially	adv. 특별히 The cabinet was made *especially* for the dining room. 캐비닛이 식당용으로 특별히 제작되었다.
particular	adj. 특이한, 특유의 She is so *particular* that no one can please her. 그녀는 너무 특이해서 아무도 그녀를 즐겁게 할 수 없다.
particularly	adv. 특히, 각별히 The coffee is *particularly* good today. 오늘 커피는 특별히 좋다.

sensible	adj. 사리분별 있는 = thoughtful, intelligent, wise, prudent Donald is a *sensible* young man. 도널드는 분별 있는 젊은이다.
sensitive	adj. 민감한, 예민한 = perceptive, delicate, keen The tips of the fingers are particularly *sensitive*. 손가락 끝이 특히 예민하다.
sensational	adj. 선풍적인 = outstanding, striking, spectacular The boy was reading a *sensational* paperback novel. 소년은 선풍적인 인기소설을 읽고 있었다.
sensual	adj. 관능적인, 육감적인 = erotic, lustful, sexy He has a *sensual* appreciation of fine wine. 그는 좋은 포도주에 대한 육감적인 감상능력을 가지고 있다.
sensuous	adj. 감각적인 = strongly appealing, exquisite, delicious A meadow in spring is full of *sensuous* delights. 봄의 풀밭은 감각적인 기쁨으로 가득하다.

set	vt. 두다, 배치하다, 정하다 (set-set-set-setting) She *set* the flowers on the table. 그녀는 탁자 위에 꽃을 놓았다.
sit	vi. 앉다, 자리잡다 (sit-sat-sat-sitting) They were *sitting* on the porch. 그들은 현관에 앉았다.
seat	vt. 앉히다, 수용하다 (seat-seated-seated-seating) *Seat* that lady in an armchair. The hall will seat 5,000. 저 숙녀를 안락의자에 앉혀라. 그 홀은 5,000명을 수용한다.

stationary	adj. 정지된 = immovable, fixed, motionless After remaining *stationary* for two days, the cold front finally moved west. 이틀 간 머물러 있다가 한랭전선이 드디어 서쪽으로 이동하였다.
stationery	n. 문구류 She wrote the letter on the university *stationery*. 그녀는 대학 문구로 편지를 썼다.

successive	adj. 연속적인, 이어지는 = following He underwent four *successive* operations in two weeks. 그는 2주일 간 4번이나 연속으로 수술을 받았다.
successful	adj. 성공적인 = achieved, fruitful She is a *successful* businesswoman. 그녀는 성공적인 비즈니스 우먼이다.

take	vt. …을 가지고/데리고 가다 Please *take* a cookie from the bowl. 그릇에서 쿠키를 하나 가져오너라.
bring	vi. …을 가지고/데리고 오다 April showers *bring* May flowers. 4월의 비는 5월에 꽃을 가져온다.
fetch	vt. 가서 …을 가지고/데리고 오다 The man was training his dogs to *fetch* a ball. 그 남자는 자기 개를 훈련시켜 공을 가져오도록 하였다.

thank	v. 고맙게 생각하다, 사례하다 * thank +사람 (+for+ 행위/사물) There is no need to *thank* me. Thank you very much. 나에게 고마워할 필요 없다. 대단히 감사합니다.
appreciate	v. 고맙게 생각하다, 감상하다 * appreciate + 행위/사물 I greatly *appreciate* your kindness. 친절히 대해주셔서 대단히 감사합니다. Van Gogh's paintings weren't *appreciated* until after his death. 반 고흐의 그림은 사망 이후까지도 제대로 감상되지(평가받지) 못했다.

thorough	adj. 철저한, 완전한 = complete, exhaustive, perfect The report was very *thorough*. 보고서는 매우 완벽하였다.
through	prep. 통과 He walked *through* the room. 그는 방을 통과하여 걸어갔다.
throughout	prep. 처음부터 끝까지, 온통 = all over, all the time The factory was painted green *throughout*. 공장은 온통 녹색으로 칠해져 있었다.

uninterested	이해관계가 없는, 무관심한 = indifferent She is entirely *uninterested* in political problems. 그녀는 정치적인 문제에 완전히 무관심하다.
disinterested	사심이 없는, 공평한 = impartial, unprejudiced We need a *disinterested* party to settle the argument. 우리는 논쟁을 해결할 공평한 단체를 원한다.

use	n. 사용 행위 The *use* of the computer is growing very rapidly. 컴퓨터의 사용은 매우 급속히 성장하고 있다.
usage	n. 사용 방법, 용법 In British *usage*, 'lift' means 'elevator'. 영국식 용법으로는 lift가 elevator를 뜻한다.

COMMONLY MISUSED WORDS

Practice Test 16

DIRECTIONS Select the word in parentheses that completes the meaning in each sentence.

1. Betty's insulting remark greatly (effected/affected) Kurt, who is a very sensitive person.

2. Detroit manufacturers hope to develope an easily attachable (device/devise) for the carburetor to improve gas mileage.

3. While doing the experiment, we asked the lab technician's (advice/advise).

4. After declaring bankruptcy, the company was forced to (liquefy/liquidate) its assets.

5. Keith's company's headquarters were (formerly/formally) located in philadelphia.

6. (Especially/Special) attention must be given to the questions at the end of each chapter.

7. George was (among/between) those students selected to participate in the debate.

| ANSWER |

1. 베티의 모욕적인 말은 아주 민감한 사람인 커트에게 심하게 영향을 미쳤다.
2. 디트로이트 기업체들은 연료 연비를 향상시키도록 내연기관에 쉽게 부착할 수 있는 장치를 개발하려고 한다.
3. 실험을 하는 동안 우리는 연구실 전문가의 조언을 구하였다.
4. 파산을 선고한 후에 회사는 자산을 청산하도록 강요받았다.
5. 케이스사의 본사가 전에는 필라델피아에 위치해 있었다.
6. 각 장의 끝에 있는 문제들에 특별한 관심을 기울여야 한다.
7. 조지는 저 학생들 가운데 토론에 참가하기로 선발되었다.

1. affected
2. device
3. advice
4. liquefy
5. formerly
6. Special
7. among

8. They were (already/all ready) to leave when a telegram arrived.

9. By asking many questions, the instructor tried to (elicit/illicit) information from the students.

10. You should not say things that might makes a highly (sensitive/ sensible) person upset.

11. The United States is a 'melting pot', a land of (emigrants/immigrants).

12. A large (number/quantity) of whales beached and died last year.

13. When Luise set the table, she placed the silverware (besides/beside) the plates.

14. Mark is (sensible/sensitive) enough to swim close to shore.

15. In 1969 the astronauts who landed on the moon collected (examples/samples) of rocks and soil.

16. These birds are (beneficial/beneficient) to man.

ANSWER

8. 그들은 전보가 도착했을 때 모두 떠날 준비를 하고 있었다.
9. 많은 질문을 하면서 강사는 학생들로부터 정보를 유도해내려고 애썼다.
10. 너는 매우 예민한 사람을 흥분하게 만들 수 있는 것을 말해서는 안 된다.
11. 미국은 이민의 나라, '도가니' 이다.
12. 작년에는 많은 고래가 물가에 올라와 죽었다.
13. 루이스가 탁자에 앉자, 그녀는 접시 옆에 수저들을 놓았다.
14. 마크는 분별력이 있어서 육지 가까이 헤엄쳐 갈 수 있다.
15. 1969년에 달에 도착한 우주인들이 돌과 흙의 표본을 수집해왔다.
16. 이 새들은 인간에게 이롭다.

8. all ready
9. elicit
10. sensitive
11. immigrants
12. number
13. beside
14. sensible
15. samples
16. beneficial

17. The government will (persecute/prosecute) the guilty parties for polluting the waters.

18. Every time Maria travels with her children, she carries (access/excess) baggage.

19. Dante's (immoral/immortal) literary masterpieces are read in universities across the country.

20. An explanation will (precede/proceed) each section of the test.

21. Eric's courageous rescue of the drowning child was a (credulous/creditable) deed.

22. Parry's spare flashlights was (helpless/useless) the night of the storm because the batteries were corroded.

23. The gaudy decoration in the hall (detracted/distracted) from the beauty of the celebration.

24. Everything (accept/except) our swimwear is packed and ready to go.

25. Her essay is very (imaginary/imaginative).

ANSWER

17. 정부는 수질오염의 혐의가 있는 단체들을 기소할 것이다.
18. 마리아는 아이들을 데리고 여행할 때마다 너무 많은 짐을 가지고 간다.
19. 단테의 불멸의 문학작품들은 세계의 대학에서 읽혀지고 있다.
20. 시험의 각 장에 앞서 설명이 있을 것이다.
21. 물에 빠진 아이를 구한 에릭의 용감한 구조는 훌륭한 행동이었다.
22. 페리의 예비 손전등은 배터리가 나가서 폭풍이 치는 밤에 소용없었다.
23. 그 홀의 빛나는 장식은 축전의 아름다움을 떨어뜨렸다.
24. 우리 수영복을 제외한 모든 것을 챙겼고 떠날 준지가 되었다.
25. 그녀의 작문은 아주 상상력이 풍부하다.

17. prosecute
18. excess
19. immortal
20. precede
21. creditable
22. useless
23. detracted
24. except
25. imaginative

26. On halloween night, most children dress in (costumes/customs) and go from house to house asking for treats.

27. Jane said that she would arrive (later/latter) than the rest of us.

28. This report is (quite/quiet) complete and needs no revision.

29. Julie's skirt will be too (loose/lose) for her sister to wear.

30. No other power is (comparable/comparative) to that of the press.

31. He is (contemptible/contemptuous) for his meanness.

32. (Disease/Decease) may be aggravated by anxiety.

33. Mary is entirely (uninterested/disinterested) in economic problems.

34. The children were (pleasant/pleased) when they got presents.

ANSWER

26. 할로윈 밤에는 아이들 대부분이 의상을 차려입고 집집마다 겁주며 돌아다닌다.
27. 제인은 그녀가 우리들보다 더 늦게 도착할 것이라고 말했다.
28. 이 보고서는 상당히 완벽해서 수정할 필요가 없다.
29. 줄리의 치마는 너무 느슨해서 동생이 입을 수가 없을 것이다.
30. 어떤 권력도 언론의 그것에 비교할 수 없다.
31. 그는 천박함 때문에 경멸할 만하다.
32. 화를 내면 질병이 악화될 수 있다.
33. 메리는 경제문제에 완전히 무관심하다.
34. 아이들은 선물 받을 때 기뻐하였다.

26. costumes
27. later
28. quite
29. loose
30. comparable
31. contemptible
32. Disease
33. uninterested
34. pleased

35. An (ingenious/ingenuous) smile brightened her lovely face.

36. The solution of the problem is very (momentary/momentous) to the development of our economy.

37. I have no (object/objection) to your proposal.

38. He is an expert in physics. He is a (physician/physicist).

39. He is (regretful/regrettable) for what he has done.

40. The school team has won five (successive/successful) games.

| ANSWER |

35. 순수한 미소가 그녀의 예쁜 얼굴을 밝게 하였다.
36. 문제의 해법은 우리 경제의 발전에 중요하였다.
37. 나는 당신의 제안에 이의가 없어요.
38. 그는 물리학 전공자이다. 그는 물리학자이다.
39. 그는 자신이 한 일에 대해 후회하고 있다.
40. 학교팀이 5게임을 연속으로 이겼다.

35. ingenuous
36. momentous
37. objection
38. physicist
39. regretful
40. successive

Mastery Test Answers

STEP 1

Synonym Test

1. diversity 다양성
   (A) 유사성 (B) 가치
   (C) 평범함, 하찮음 **(D) 다양성**

2. degraded 타락한, 전락한
   (A) 조화롭지 못한
   (B) 기밀분류를 해제하다
   (C) 줄어든, 물러난 **(D) 타락한**

3. coherent 일관성 있는
   (A) 분명치 않은 (B) 정중한
   (C) 특정한 **(D) 논리적으로 관련된**

4. ideology 이데올로기, 개념
   (A) 파괴적인 철학 **(B) 개념**
   (C) 사고과정의 학문 (D) 완벽의 신념

5. ignoble 천박한, 비열한
   (A) 소유를 부인하다 **(B) 비천한**
   (C) 상속이 박탈된 (D) 모르는

6. laudable 칭찬할 만한
   (A) 거만한 (B) 깨끗한
   (C) 거친, 난폭한 **(D) 칭찬할 만한**

7. legible 읽기 쉬운, 명료한
   (A) 인쇄된 (B) 허용된
   (C) 타이프 **(D) 읽을 수 있는**

8. 그는 손님을 진정시키도록 요청받았다.
   (A) 안내하다 (B) 면담하다
   (C) 진정시키다 (D) 억류하다

9. yearn 그리워하다, 갈망하다
   (A) 갈망하다 (B) 입을 크게 벌리다
   (C) 졸음을 느끼다 (D) 따분해 하다

10. supervise 감독하다, 관리하다, 지휘하다
    (A) 습득하다 (B) 압박하다
    (C) 내려다 보다, 감독하다 (D) 제지하다

11. uniformity 균일함, 동일함
    (A) 의복 **(B) 동일함**
    (C) 관습 (D) 권태

12. 그는 대화를 끝내기를 원한다.
    (A) 끝내다 (B) 연기하다
    (C) 무시하다 (D) 계속하다

13. 재발하는 문제란
    (A) 전에 존재하던 문제를 대체시키는 것이다.
    (B) 예기치 못하는 것이다.
    (C) 오래 간과되어 오던 것이다.
    (D) 때때로 나타나는 것이다.

Antonym Test

1. except 빼다, 제외하다
   (A) 받다 (B) 기대하다
   (C) 인정하다 (D) 전달하다

2. finite 유한한, 한정된
   (A) 규정된 (B) 끝나는
   (C) 이기적인 **(D) 무한한**

3. objective 객관적인
   (A) 치우친 (B) 개인적인
   (C) 목표 없는 (D) 동양의

4. submission 포기; 제출
   (A) 권한위임 **(B) 도전, 반항**
   (C) 숙제, 임무 (D) 패배, 좌절

Sentence Completion Test

1. 코흐 시장이 연설을 3분도 안 되는 시간에 끝냈기에 참석자들은 그의 _____에 박수를 보냈다.
   (A) 간결함 (B) 인유, 암시
   (C) 시간 적절함 (D) 유머 감각

2. _____는 민주주의 안에 존재할 수 없으니, 민주주의란 정부라는 하나의 구조적인 형태이기 때문이다.
   (A) 무정부 상태 (B) 억압
   (C) 사회주의 (D) 자유주의

ANSWERS

3. 불행히도 이 좋은 영향들은 앞으로 수년 내에 줄어들거나 심지어 없어질 것으로 예상된다.
   (A) 증가하다 (B) 재발하다, 되돌아가다
   (C) 줄어들다 (D) 사라지다

4. 그 관습이 아이들에게 위험하기 때문에 그 지역 지도자들은 그것을 _____ 하기로 결정하였다.
   (A) 이행하다 (B) 폐지하다
   (C) 완수하다 (D) 지속하다

5. 우표와 동전의 수집은 아주 심각한 측면이 있는 일상생활에 오락거리를 제공하기 때문에 _____ 이다.
   (A) 취미 (B) 간통의
   (C) 모험의 (D) 계몽적인

6. 위대한 발명은 흔히 통찰 또는 _____ 의 순간에 일어난다.
   (A) 인지 (B) 상대성 (C) 인식 (D) 관련

7. _____ 한 부부는 휴일 쇼핑객들로부터 도움을 간청하였다.
   (A) 변덕스러운 (B) 가난한
   (C) 독자적인 (D) 부유한

8. 어떤 사람의 자신의 정신적인 삶에 완전히 빠져드는 경향을 _____ 이라고 한다.
   (A) 내성, 자기반성 (B) 음향학
   (C) 자극 (D) 내향성

9. 정치위원회는 진보 집회에서 우익 시위대를 _____ 하려고 하였다.
   (A) 억제하다 (B) 배제하다
   (C) 부인하다 (D) 격분시키다

10. 노인은 퇴직 후에 부정기적인 사회보장 수표에 의존하지 않기 위해 교직기간 동안 저축하는 _____ 이 있었다.
    (A) 검소함 (B) 인색함
    (C) 선견지명 (D) 점쟁이 능력

11. 과학사상의 한 학파에 따르면, 변화하는 환경에 서서히 적응하는 인간은 원숭이와 같은 종에서 _____ 하였다.
    (A) 진화하였다 (B) 불러일으켰다
    (C) 뒤집었다 (D) 복귀하다

12. 겉으로 보기에는 반대인데도 진실일 수 있는 표현을 _____ 라고 부른다.
    (A) 모범, 보기
    (B) 시차, 패럴렉스(파인더와 렌즈의 시차)
    (C) 역설, 패러독스 (D) 정부, 애인

13. 우리는 오랜 기간에 걸쳐 급여를 _____ 할 수 있다.
    (A) 공제하다 (B) 연장하다
    (C) (나쁜 짓을) 범하다 (D) 철폐하다

14. 아이의 학비를 벌기 위해 부업을 갖는 젊은 아버지의 행동은 칭송받아야 하고 _____ 할만한 행동이다.
    (A) 칭찬받아야 할 (B) 경멸하는, 비웃는
    (C) 싫증나는 (D) 바보 같은

15. 태양이 해마다 매일 같은 시각에 규칙적으로 떠오르기 때문에 그 외연적인 활동을 _____ 하다고 할 수 있다.
    (A) 정기적으로 되풀이되는, 순환하는
    (B) 직선의
    (C) 만연한, 마구 퍼지는
    (D) 반동적인, 보수적인

STEP 2

Synonym Test

1. **analogous** 유사한, 비슷한
   (A) 서로 같은 (B) 숨겨진
   (C) 금속성의 (D) 비이성적인

2. **adroit** 능숙한, 솜씨 좋은
   (A) 똑똑한, 재주 있는 (B) 축축한
   (C) 목표 없는 (D) 예술적인

3. **abhor** 싫어하다
   (A) 회합하다 (B) 저지하다
   (C) 칭찬하다 (D) 혐오하다

4. **dogmatic** 독단적인, 임의대로의, 교리에 얽매인
   (A) 교범 (B) 교조주의의, 공론주의의
   (C) 개의 (D) 부도덕한, 파렴치한

5. garrulous 수다스러운, 말 많은
   (A) 초조한, 까다로운 (B) 예술적인
   (C) 살인적인 (D) 수다스러운

6. fallacious 불합리한, 틀린
   (A) 비틀거리는, 말더듬는 (B) 비틀거리는
   (C) 거짓의 (D) 바보 같은

7. indolence 나태, 게으름
   (A) 대담함, 뻔뻔스러움 (B) 거만함
   (C) 게으름 (D) 가난

8. mitigate 경감하다, 완화하다
   (A) 줄이다 (B) 자극하다
   (C) 측정하다 (D) 기소하다

9. reprimand 비난하다
   (A) 약속을 어기다, 취소하다 (B) 재주문하다
   (C) 비난하다 (D) 소급하는

10. subversive 전복하는, 파괴적인
    (A) 비밀의 (B) 외국의
    (C) 회피하는, 둘러대는 (D) 파괴적인

11. subdue 정복하다, 억제하다, 가라앉히다
    (A) 지하의 (B) 중량이 부족한
    (C) 정복하다, 극복하다
    (D) 기한이 지난, 늦은

Antonym Test

1. apathy 무관심, 냉담
   (A) 잠 (B) 유혹 (C) 열정 (D) 환대

2. agitate 동요시키다
   (A) 무효화하다 (B) 화해시키다
   (C) 진정시키다 (D) 표현하다

3. apprehensive 염려하는
   (A) 감상할 줄 아는, 감사하는 (B) 침략적인
   (C) 멀어진 (D) 확실한

4. avert 돌리다, 피하다
   (A) 숨기다 (B) 원인이 되다, 일으키다
   (C) 변명하다 (D) 부인하다

5. animosity 악의, 원한
   (A) 사려 깊음 (B) 우호
   (C) 신뢰 (D) 분노

6. apathetic 냉담한, 무심한
   (A) 방심 않는, 경계하는 (B) 슬픈
   (C) 감염된 (D) 마음 아픈, 비참한

7. derisive 조소하는
   (A) 분리하는 (B) 가구 비치
   (C) 반영하는 (D) 칭찬하는

8. deride 조소하다, 비웃다
   (A) 날다 (B) 칭찬하다
   (C) 수정하다 (D) 인정하다

9. latent 잠재적인
   (A) 분명한 (B) 조작된, 발명한
   (C) 말썽이 된 (D) 독특한

10. recessive 퇴행하는, 역행하는
    (A) 주는 (B) 끌로 깎은
    (C) 천천히 치료되는 (D) 지배적인, 유력한

11. tangible 만져서 알 수 있는, 명백한
    (A) 필수의 (B) 만져서 알 수 없는
    (C) 남 앞에 내놓을 만한, 보기에 부끄럽지 않은
    (D) 불법적인

Sentence Completion Test

1. 그는 자기 삼촌 유언의 주요한 _____이었다. 세금을 납부하고 그에게는 2만달러 상당의 유산이 남았다.
   (A) 집행인 (B) 연금 수령자
   (C) 보험이나 연금 수령인 (D) 경쟁자

2. _____한 조수는 고용주에게는 큰 도움이 된다.
   (A) 졸리는 (B) 숙련된
   (C) 결근한 (D) 왼손잡이인

3. 다른 사람을 _____ 하는 사람은 그와 함께 웃는 것이 아니라, 그를 비웃는 것이다.
   (A) 조소하다 (B) 모독하다
   (C) 몹시 꾸짖다 (D) 연기하다

ANSWERS

4. 그리도 아름다운 음악이 쇳소리가 났다. 그것은 음악이 야외극장의 강풍에 _____되었기 때문이었다.
   (A) 부러진   **(B) 일그러진**
   (C) 뒤죽박죽 된   (D) 흩뜨려진

5. 야생동물이므로 이리는 _____한 동물이 아니다.
   (A) 고양이과의   (B) 사랑스러운
   (C) 유순한, 다루기 쉬운   (D) 즐거운

6. 그녀는 _____하게 완전한 여성이라서 아무도 그녀의 기준에 의의를 제기하지 않았다.
   (A) 어렴풋한   **(B) 의심의 여지가 없는**
   (C) 의심스러운   (D) 신비한

7. 노동협상의 _____한 중재자는 유사한 사건에서 공명정대한 것으로 알려져 있었다.
   (A) 수지 맞는   **(B) 현명한**
   (C) 뜻밖의 발견을 하는   (D) 익살맞은

8. 약사는 의사가 _____하는 주문에 따라 투약할 것이다.
   (A) 처방하다   (B) 금지하다
   (C) 계획하다   (D) 인권을 박탈하다, 금지하다

9. 눈이 많이 와서 운전을 _____하게 하였다.
   (A) 달래다, 화해시키다   (B) 편견에 사로잡힌
   (C) 배제하다, 못하게 하다   (D) 선점한

10. 오로지 사실만을 기사화해야 하는 기자는 언제나 마감시간 전에 기사를 _____한다.
    (A) 동사화하다   **(B) 입증하다**
    (C) 확인하다   (D) 방해하다

11. 일상생활에 관한 문제들은 종교적인 것에 반하는 _____한 것이라 한다.
    (A) 종파적인   (B) 격려된
    (C) 세속적인   (D) 이차적인

12. 일부 공산국가들에서는 주민들이 정부를 전복시키려 한다고 당국이 느낄 때 주민들은 _____로서 구속된다.
    (A) 불치병자   (B) 상습자
    (C) 나쁜 길로 인도하는 사람   **(D) 위험인물**

STEP 3

Synonym Test

1. abet 부추기다, 선동하다
   (A) 도박하다   (B) 신성시하다, 정화하다
   (C) 부추기다, 선동하다   (D) 비난하다

2. acumen 예민함, 총명
   (A) 강렬함   (B) 정확성
   (C) 통찰력   (D) 본능

3. ambiguous 애매 모호한
   (A) 강력하고 확신을 주는
   (B) 한 가지 의미 이상으로 이해될 수 있는
   (C) 훌륭한 판단과 건전한 추론과정에 바탕을 둔
   (D) 재미없고 너무 장황한

4. 감독은 서기의 태만함을 꾸짖었다.
   (A) 꾸짖었다   (B) 용서하였다
   (C) 이동시켰다   (D) 처벌하였다

5. divergent 분리하는, 차이나는
   (A) 동시에 발생하는   **(B) 차이나는**
   (C) 접근하는   (D) 평행의, 나란한

6. concede 시인하다, 인정하다
   운전자는 자신이 잘못했음을 시인했다.
   (A) 부인했다   (B) 설명했다
   (C) 암시했다   **(D) 인정했다**

7. cognizant 인식하고 있는
   (A) 드문   (B) 꺼리는
   (C) 알고 있는, 인지하는   (D) 우연한

8. congruent 일치하는
   (A) 시끄러운   **(B) 동의하는**
   (C) 싸우기 좋아하는   (D) 끈끈한, 달라붙는

9. congenital 타고난, 선천적인
   (A) 조화로운   (B) 동정적인
   (C) 타고난   (D) 술 장식이 있는

10. culpable 과실이 있는
    (A) 위험한   (B) 부드러운
    (C) 비난받을 만한   (D) 쉽게 알 수 있는

11. edify 교화하다, 계몽하다
    (A) 선언하다, 포고하다 (B) 개정하다
    (C) 회전하다 (D) 계몽하다

12. equanimity 평정, 침착
    (A) 평정 (B) 한결같음, 일치, 균등
    (C) 동등한 정의 (D) 무관심

13. enervated 힘없는, 연약한
    (A) 신경의 (B) 연약한
    (C) 겁 많은 (D) 강화된

14. hypothetical 가설적인, 가정의
    (A) 반박할 수 없는 (B) 가정적인, 잠정적인
    (C) 삼각형의 (D) 마법에 걸린

15. engender 발생시키다, 일으키다
    (A) 활력을 죽이다 (B) 위험하게 하다
    (C) 교묘하게 다루다 (D) 생산하다, 발생시키다

16. inception 시작
    프로그램 시작 때 그는 나타나지 않았다.
    (A) 시작 (B) 종국
    (C) 결론 (D) 거절

17. impede 방해하다
    그는 자기 조의 작업을 방해할 생각이 없었다.
    (A) 수행하다 (B) 비난하다
    (C) 칭찬하다 (D) 방해하다

18. peccadillo 가벼운 죄나 과오, 작은 결점
    (A) 멧돼지 (B) 굴을 파는 동물
    (C) 작은 잘못 (D) 골동품

19. levity 경솔함, 경거망동
    (A) 지중해의 (B) 물에 뜰 수 있는
    (C) 천박, 경솔 (D) 조명

20. malign 비난하다; 유해한, 악의적인
    (A) 비난하다 (B) 깨트리다
    (C) 분리하다 (D) 상처를 입히다

21. loquacious 말 많은, 수다스러운
    (A) 새 같은, 민첩한 (B) 감겨지는, 꼬불꼬불한
    (C) 풍부한 (D) 수다스런

22. tenacity 고집, 끈기, 불굴의 의지
    (A) 견고함, 확고부동 (B) 무모, 만용
    (C) 총명, 영민 (D) 실망

23. renounce 포기하다, 단념하다, 부인하다
    (A) 중얼거리다 (B) 반복하다
    (C) 흉내내다 (D) 단념하다, 부인하다

24. 직원들은 경계 훈련을 하도록 지시받았다.
    (A) 엄격한 규율 (B) 일상적인 예방
    (C) 체계적 연습 (D) 방심 없는 경계

Antonym Test

1. benign 다정한, 친절한
   (A) 비난하는 (B) 관련된, 적절한
   (C) 로봇 (D) 악의적인, 심술궂은

2. adjourn 휴회하다
   (A) 회의를 소집하다 (B) 무효를 선언하다
   (C) 조사하다 (D) 번역하다

3. capricious 변덕스러운, 변하기 쉬운
   (A) 활동적인 (B) 안정된
   (C) 반대되는 (D) 온순한

4. condone 용서하다
   (A) 비난하다 (B) 무시하다
   (C) 처벌하다 (D) 실수하다

5. discern 분별하다, 식별하다
   (A) 인지하지 못하다 (B) 방출하다
   (C) 확장하다 (D) 배치시키다

6. discrete 분리된
   (A) 신중한 (B) 결합된
   (C) 꼬부라진 (D) 성장이 저지된

7. dissonance 불협화음, 부조화
   (A) 거부 (B) 재난
   (C) 조화 (D) 불일치, 부동

8. disparage 깔보다
   (A) 칭찬하다 (B) 비난하다
   (C) 지우다 (D) 개혁하다

ANSWERS

9. itinerant 순회하는, 이동하는
   (A) 원한 (B) 은유
   (C) 가해자, 범죄자 (D) 거주하는

10. eulogize 칭송하다
    (A) 매혹시키다, 끌다 (B) 주의하다
    (C) 비방하다 (D) 피하다

11. imputation 덮어씌우기, 전가, 비난
    (A) 근면 (B) 옹호
    (C) 샬리천(옷감) (D) 의류

12. equivocal 모호한
    (A) 확실한, 단정적인 (B) 중간의
    (C) 단조로운 (D) 음악적인

13. lassitude 나른함, 권태, 피로
    (A) 얽힘 (B) 긴 숨결 (C) 결정 (D) 활력

14. obviate 방지하다, 제거하다, 회피하다
    (A) 움켜쥐다 (B) 개혁하다
    (C) 필요하게 하다 (D) 진정시키다

15. placate 달래다
    (A) 즐겁게 하다 (B) ...을 적으로 만들다
    (C) 연루시키다 (D) 동정

16. mollify 달래다
    (A) 요새화하다, 강하게 하다 (B) 달래다
    (C) 창피를 주다 (D) 격렬하게 하다

17. reticent 삼가는, 절제된, 과묵한
    (A) 들뜬, 안절부절못하는 (B) 되풀이되는
    (C) 수다스런 (D) 편안한

18. reactionary 반동적인, 보수적인
    (A) 화학적으로 유도된 (B) 일상적인
    (C) 혁신적인 (D) 순진한, 소박한

19. sentient 감각이 있는
    (A) 감성적인 (B) 감각이 없는
    (C) 적대적인 (D) 동정적인

20. wily 계략을 쓰는, 교활한
    (A) 얇은 (B) 기민한, 날랜
    (C) 고집 센 (D) 부적절한, 어리석은

Sentence Completion Test

1. 그의 소견은 아주 _____해서 우리는 가능한 의미 가운데 어느 것이 맞는지 판단할 수가 없었다.
   (A) 애매모호한 (B) 익살스런, 유쾌한
   (C) 감지할 수 없는 (D) 어울리는

2. 죽은 용 주위로 젊은 처녀들의 머리, 팔, 몸통 등 _____의 잔해들이 흩어져 있었다.
   (A) 전투 (B) 유해 (C) 축제 (D) 살육

3. 워터게이트 사건은 닉슨이 대통령직을 _____하기로 결정한 표면적인 원인이었다.
   (A) 버리다 (B) 포기하다, 양위하다
   (C) 열망하다 (D) 유산시키다

4. 델피 오라클은 지중해에서 아가멤논에게 폭풍을 경고하였으나, 그는 그 _____를 유념하지 않았고, 그의 함대는 파괴되었다.
   (A) 허가 (B) 경고 (C) 지식 (D) 제안

5. 휴가가 _____하도록 우리가 계획을 조정할 수 있다면, 우리는 여행을 함께 할 수 있을 것이다.
   (A) 협동하다 (B) 연합하다
   (C) 강요하다 (D) 일치하다

6. 그 약의 효능은 임산부들에게 _____한 것으로 알려져 있어서, 어떤 의사도 그녀에게 그것을 처방하지 않을 것이다.
   (A) 해독하는 (B) 작은
   (C) 유독한 (E) 불법인

7. 후보 가운데 한 사람이 토론 도중에 이슈를 회피하였을 때 다른 사람이 그의 _____를 비난하였다.
   (A) 분위기 (B) 귀에 거슬리는 소리
   (C) 완곡 표현 (D) 일관성

8. 교회성가대의 _____은 베이스의 감기와 테너의 연습부족의 결과였다.
   (A) 불통일 (B) 조화 (C) 불협화음 (D) 부조화

9. 그의 결론은 너무 _____해서 그들이 아무도 도울 수 없었다.
   (A) 불명확한 (B) 헤아릴 수 없는
   (C) 알려지지 않은 (D) 돈이 없는

10. 부모님의 _____통증은 약으로 누그러질 수 없었다.
    (A) 붕대를 감은 (B) 찾아낼 수 없는
    (C) 고집 센, (병이) 잘 낫지 않는 (D) 침착한

11. 언제나 다른 즐거운 젊은 여성들의 모임을 추구하는 젊은 사교계의 명사는 지극히 _____했다.
    (A) 사교적인 (B) 보이는
    (C) 은혜를 모르는 (D) 명시적인

12. 그의 해설은 불필요하고 _____해서 아무도 그가 왜 그 말을 덧붙이는지 이해하지 못했다.
    (A) 호의적인 (B) 불필요한, 이유 없는
    (C) 기괴한 (D) 사교적인

13. 판사는 그 계약의 모든 법률적인 힘을 박탈하며 무효화하여, 그것을 _____하였다.
    (A) 폐기하다 (B) 완화시키다
    (C) 폐지하다 (D) 철폐하다

14. 그녀는 타의에 의해서가 아니라 자신의 강한 의지를 자부하였기에 자신의 _____으로 금연하였다.
    (A) 악의 (B) 의지력, 결단력
    (C) 편집증 (D) 직업

15. 거울에 번쩍이게 보이게 하는 금박의 _____가 있었다.
    (A) (건물의) 정면, 외관 (B) 양
    (C) 억압 (D) 과음 과식

16. 돌고래들이 활개치고 있어서 물결이 사나웠다.
    (A) 고요한 (B) 물에 잠기는
    (C) 사나운 (D) 달래는

17. 양심적인 사장은 문제를 일으킨 직원을 다른 사람들 앞에서 _____하지 않는다.
    (A) 야단치다 (B) 무시하다
    (C) 칭찬하다 (D) 승급시키다

18. 경비원은 달빛이 없는 밤에는 각별히 _____하는 것이 필요하다.
    (A) 차가운 (B) 경계하는
    (C) 진동하는 (D) 비우호적인

STEP 4

Synonym Test

1. acclimate 익숙해지다
   (A) 날씨를 예고하다 (B) 익숙해지다
   (C) 좋은 기후를 즐기다 (D) 완전히 뚫다

2. augment 증대시키다
   (A) 채택하다 (B) 증가시키다
   (C) 수정하다 (D) 예상하다

3. auspicious 길조의, 행운의
   (A) 의문의 (B) 유명한 (C) 자유로운 (D) 좋은

4. dilatory 늦은, 지연하는
   (A) 늦은 (B) 확대된
   (C) 목표 없는 (D) 팽창하는

5. deprecate 비난하다
   (A) 가치를 떨어뜨리다 (B) 비판하다
   (C) 사과하다 (D) 칭찬하다

6. erudition 학식, 박식
   (A) 조잡함, 상스러움 (B) 학식
   (C) 거만함, 화려함 (D) 배제

7. expedient 편의적인, 편한
   (A) 정당한 (B) 노련한
   (C) 편의적인 (D) 반대할 만한

8. mendacious 허위의, 거짓말을 잘 하는
   (A) 거지가 된 (B) 거짓된
   (C) 지적인 (D) 칭찬할 만한

9. miscreant 이단의, 사악한
   (A) 유산된 (B) 변형된
   (C) 사악한 (D) 잘못된

10. 그의 부하들은 그의 관대한 행위를 잘 알고 있었다.
    (A) 거만한 (B) 영리한
    (C) 이타적인 (D) 위협적인

11. 손님은 침울하였다.
    (A) 호기심 있는 (B) 우울한
    (C) 성급한 (D) 소심한

ANSWERS

12. **specious** 그럴듯한, 허울좋은
    (A) 특별한 (B) 거짓의, 사기의
    (C) 진짜의 (D) 산발적인, 때때로 일어나는

13. **salient** 현저한, 두드러진
    (A) 군침을 흘리게 하는, 맛있어 보이는 (B) 짠
    (C) 바다의 (D) 눈에 띄는, 현저한

14. **sedulous** 근면한, 정성을 다하는
    (A) 부지런한 (B) 배반하는, 불충의
    (C) 매혹적인, 유혹하는 (D) 순진한, 솔직한

Antonym Test

1. **ambulatory** 이동하는, 걸을 수 있는
   (A) 침대에 틀어박혀 있는 (B) 걸을 수 있는
   (C) 다친 (D) 격리된

2. **cataclysm** 지각변동, 격변
   (A) 큰 실수 (B) 현상
   (C) 배반 (D) 승리

3. **auspicious** 길조의, 경사스런
   (A) 비난의, 처벌의 (B) 눈에 띄는
   (C) 좋지 않은 (D) 의문의

4. **dilatory** 더딘, 꾸물거리는
   (A) 털이 난 (B) 낙천적인
   (C) 폐허가 된 (D) 시간을 지키는

5. **conversant** 정통하고 있는, 관련이 있는, 친한
   (A) 간결한 (B) 강하게 밀어붙이는
   (C) 확신하는 (D) 낯선

6. **derogatory** 손상시키는, 경멸하는
   (A) 균등하지 않은 (B) 동등한
   (C) 반대의 (D) 아첨하는

7. **feckless** 무기력한
   (A) 용감한 (B) 얼룩이 없는
   (C) 근면한 (D) 변덕스러운

8. **ingenuous** 솔직한, 꾸밈없는
   (A) 재빠른 (B) 악의 없는
   (C) 재능 있는 (D) 음모를 꾸미는, 계략적인

9. **extrinsic** 외부로부터의, 본질이 아닌
   (A) 병원균검사 (B) 기이한
   (C) 교육되지 않은 (D) 내부의

10. **laconic** 간결한, 말 수 적은
    (A) 물기 많은 (B) 음악의
    (C) 쾌활한 (D) 말이 많은, 장황한

11. **languid** 나른한, 활기 없는, 느린
    (A) 유창한 (B) 습기 있는
    (C) 병약한 (D) 정력 왕성한

12. **obfuscate** (마음을) 어둡게 하다, (판단을) 흐리게 하다
    (A) 불구로 만들다 (B) 달래다, 화해시키다
    (C) 타락시키다 (D) 분명하게 하다

13. **petulant** 토라진, 성마른
    (A) 성을 잘 내는 (B) 즐거운
    (C) 거친, 난폭한 (D) 보통과 다른

14. **lucrative** 유리한, 수지 맞는
    (A) 가치를 떨어뜨리다
    (B) 수지가 맞지 않는
    (C) 영향력 있는
    (D) 통화의

15. **ostensible** 외면적인, 표면적인
    (A) 화려한, 허영의
    (B) 이해하기 어려운, 분명치 않은
    (C) 녹슬지 않는
    (D) 섞인

16. **renege** (약속을) 어기다, 취소하다
    (A) 도망
    (B) 명예를 주다, 승낙하다
    (C) 가볍게 하다
    (D) 부인하다

17. **sedulous** 근면한, 정성을 다하는
    (A) 사기의, 속이는 (B) 종교적인
    (C) 부주의한 (D) 미운

18. **usurp** 권리를 침해하다, 강탈하다
    (A) 버리다, 포기하다 (B) 예언하다
    (C) 진정시키다 (D) 변론하다

Sentence Completion Test

1. 테러리스트들의 요구를 들어주는 것은 우리의 책임을 배반하는 것이다. 그런 _____은 자신들의 목적을 얻기 위해 비슷한 수단을 사용할 다른 사람들을 고무시키기만 할 것이다.
   (A) 패배 (B) 유화
   (C) 호소 (D) 핑계, 속임수

2. 그녀는 자신의 목표를 이루기 위한 결심이 _____하다.
   (A) 예쁜 (B) 확고한
   (C) 초도덕적인 (D) 유익한

3. 비록 수년 간 실질적인 자원이 문제를 해결하는 데 바쳐졌지만, 만족스러운 해결은 여전히 _____ 남아있었다.
   (A) 고비용으로
   (B) 가능하게
   (C) 잘 피하는, 알 수 없는
   (D) 비법을 이어받는

4. 고대 로마인들은 황제들을 너무나 존경해서 _____하기까지 했다.
   (A) 질문하다 (B) 숭배하다
   (C) 폐위시키다 (D) 겁나게 하다

5. 비록 자기는 일자리를 잡았지만 몇몇 사람들이 해고될 것이라는 것을 듣고 그는 _____하기로 결심하였다.
   (A) 웃다 (B) 위임하다
   (C) 바치다 (D) 반대하다

6. 곡예사가 막대기를 부드럽게 흔들자 접시는 곡예사의 막대기 꼭대기에서 _____하기 시작했다.
   (A) 흔들다 (B) 매달리다
   (C) 질주하다 (D) 회전하다

7. 그녀가 흥분하면 과장하는 경향이 있음을 모두가 알고 있었기에, 아무도 그녀의 _____를 진지하게 받아들이지 않았다.
   (A) 과장 (B) 고혈압
   (C) 저혈압 (D) 유쾌한 기분

8. 그 용감한 경찰관은 _____한 봉사로 존경을 받았다.
   (A) 허위의 (B) 평범한
   (C) 야한, 저속한 (D) 칭찬할 만한

9. 전에는 반듯했던 아이에게 그가 _____한 영향을 끼쳤다.
   (A) 밀접한 관계의 (B) 광범위한
   (C) 해로운 (D) 까다로운

10. _____한 어린이는 부모님이 계속 아니라고 말했음에도, 폭풍우가 치는 동안 하늘이 무너질 거라는 자기 의견을 고치기를 거절하였다.
    (A) 싫은, 얄미운 (B) 억지의, 고집 센
    (C) 못마땅한, 반대할 만한 (D) 의무적인

11. 그녀의 발언은 너무 _____해서 우리는 토론의 진짜 요점을 기억할 수 없었다.
    (A) 노골적인 (B) 비우호적인
    (C) 주저하는 (D) 지엽적인, 옆길로 새는

12. 그 한 첩의 약은 _____되게 만들어 적들이 무사히 지나갈 수 있게 허용하였다.
    (A) 속도 (B) 마비
    (C) 거만 (D) 주저

13. 그 연사의 요점은 너무 _____해서 청중들이 납득을 하였다.
    (A) 모호한 (B) 빈약한
    (C) 명확한 (D) 반동적인, 보수적인

14. 의붓 부모는 친부모의 권리를 _____할까봐 아이들에 대한 통제를 거의 행사하지 않을 수 있다.
    (A) 정복하는 (B) 비방하는
    (C) 침해하는 (D) 야단치는

STEP 5

Synonym Test

1. **adventitious** 우연의, 우발적인, 외래의
   (A) 재미있는 (B) 위험한
   (C) 우연한 (D) 주제넘은

ANSWERS

2. **acerbic** 거친, 신랄한
   (A) 거친 (B) 절제하는
   (C) 조롱하는 (D) 호전적인

3. **ameliorate** 개선하다, 개량하다
   (A) 개선하다
   (B) 확대하다
   (C) 개정하다, 수정하다
   (D) 치료하다

4. **captious** 헐뜯는, 비난하는
   (A) 고집 센 (B) 욕심 많은
   (C) 매혹적인 (D) 비평하는

5. **bellicose** 호전적인
   (A) 재미있는 (B) 싸움을 좋아하는
   (C) 반항의, 널리 알려진 (D) 살찐

6. **corroboration** 확증
   (A) 지출 (B) 편집
   (C) 확정 (D) 경감

7. **desultory** 산만한, 변덕스러운, 일관성 없는
   (A) 길을 잘못 든 (B) 낙담한
   (C) 목표 없는, 정처 없는 (D) 빈곤한

8. **imprecation** 저주
   (A) 즉흥작곡 (B) 방탕
   (C) 암시 (D) 저주

9. **indigenous** 타고난, 본래의
   (A) 화난 (B) 가난해진
   (C) 본래의 (D) 모욕적인

10. **lethargic** 혼미한, 혼수상태의
    (A) 낭만적인 (B) 나른한, 활발하지 못한
    (C) 기름칠한 (D) 선율이 아름다운

11. **nebulous** 흐린, 모호한, 불투명한
    (A) 흐린 (B) 복종된
    (C) 어색한 (D) 부주의한

12. **nonchalant** 무관심한, 태연한
    (A) 얻기 어려운 (B) 격분하기 쉬운
    (C) 중요하지 않은 (D) 무관심한

13. **spurious** 가짜의, 위조의, 겉치레의
    (A) 주저하는, 망설이는
    (B) 거짓의
    (C) (질병이) 급속히 진행하는
    (D) 심리중인, 미결의

Antonym Test

1. **calumnious** 중상하는, 비방하는
   (A) 비참한 (B) 음모의
   (C) 불평하는, 트집잡는 (D) 칭찬의

2. **alacrity** 활발함, 민활함
   (A) 공포 (B) 권태, 무기력
   (C) 명성 (D) 절제

3. **acrimonious** 매서운, 신랄한
   (A) 쾌활하게 (B) 지적인
   (C) 마음을 진정시키는 (D) 심한, 호된

4. **cursory** 서두른, 엉성한
   (A) 철저한 (B) 무례한
   (C) 정직한 (D) 신속하게

5. **debilitate** 쇠약하게 하다
   (A) 격려하다 (B) 은근히 주입시키다
   (C) 준비하다 (D) 강화시키다

6. **eclectic** 폭넓은, 선택적인, 얽매이지 않는
   (A) 화려한 (B) 독점적인
   (C) 목가적인 (D) 결론적인

7. **corroborate** 확증하다, 입증하다
   (A) 옳은
   (B) 강화하다
   (C) 확장하다
   (D) 근본을 훼손하다, 손상시키다

8. **depredation** 약탈, 침식
   (A) 다혈질 (B) 총체적인
   (C) 회복 (D) 매력

9. **flaunt** 자랑하다, 과시하다
   (A) 조롱하다 (B) 숨기다
   (C) 격분시키다 (D) 방어하다

10. gauche 세련되지 못한
    (A) 서구의 (B) 경솔한
    (C) 세련된 (D) 간결한

11. germane 적절한 관련이 있는
    (A) 튜튼족의 (B) 씨뿌린
    (C) 겁이 많은 (D) 상관없는

12. extemporaneous 즉흥의
    (A) 정력적인 (B) 외국의
    (C) 엄숙한 (D) 준비된, 연습한

13. intransigent 비타협적인
    (A) 통행할 수 없는 (B) 화해할 수 있는
    (C) 거친 (D) 믿을 수 없는

14. extirpate 전멸시키다, 근절시키다
    (A) 더럽히다
    (B) 깨끗이 하다
    (C) 심다, 주입시키다
    (D) 호의를 보이다

15. polemic 논쟁을 좋아하는
    (A) 북극의 (B) 전기화학의
    (C) 동의하는 (D) 통계상의

16. obsequious 아첨하는, 비굴한, 순종하는
    (A) 존경스러운 (B) 건방진
    (C) 유전적인 (D) 어두운, 음울한

17. parsimony 인색함
    (A) 반박 (B) 낭비
    (C) 구부림 (D) 빈곤

18. sagacious 총명한, 현명한
    (A) 무지한, 모르는 (B) 위험한
    (C) 분명한 (D) 말이 많은

19. rectitude 정직, 청렴
    (A) 비도덕 (B) 용기, 불굴의 정신
    (C) 비겁 (D) 태도

20. satiated 물린, 배부른
    (A) 풍자적인 (B) 배고픈
    (C) 호화로운 (D) 즐거운

21. truculent 야만스런, 모질고 사나운, 가혹한
    (A) 화려한
    (B) 아첨하는
    (C) 자동차의
    (D) 다루기 어려운, 제멋대로 구는

22. risibility 잘 웃는 성질, 웃는 버릇
    (A) 우울증 (B) 소심
    (C) 건방짐, 거만 (D) 흥분

Sentence Completion Test

1. 달콤한 것을 좋아하는 여성은 _____ 때문에 피클의 맛을 싫어한다.
   (A) 민첩함 (B) 독신
   (C) 신맛 (D) 즙이 많음

2. 어떤 역사가들은 _____인 통치자로 여겨졌던 프랭클린 루스벨트와는 달리 히틀러는 독재자였다고 주장한다.
   (A) 이기적인 (B) 열중한
   (C) 부조리한 (D) 이타적인

3. 사람들은 무신론자들이 조각상에 진흙을 던지는 행위가 _____한 것으로 느꼈다.
   (A) 혐오 (B) 신성모독
   (C) 직무태만 (D) 대표단

4. 정문이 떨어지는 잔해에 막힌 후에 밖으로 난 창을 통해서 도로로 나 있는 _____가 발견되었다.
   (A) 출구 (B) 복귀
   (C) 집단이주 (D) 애정 도피행각

5. 감독은 오늘 _____한 읽기뿐만 아니라 보고할 시간조차 없었다.
   (A) 주변의 (B) 집중된
   (C) 수상한 (D) 몹시 서두른

6. 석탄은 지구표면 아래로부터 용해된 물질이 건조될 때 형성되기 때문에 _____암이다.
   (A) 타고난
   (B) 필수적인
   (C) 불의, 화성의
   (D) 불가사의한, 헤아릴 수 없는

ANSWERS

7. 노인부부에 대한 사악한 공격이 _____하고, 끔찍하고, 용서할 수 없는 것으로 비난받았다.
   (A) 우연한 (B) 주저하는
   (C) 우연한 일 (D) 흉악한

8. 부모는 다른 사람들에 대한 도덕과 존경심으로 아이를 _____하려고 한다.
   (A) 주입시키다, 가르치다 (B) 계산하다
   (C) 부화시키다 (D) 접목하다

9. 자유시간이 좀 있어서 그녀는 백화점에서 모자를 _____하려고 작정했다.
   (A) 훔치다 (B) 투자하다
   (C) 읽다, 음미하다 (D) 추진하다

10. 여기저기 거닐고 산책하는 사람은 _____ 이다.
    (A) 충격의 (B) 유랑성의, 순회하는
    (C) 소요하는, 배회하는 (D) 진보적인

11. 학부모에게 아첨하는 선생님의 행동은 교장선생님으로 하여금 왜 그렇게 학부모에게는 _____하고, 학생들에게는 그렇게 엄격할까 의문을 갖게 만들었다.
    (A) (열매가) 달걀을 거꾸로 세운 모양의
    (B) 부주의한
    (C) (귀신이나 망상이) 붙다
    (D) 아첨하는, 비굴한

12. 기독교의 신은 무한하고 우주적인 힘을 가지고 있어서 _____하다.
    (A) 언제 어디든 있는
    (B) 무엇이든 알고 있는, 전지의
    (C) 잡식성의
    (D) 전능한, 무엇이든 할 수 있는

13. _____는 인간이 자신에게 악의적인 행위들을 한다고 생각하여 인간을 미워하고 불신하였다.
    (A) 염세주의자 (B) 거물, 실력자
    (C) 구두쇠 (D) 악한, 이단자

14. 고치에서 나온 다음에 나방은 나비로의 _____을 완성하였다.
    (A) 직역하다 (B) 중기(中期)
    (C) 변태, 변신 (D) 은유

15. 재정에 대한 우리의 이해가 너무 _____해서 우리는 외부의 자문을 필요로 한다.
    (A) 빈약한 (B) 기민한, 빈틈없는
    (C) 확신하는 (D) 걱정하는

16. 그의 _____한 태도는 여주인을 불쾌하게 하였다.
    (A) 눈에 안 띄는 (B) 노출된
    (C) 풀어진 (D) 거친